IT HAPPENED ON
BROADWAY

IT HAPPENED ON

BROADWAY

AN ORAL HISTORY
of the
GREAT WHITE WAY

MYRNA KATZ FROMMER | HARVEY FROMMER

Harcourt Brace & Company

New York   San Diego   London

To the gifted and generous members of the Broadway community.
Thanks for your memories.

And to the memory of Fred Golden, a most gifted, generous, and also gallant man who became,
during the time we researched and wrote this book, our counsel and friend.

Library of Congress Cataloging-in-Publication Data
It happened on Broadway: an oral history of the great white way /
   [compiled by] Myrna Katz Frommer, Harvey Frommer.—1st ed.
      p.   cm.
   Includes index.
   ISBN 0-15-100280-0
   1. Theater—New York (State)—New York—History—20th century.
2. Entertainers—United States—Interviews.   3. Theater—New York
(State)—New York—Interviews.   I. Frommer, Myrna. II. Frommer, Harvey.
PN2277.N5I8   1998
792'.09747'1—dc21   98-15469

Designed by Susan Shankin

Printed in the United States of America
First edition
E D C B A

CONTENTS

INTRODUCTION

Seven in the evening, midtown Manhattan. The message board on Times Square spells out the news headlines in electronic amber while below Broadway and Seventh Avenue converge in a riot of neon billboards, swirling crowds, and gridlocked traffic. Yet just to the west, a quieter drama is beginning as small groups of people drift onto a dozen side streets and assemble beneath the marquees of an irregular collection of soot-stained buildings. Within the next half hour their number will grow until they are too many to be contained by the sidewalks, and they will spill out into gutters by now congested with yellow cabs, police on horseback, stretch limos, tour buses, and late-model cars from the suburbs lined up for space in the nearest parking lot. The stately and slovenly, dressed in grimy grunge and haute couture, speaking in the accents of New York and Texas, Paris and Rome, Moscow and Munich, they will gather and wait.

On West Forty-fourth Street half a dozen girls pose for photographs along the wall of the Majestic Theater, where *Phantom of the Opera* is still drawing capacity audiences after all these years. And down the block, at the Shubert Alley intersection, in the same Shubert Theater where *Hamlet* opened on October 2, 1913, and *A Chorus Line* closed on April 28, 1990—after what was then the longest run in Broadway history—a theater party crowd convenes for the revival of *Chicago,* playing to full houses into its fourth year.

Out-of-towners fingering their full-price tickets and savvy New Yorkers pocketing the half-pricers they picked up at the TKTS booth at Duffy Square hours ago commingle in a ritual of anticipation that abruptly ends at the eight o'clock curtain hour. Moments later the streets stand silent and empty, while within the Lunt-Fontanne, the Royale, the Broadhurst, the Gershwin, the Richard Rodgers, the Ethel Barrymore, the Shubert, the Martin Beck, the St. James, the Music Box, the Booth, the Neil Simon, the Imperial, and the rest—the making of magic begins.

There are other neighborhoods in New York City and in cities all across America where audiences are being seated, where curtains are rising and performers are poised to play their roles. But here is the apex, the acme, the one singular sensation: BROADWAY.

There are other books about Broadway, but like the place itself, this one is unique, its singularity lying in the tellers of its tales. There is Carol Channing reliving the moment she realized the safest place for her would be the center of a stage. There is Robert Whitehead thinking back to the time he convinced Ethel Waters to take the role of Berenice Sadie Brown in *The Member of the Wedding* and the time Judith Anderson convinced him to give her the role of the nurse their second time around with *Medea*. There is John Raitt recalling how he opened a pleated width of sheet music folded like an accordion to find the "Soliloquy" from *Carousel*. There is Cy Feuer reminiscing about the time Frank Loesser snatched a line of Abe Burrows's dialogue and wrote "The Oldest Established Permanent Floating Crap Game in New York" for *Guys and Dolls*. There is Mary Rodgers remembering the times she'd pass by the living-room doorway and hear another gorgeous refrain as her father tried out new melodies on the piano, Kim Hunter remembering her onstage mishaps with Marlon Brando in the original production of *A Streetcar Named Desire,* Gwen Verdon remembering her first dance encounter with Bob Fosse, when he worked her through the steps of "Whatever Lola Wants." There is Joel Grey describing how he found his way into the diabolical character of the emcee in *Cabaret;* Len Cariou recounting how he sat down to lunch one day with a script that had just arrived from Stephen Sondheim, *Sweeney Todd*; Charles Durning playing *Inherit the Wind* opposite George C. Scott and recalling how George would turn and tell him, "I'll see you in reality," just as he stepped onto the stage.

And the hundred other Broadway babies, bards, balladeers, and boulevardiers whose dreams and defeats, trials and triumphs, are woven together into this multiple memoir: Each of them, once upon a time, fell in love with the theater and through these pages remembers the journey propelled by that love. Bringing the reader through the stage door, into a world of dressing rooms and rehearsal halls, flies and projection booths, around pianos in angels' living rooms and conference tables in producers' offices, they reimagine the auditions, readings, rehearsals, openings, runs, closings, and lived-for moments of glory under the bright lights, center stage.

Out of the particulars of their lives, the larger story of American theater is told. The evolvement of musical theater emerges, from the waning days of vaudeville and burlesque to the midcentury musicals anchored in increasingly strong books and believable characters, to the sung-through spectaculars that have dominated in recent years. The evolvement of serious drama emerges, from the early Eugene O'Neill productions through the imports of European dramas and the development of a body of uniquely American dramatic literature: plays of social purpose, impressionistic works, plays that gnaw at the troubled essences deep within this society.

An account of Broadway vis-à-vis the moods and issues that have engaged the nation over the past fifty years emerges as well. There is Broadway blossoming in the victorious euphoria of the postwar period, Broadway asserting itself in the midst of Cold War hysteria and the blacklist, Broadway reflecting the disruptions and unrest of the 1960s and 1970s and the post-Vietnam disillusionment, Broadway embracing the ideals of a more inclusive society, Broadway positioning itself in the forefront of the battle against AIDS, Broadway reacting to the challenges posed by alternative entertainment media and changing audiences— Broadway struggling forever, it would seem, between the pulls of art and commerce, Broadway playing back to us the mirror of our collective selves.

Finally, Broadway as myth and metaphor is evoked. Still the big time, still the pinnacle, still the dreamed-of, longed-for destination of some of the most talented among us, this collection of midtown Manhattan sidestreets continues to present America's glorious gift to the world in all its joy and energy, hilarity and heartbreak, and humanity.

All the world may be a stage, but there is only one Broadway.

All the world may be a stage, but there is only one Broadway.

WHO'S WHO IN THE CAST

BILLIE ALLEN

has appeared in *On the Town, Mamba's Daughters,* and *A Raisin in the Sun.* She is a director and writer as well as an actress, and the wife of Luther Henderson.

MICHAEL "MICKEY" ALPERT

has represented hundreds of shows in his more than four decades of experience as a Broadway press agent.

EMANUEL "MANNY" AZENBERG

has produced every Neil Simon play since 1972. Among his other production credits are *The Lion in Winter, Mark Twain Tonight!, Scapino, Ain't Misbehavin', Master Harold and the Boys, Joe Egg, Long Day's Journey into Night, A Moon for the Misbegotten, Sunday in the Park with George, Molly Sweeney,* and *Side Show.*

CLIVE BARNES

is the drama critic of the *New York Post.*

MARY ELLIN BARRETT,

the daughter of Irving Berlin, is the author of *A Daughter's Memoir.*

NORMAN BEIM

is an actor and playwright. He appeared on Broadway in the original production of *Inherit the Wind.*

MICHEL BELL,

formerly a member of the vocal group The Fifth Dimension, spent many years on the opera and concert circuit. He made his Broadway debut in the 1994 revival of *Showboat.*

PRICE BERKLEY

is the publisher of the *Theatrical Index,* the authoritative publication about Broadway, off-Broadway, regional, and West End shows.

THEODORE BIKEL,

a major personality on the stage, screen, and concert circuit, made his Broadway debut as Captain von Trapp in *The Sound of Music.* He went on to starring Broadway roles in *Zorba* and *Fiddler on the Roof.*

BETTY BUCKLEY,

star of stage, screen, and television, made her Broadway debut as Martha Jefferson in *1776.* Among her other Broadway roles are Catherine in *Pippin,* Grizabella in *Cats,* and Norma Desmond in *Sunset Boulevard.*

LEONARD "LEN" CARIOU

has starred on Broadway in such plays as *Henry V, A Little Night Music, Sweeney Todd, Teddy and Alice,* and *Applause.*

MARGE CHAMPION,

dancer, actress, and choreographer, was married to Gower Champion.

CAROL CHANNING,

Broadway legend, made her Broadway debut in *Lend an Ear.* Her best-known roles are Lorelei Lee in *Gentlemen Prefer Blondes* and Dolly Levi in *Hello, Dolly!*

TED CHAPIN

is president and executive director of the Rodgers & Hammerstein Organization.

MARTIN CHARNIN

appeared in the original *West Side Story.* He conceived and wrote the lyrics for *Annie* and directed the original Broadway production in 1977 and the twentieth-anniversary revival in 1997.

WAYNE CILENTO

originated the role of Mike Costa in *A Chorus Line* and starred in *Dancin'.* He was the choreographer of *Jerry's Girls, Tommy,* and the revival of *How to Succeed in Business without Really Trying!,* and the choreographer-director of *Dream.*

CY COLEMAN

wrote the scores for such Broadway hits as *Wildcat, Little Me, Sweet Charity, Seesaw, On the Twentieth Century, I Love My Wife, Barnum, City of Angels, The Will Rogers Follies,* and *The Life.*

ALVIN COLT

designed the costumes for *On the Town, Mary Stuart, Elizabeth the Queen,* the original production of *Guys and Dolls, Fanny, Wildcat,* and *Li'l Abner,* among others, in a career that began in 1938.

BETTY COMDEN

is half of the Comden and Green book-and-lyric-writing team. They are represented on Broadway in such shows as *On the Town; Bells Are Ringing; Two on the Aisle; Wonderful Town; Do Re Mi; Hallelujah, Baby!; Applause; On the Twentieth Century;* and *The Will Rogers Follies.*

HELEN DARION

is the editor and researcher for her husband, Joe Darion.

JOE DARION

is a librettist, playwright, and lyricist whose work runs the gamut from popular songs to the concert stage. His Broadway credits include *Man of La Mancha, Ilya Darling,* and *The Megilla.* His opera *Archy and Mehitabel* was turned into the Broadway musical *Shinbone Alley.*

MERLE DEBUSKEY

was a press agent for almost fifty years. Among the shows he worked on were the original production of *How to Succeed in Business without Really Trying!; A Chorus Line; The Diary of Anne Frank; Mary, Mary; Jesus Christ Superstar; Scapino;* and the revival of *Carousel.*

CHARLES DURNING,

stage and screen personality, has been seen on Broadway in such shows as *That Championship Season,* the revivals of *Cat on a Hot Tin Roof* and *Inherit the Wind,* and *The Gin Game.*

FRED EBB,

a lyricist, has collaborated with John Kander to write songs for film and theater. His Broadway credits include *Flora, the Red Menace; Cabaret; Zorba; Chicago; The Act; Woman of the Year; The Rink;* and *Steel Pier.*

SCOTT ELLIS

directed *A Month in the Country, She Loves Me, Steel Pier,* and the 1997 revival of *1776.*

BOB EMMETT,

an actor and writer, is the husband of Kim Hunter.

CY FEUER

teamed with Ernie Martin to produce such Broadway hits as *Where's Charley?, Guys and Dolls, Can-Can, The Boy Friend, Silk Stockings,* and *How to Succeed in Business without Really Trying!*

JULES FISHER

has designed the lighting for many Broadway productions, including *Spoon River Anthology; La Cage aux Folles; Chicago; Hair; Jesus Christ Superstar; The Will Rogers Follies; Dancin'; Pippin; Ulysses in Nightgown; Grand Hotel;* and *Bring in 'Da Noise, Bring in 'Da Funk.* He was the producer of *The Rink, Dancin',* and *Big Deal.*

JOAN FONTAINE,

the celebrated movie actress, starred on Broadway in *Tea and Sympathy.*

JANET GARI

is a composer and lyricist and the daughter of Eddie Cantor.

FREDDIE GERSHON

is an entertainment attorney; a film and theater producer; the author of *Sweetie Baby Cookie Honey;* the chairman and CEO of Music Theater International, which licenses musicals; and the cochairman and principal of SESAC, which represents music publishers and songwriters. His Broadway credits include *Evita* and *La Cage aux Folles.*

BERNARD GERSTEN

is the executive producer at Lincoln Center and was associate producer of the New York Public Theater during the Joseph Papp years.

MADELINE GILFORD,

the widow of actor Jack Gilford, is a writer and performer.

FRED GOLDEN,

dubbed by *Variety* "the dean of theatrical advertising," enjoyed a sixty-six-year Broadway career. He was a partner in the Blaine-Thompson Advertising Agency and handled all the David Merrick productions.

FRANK GOODMAN,

a former press agent, worked on over five hundred shows, including *Funny Girl, Gypsy,* and *The Sound of Music.*

MORTON GOTTLIEB

produced such Broadway hits as *Sail Away, Arms and the Man, Enter Laughing, Tribute, Sleuth, Edward My Son, Same Time Next Year, The Promise,* and *The Killing of Sister George.*

DOLORES GRAY

has appeared in many movies and Broadway shows such as *The Seven Lively Arts, Two on the Aisle, Carnival in Flanders,* and *Destry Rides Again.*

ADOLPH GREEN

is half of the Comden and Green book-and-lyric-writing team. They are represented on Broadway in such shows as *On the Town; Bells Are Ringing; Two on the Aisle; Wonderful Town; Do Re Mi; Hallelujah, Baby!; Applause; On the Twentieth Century;* and *The Will Rogers Follies.*

JOEL GREY

created the role of the emcee in the original Broadway production and revival of *Cabaret.* He also starred in *George M., Come Blow Your Horn, Stop the World—I Want to Get Off,* and the 1996 revival of *Chicago.*

JOHN GRIESEMER,

an actor on stage and screen, appeared in the 1996 revival of *Inherit the Wind.*

JAMES HAMMERSTEIN

has been a stage manager, director, producer, and president of the Society of Stage Directors and Choreographers. The son of Oscar Hammerstein II and a director of the Rodgers & Hammerstein Organization, he was the director of *State Fair.*

KITTY CARLISLE HART,

actress, opera singer, and television personality, is the widow of Moss Hart. The former chair of the New York State Council on the Arts, she has appeared on Broadway in *Champagne Sec, Three Waltzes,* and *Walk with Music.*

LUTHER HENDERSON

has composed, arranged, orchestrated, or performed the musical direction for more than fifty Broadway shows, including *Ain't Misbehavin'; Hallelujah, Baby!; Flower Drum Song; Funny Girl; Purlie; No, No, Nanette;* and *Jelly's Last Jam.*

JERRY HERMAN

is the composer-lyricist of *Milk and Honey; Hello, Dolly!; Mame; Dear World; Mack and Mabel; The Grand Tour;* and *La Cage aux Folles. Jerry's Girls,* a revue based on his songs, was produced in 1981.

SHIRLEY HERZ

has been a Broadway press agent for more than forty years.

PAM KOSLOW HINES

produced *Jelly's Last Jam.*

FOSTER HIRSCH,

film and theater historian, is the author of *Harold Prince and the American Musical.*

AL HIRSCHFELD,

the famed caricaturist, has been plying his trade since the 1920s.

HAL HOLBROOK

first performed his one-man show *Mark Twain Tonight!* in 1955. He has appeared on Broadway in such shows as *Marco Millions, After the Fall,* and *I Never Sang for My Father.*

GEOFFREY HOLDER,

a performing and visual artist, played in *House of Flowers* and *Waiting for Godot.* He directed and designed the costumes for *The Wiz.*

CELESTE HOLM,

star of stage and screen, was the original Ado Annie in *Oklahoma!* She appeared in many other Broadway productions, including *The Time of Your Life, Invitation to a March, The King and I,* and *Bloomer Girl.*

KIM HUNTER

played Stella in the original Broadway production and film version of *A Streetcar Named Desire.* She also performed on Broadway in such plays as *The Children's Hour, Darkness at Noon, The Tender Trap, Write Me a Murder, The Women, Weekend,* and the 1996 production of *An Ideal Husband.*

MARTY JACOBS

is the archivist for the New York Theater Collection of the Museum of the City of New York.

JOHN KANDER,

a composer, has collaborated with Fred Ebb to write songs for film and theater. His Broadway credits include *Flora, the Red Menace; Cabaret; Zorba; Chicago; The Act; Woman of the Year; The Rink;* and *Steel Pier.*

JUDY KAYE,

singer and actress, appeared in *Grease* and starred on Broadway in *On the Twentieth Century* and *Phantom of the Opera.*

RICHARD KILEY

renowned for his portrayal of Miguel de Cervantes/Don Quixote in *Man of La Mancha,* also appeared on Broadway in *Misalliance, Kismet, I Had a Ball, Redhead, Absurd Person Singular,* and *No Strings.*

HOWARD KISSEL

is the drama critic for the *New York Daily News* and the author of *David Merrick: The Abominable Showman.*

V. MAX KLIMAVICIUS

is the president of Sardi's.

FLORENCE KLOTZ

has designed the costumes for such Broadway shows as *Side by Side by Sondheim, On the Twentieth Century, Follies, The Little Foxes, A Little Night Music, Pacific Overtures, Jerry's Girls, Kiss of the Spider Woman, City of Angels,* and the 1994 revival of *Showboat.*

MARVIN KRAUSS

is a producer whose credits include the revival of *Death of a Salesman, The Poison Tree, Merlin,* and *La Cage aux Folles.* He has been general manager for such shows as *Woman of the Year, Dancin', Butterflies Are Free, Beatlemania, Dreamgirls,* and *The Life.*

JOHN LAHR

is the drama critic of the *New Yorker* and the son of comedian Bert Lahr.

PHILIP LANGNER

is the head of the Theater Guild, the prolific theatrical producing company founded by his parents.

LOUISE LASSER,

familiar to television audiences for her portrayal of Mary Hartman, appeared on Broadway in *I Can Get It for You Wholesale* and *Henry, Sweet Henry.*

LINDA LAVIN

has starred in *The Last of the Red Hot Lovers, Little Murderers, Broadway Bound,* and the 1997 revival of *The Diary of Anne Frank.*

RONNIE LEE

appeared in the original productions of *The King and I, Peter Pan,* and *West Side Story.* He is a producer and the founder-president of Group Sales Box Office, a theater-group tickets agency.

MITCH LEIGH

wrote the music to *Man of La Mancha* and is the founder of Music Makers, Inc., which creates radio and television commercial music.

PAUL LIBIN,

longtime producer for Circle in the Square, is currently producing director for Jujamcyn Theatres.

CHARLES LOWE

was formerly the manager of Carol Channing.

RICHARD MALTBY, JR.

cowrote the lyrics for *Miss Saigon,* directed and conceived *Ain't Misbehavin',* directed *Song and Dance,* and wrote the lyrics for *Big.*

ANDREA MCARDLE,

the original Annie, has also appeared in *Les Mis, Starlight Express,* and *State Fair.*

DONNA MCKECHNIE

is best known for her role as Cassie in the original *A Chorus Line.* Her other Broadway appearances include roles in *How to Succeed in Business without Really Trying!; Company; On the Town; Promises, Promises;* and *State Fair.*

WARD MOREHOUSE III

is an author and the Broadway columnist for the *New York Post.*

PATRICIA NEAL,

film and stage actress, appeared on Broadway in such works as *Another Part of the Forest, The Children's Hour,* and *The Miracle Worker.*

BARRY NELSON

was in such Broadway plays as *Light Up the Sky; The Moon Is Blue; The Rat Race; The Fig Leaves Are Falling; Cactus Flower; Mary, Mary; Everything in the Garden; Seascape;* and *The Act.* He has also acted on television and directed *The Only Game in Town.*

JOHN RAITT,

Broadway star and recording and concert artist, was the original Billy Bigelow in *Carousel.* He starred on Broadway in *Magdalena, Three Wishes for Jamie, Carnival in Flanders, Pajama Game,* and *A Musical Jubilee.*

LEE ROY REAMS

has appeared in *Sweet Charity, Lorelei, 42nd Street, Applause,* and *Beauty and the Beast.* He played Will Parker in the Lincoln Center revival of *Oklahoma!* and directed the 1996 Broadway revival and international tour of *Hello, Dolly!*

MARTIN RICHARDS,

producer for both stage and screen, formed the Producers Circle Company with his late wife, Mary Lea Johnson. His Broadway productions include *Chicago, On the Twentieth Century, Sweeney Todd, Crimes of the Heart, Foxfire, La Cage aux Folles, Grand Hotel, The Will Rogers Follies,* and *The Life.*

FLORA ROBERTS

is a theatrical agent whose clients include Stephen Sondheim and Maury Yeston. She has been on the Broadway scene since the late 1940s.

MARY RODGERS,

the daughter of Richard Rodgers, is a composer and author who wrote the music to *Once Upon a Mattress.* She is a director of the Rodgers & Hammerstein Organization and chair of the board of the Juilliard School.

HARVEY SABINSON

is a former Broadway press agent who worked on nearly 250 shows over a fifty-year career. He was also the executive director of the League of American Theaters and Producers.

VINCENT SARDI, JR.

is the owner of the restaurant Sardi's, founded by his parents.

IRVING SCHNEIDER

was a production manager and producer, and the associate of Irene Selznick.

ANNE KAUFMAN SCHNEIDER

is a theatrical consultant and the daughter of playwright Irving Kaufman.

SUSAN L. SCHULMAN

is a press agent whose credits include *Applause, Death of a Salesman, Scapino, Dancin', Death and the Maiden, State Fair,* and *Dream.*

ARTHUR SEELEN

is co-owner of the Drama Book Shop.

ROZANNE SEELEN

is the wife of Arthur Seelen and co-owner of the Drama Book Shop.

CAROLE SHELLEY

played the role of Gwendolyn Pigeon in the play, movie, and television series versions of *The Odd Couple.* On Broadway she appeared in *The Miser, Stepping Out, Noises Off, The Elephant Man, Hay Fever, Absurd Person Singular, London Suite,* and the revival of *Showboat.*

DAVID SHIRE

has composed music for both film and theater, including the Broadway show *Big.*

ROY SOMLYO

is president of the American Theater Wing. He was managing producer of the Tony Awards, and among his producing theatrical credits is *A Day in Hollywood, a Night in the Ukraine.*

MAUREEN STAPLETON,

theatrical and movie star, made her Broadway debut in *The Playboy of the Western World* in 1946. She starred in such Broadway productions as *The Rose Tattoo, Orpheus Descending, Cold Wind and the Warm, Toys in the Attic, Plaza Suite,* and *The Gingerbread Lady.*

ELAINE STEINBECK

is a former stage manager and the widow of John Steinbeck.

ERIC STERN

is a musical director whose credits include *The Will Rogers Follies, Legs Diamond, Rags, Sunday in the Park with George,* and the revivals of *The Most Happy Fella, Carousel, Gypsy, Showboat,* and *The King and I.*

PETER STONE

is president of the Dramatists Guild. He has written the books for *Kean, Skyscraper, 1776, Two by Two, Woman of the Year, The Will Rogers Follies, My One and Only, Sugar,* and *Titanic.*

ELAINE STRITCH,

renowned for her "Ladies Who Lunch" number in *Company,* also appeared on Broadway in *Sail Away, Bus Stop, Who's Afraid of Virginia Woolf?, Pal Joey, On Your Toes,* the 1994 revival of *Showboat,* and the 1996 revival of *A Delicate Balance.*

SUSAN STROMAN

choreographed the dances for *Crazy for You, Showboat, Big,* and *Steel Pier.*

CHARLES STROUSE

wrote the scores for *Bye Bye Birdie, Golden Boy, Annie, Rags,* and *Applause.*

JANE SUMMERHAYS

has appeared on Broadway in such shows as *Me and My Girl, Lend Me a Tenor,* and *A Chorus Line.*

JOSEPH TRAINA

is the house manager of the Belasco Theater.

LESLIE UGGAMS

began her show business career when she was five years old and is a star of stage and television. Her Broadway credits include *Camelot; Hallelujah, Baby!; Anything Goes;* and *Jerry's Girls.*

GWEN VERDON

is renowned for her creation of Lola in the original production of *Damn Yankees.* She has also starred on Broadway in *Can-Can, New Girl in Town, Redhead, Sweet Charity,* and *Chicago.*

SHIRLEY VERRETT

dramatic/mezzo-soprano, has performed at the Metropolitan Opera, the San Francisco Opera, La Scala, and Covent Garden. She made her Broadway debut as Nettie Fowler in the 1994 revival of *Carousel*.

TONY WALTON

designed the costumes and sets for *Golden Boy* and both the original 1962 and the 1996 revival productions of *A Funny Thing Happened on the Way to the Forum*. He was the set designer for *Pippin*, and the original productions of *Chicago, The Act, Sophisticated Ladies,* and *Steel Pier.*

DOUGLAS WATT

is the former drama critic for the *New York Daily News*.

ROBERT WHITEHEAD

has more than fifty years of production experience on the Broadway stage, starting with *Medea* (starring Judith Anderson) and including *The Member of the Wedding; The Waltz of the Toreadors; The Visit; A Man for All Seasons; A Touch of the Poet; Bus Stop; The Prime of Miss Jean Brodie;* eight plays by Arthur Miller, including the 1984 revival of *Death of a Salesman;* and *Master Class,* starring his wife, Zoe Caldwell, whom he also directed in a revival of *Medea*.

GEORGE C. WOLFE,

playwright, producer, director, and author, is currently the producer of the New York Shakespeare Festival/Joseph Papp Public Theater. His recent Broadway productions include *Angels in America* and *Bring in 'Da Noise, Bring in 'Da Funk*.

MAURY YESTON

is a composer and lyricist who straddles the popular and classical worlds and who directed undergraduate studies in music at Yale. He wrote the music and lyrics to such Broadway shows as *Nine, Grand Hotel,* and *Titanic*.

JERRY ZAKS

is director-in-residence of Jujamcyn Theatres. He has directed *House of Blue Leaves, Six Degrees of Separation, Smokey Joe's Café,* and the revivals of *Anything Goes, Guys and Dolls,* and *A Funny Thing Happened on the Way to the Forum*. He has performed on Broadway in *Grease, Tintypes,* and *Fiddler on the Roof.*

1 | BROADWAY CALLING

CAROL CHANNING: The first time I ever set foot onstage was in grammar school in San Francisco. The student body sat in the audience and made nominations for next year's student body officers, and you would get up on the stage and tell your fellow students why they should vote for you. When I was in the fourth grade, I was nominated for secretary. I walked up on the stage. My knees were shaking. Naturally, I didn't know what to say, so I "did" the principal of the school, Miss Barrard. In her voice I said, "Go to the polls and vote for Carol." Everyone laughed. They recognized her. Then I did the chemistry teacher, who blew up the chemistry class on an average of once a term. They all laughed. They knew it was Mr. Schwartz. Miss Barrard laughed, too, and so did Mr. Schwartz.

It wasn't cruel. It came from adoration. I was so thrilled with them that I had to become them. I was an only child, and like other only children, I would sit in my room and become other people because I had nobody to talk to. Now, suddenly, I was no longer an only child. What I laughed at, all my fellow students laughed at. What I thought was entertaining, they thought was entertaining. "We're all alike," I said to myself. This was a grand revelation. I ran off the stage, and behind the cloakroom, I started to cry, and I said, "Oh god, I'll do anything to get back on that stage again."

I was elected secretary, and I got to get up on that stage and read the minutes I wrote. I lived for my readings on Fridays. We couldn't fit the entire student body into the auditorium, so I got to do three shows. The first time it wasn't so good. The second time it was better. When they didn't get a joke, I realized I had to build the lines. By the third show I was swinging. That's when I learned to like long runs.

Nobody cared if the minutes were accurate, as long as they were entertaining. So I read them like Marjorie Gould, the president of the

OPPOSITE PAGE

Carol Channing: From the first time she set foot on a stage, she knew she wanted to be a star.

student body and the cutest girl in the whole school. Years later, a lot of Marjorie would go into Lorelei. I had a tough audience, right from the beginning.

Children are honest. They don't care if they are rude. They would throw erasers and chalk and make paper airplanes. They would yell, "Hey, Carol, come off it. Speak up!"

After my first time on the stage, I told my father how much I loved it. And he said, "You know, there's an adage: 'Be careful what you set your heart upon, for you shall surely get it.'"

And I said, "You mean I can get it? I can lay my life down right now to being on the stage and communicating with people, and they will come to see me when I go out there? I will crawl across the desert without water. I will go without sleep. I will suffer. I will do anything. I just want to be a great star. "

And my father told me, "Don't tell anyone, because there are two ways to go. You can talk about it or you can do it." So I never told a living soul except my father—but from the fourth grade on, I had the blessing of the childhood of someone who secretly wanted to go into the theater. I knew the safest place in the world for me would be the center of the stage.

At Bennington I was a dance and drama major. But then I could not get started. I covered every single facet of theater in San Francisco and Los Angeles. Nobody would have me. They kept saying, "Who do you want to be, Eve Arden?" because I was tall. I went home to my parents with my tail between my legs.

Finally I ran into Marge Champion. She said, "Gower is casting, and he has to see you." They had been married only three weeks, and she was the most adorable thing you ever saw. Gower gave me about a minute and a quarter. I started out doing Ethel Waters. Marge said, "Now do Gertrude Lawrence," because she'd seen Gower look at his watch, "and now do Uta Hagen, and now do Lynn Fontanne." I did everybody who was on Broadway at the time, everybody that we all adored.

At the end of it, Gower said, "What else have you got?"

And I said, "I've done twelve numbers. That's all I've got. I haven't got any more."

So he said, "Go back and start again." I did it all again.

As soon as I got home there was a ring on the phone: "Report for rehearsal tomorrow morning."

I did my twelve different characters in this little revue, *Lend an Ear,* in the little Los Palmos Theater in L.A. I was one of twenty unknowns. And then it became a cult among the movie stars, so they moved us to Broadway, where it became a big hit. We were in a three-hundred-seat theater, but they took out two seats so Equity would have no jurisdiction over us and they could pay us $34.50 a week, which was under the Equity minimum, and make us do a matinee each day. But I was so happy. I would think, thank god I have a matinee tomorrow and won't have to wait twenty-four hours to correct what I did wrong in the last show.

I didn't dream about being on Broadway, I dreamed of the characters I was doing. What impressed me was that I had this opportunity to do twelve different characters that I thought were hysterically funny. One of them was the Gladiola Girl. She was a satire on all pretty girls. Anita Loos spotted me. Though I was over six feet tall in heels and had muddy brown eyes, and the character in *Gentlemen Prefer Blondes* was five feet two, eyes of blue, Anita said, "There's my Lorelei." She brought Jule Styne, and he went right home and wrote my "Battle Hymn of the Republic": "Diamonds Are a Girl's Best Friend."

I was a tremendous risk. Those on the business end wanted someone with a name. Anita couldn't get all the money together for this enormous musical, so she called in the Lunts. They thought it would be demeaning for me to audition for them, so they sat down with me and asked me questions: "What was Lorelei's mother like?" That isn't in the book but Miss Fontanne wanted to know if I'd thought about it. "And what did Lorelei do?" Well, she was a barefoot bumpkin from the foot of the Ozarks who became one of the richest women in the world.

They talked to me for about three-quarters of an hour, and then they came out and told Anita, "We will put . . . (oh, it was a great deal of money) into your show." Once the Lunts invested, everybody trusted it. Leland Hayward put money in. Rodgers and Hammerstein, Josh Logan put money in.

The Lunts told Anita, "We will give you our director John C. Wilson." He kept *Gentlemen Prefer Blondes* from being the story of a funny little whore and made it the most elegant comedy. In the book Lorelei misspells everything. We had to somehow show the misspelling orally. Like "All alone out on the big oshean" or "Bosting, Massachusetts."

After performing in *Lend an Ear,* I'd work all night long with Jule

I didn't dream about being on Broadway, I dreamed of the characters I was doing.

Styne and Leo Robin, who did the lyrics for *Gentlemen Prefer Blondes*. Jule had an apartment with a garden, and along about three in the morning, people would throw beer bottles and other things down and scream at us to shut up. So we would be very quiet. Then Jule would ask if I could hit an A at the end of "Diamonds." He'd play the note and I'd sing out "B-E-S-T F-R-I-E-N-D," and all the neighbors would yell and holler. We made so much noise, we got evicted and wound up sitting on the sidewalk.

We'd work all through the night, and the next day I'd have a matinee. But it didn't matter. I was with these two great men who were like Rodin, and I was their statue. They wrote "I'm Just a Little Girl from Little Rock" by trying it out on me. It was a privilege.

The eleven o'clock number is where the people carrying the plot stand there and bare their souls. "Diamonds Are a Girl's Best Friend" is Lorelei's eleven o'clock number. Miles White, the costume designer, realized that the more I looked like the Pope standing on the balcony outside the Vatican with the wand and everything, the funnier the song got. The girl was an idiot about everything except the one thing that mattered in those days, and that was that diamonds *were* a girl's best friend.

We opened December 8, 1949. I wore a diamond dress and the tiara that Napoleon gave Josephine. Anita had gotten it from Van Cleef & Arpels. Everyone came to see the tiara. It stopped traffic all the way up through Central Park through 110th Street. The Lunts were there in their grandest clothes. Thornton Wilder was there, like a little cherub, he was so happy.

Opening night you're either walking over a cliff into oblivion and death or you will sustain and keep walking. *Gentlemen Prefer Blondes* ran a very long time. Then I took over Rosalind Russell's role in *Wonderful Town*. I sustained and have kept on walking.

● ● ● ● ●

JERRY HERMAN: When I took piano lessons I would invent instant arrangements and chords for the pieces I was learning. I could transpose, play by ear in any key. Finally my teacher told my mother, "I don't know what to do with him," and suggested my ability just be allowed to marinate.

I was an only child growing up in Jersey City, New Jersey. My parents were teachers, people of modest means, but they adored Broadway. My father played the saxophone, my mother the accordion, and after dinner

Opening night
you're either
walking over a cliff
into oblivion
and death or you
will sustain and
keep walking.

we'd play show music together. Every Thursday or Friday night, we would go to see a show. It cost $4.40, $6.50 for the good seats. I saw every great American musical of the 1940s and 1950s.

When I was fifteen, I saw *Annie Get Your Gun* and thought what a wonderful gift Irving Berlin had given to a total stranger. I came home and played at least six of the songs from the show, even though I had never heard them before. My mother was kind of slack jawed. We sang "They Say that Falling in Love Is Wonderful" together. We knew at least the first four phrases because the song was reprised so much.

When I was about eighteen and had just started to go to Parsons School of Design, my mother made me bring a bunch of my songs to Frank Loesser. A friend of hers knew someone who knew him. I was very shy, scared to death. He said, "I want you to play everything you've ever written."

The star and the songwriter, *Dolly's* dynamic duo: Carol Channing and Jerry Herman.

When I finished, he sat me down like a Dutch uncle. "I'm not trying to tell you this is an easy business. Some people make it, and some people don't. But you can tell your parents I think you have what it takes." Then he drew a picture of a train with a caboose. "This is what makes a good song," he said. "The locomotive has to start it. The caboose has to finish it off. Those are the bookends. Then you fill in different colors for the cars in the middle." It was such a graphic, beautiful lesson about how to write a song. It stayed with me forever.

I came home filled with all this excitement. My mother was ecstatic. My father was absolutely horrified, thinking I would starve somewhere in an attic. My mother said, "Let the kid try. He's young enough to make a mistake."

I did a series of off-Broadway musicals. One of them was a revue called *Parade*. The producer came over and said, "I'm going to be doing a musical set in Israel. Would you be interested in writing the score?"

Israel was only thirteen years old at the time and really didn't have a culture of its own. I had to find a sound that Americans would accept as Israeli. Arabic wailing, American rock and roll—almost anything could qualify as an Israeli sound. So I took a lesson from Richard Rodgers, who had created a Siamese sound. *The King and I* is as American as you can get, but it's flavored by the clever use of certain chords.

My mother taught Hebrew songs at our community center and was the president of our local Hadassah. I would hear "Hatikvah" being hummed around the house. Even though that wasn't the style I had been writing in for my revues, I did not have to reach very far to find those minor chords and hora rhythms.

Watching rehearsals of *Milk and Honey* in a theater I had sat in as a child was like a fairy tale. It was the first time I heard my works orchestrated, the first time I ever worked with great stars, like the opera singers Mimi Benzel and Robert Weede, and the star of the Yiddish theater Molly Picon, who was making her Broadway debut. But it was very hard to stand in the back of the Martin Beck Theater and realize that Ruth, my mother, was not there. She had died tragically at age forty-four. My father did, however, live to an old age and enjoy my successes.

Milk and Honey opened to unanimous approval and ran for nearly two years. I was still in my twenties. "This is it," I said to myself. "This happens just once." I thought this was something that would never come again.

But David Merrick had seen *Milk and Honey*. "I don't know if you're

American enough, but I would like to consider you to write the score for a musical version of *The Matchmaker,*" he said.

I had been nominated for a Tony, I had a hit show, but I was still the new kid on the block. I had to prove to Mr. Merrick that I was the right person, that I was truly American. I wrote four songs in three days: "Put on Your Sunday Clothes," "Dancing," the whole opening number, and a fourth song for Mrs. Malloy that I replaced with "Ribbons Down My Back" a few weeks later.

Merrick petrified everybody around him. He thought it was how he could get the best work out of his people. That was his technique, and I went along with it because I wanted the job. I played my songs, which, aside from the one replacement, went into that musical version of *The Matchmaker: Hello, Dolly!,* word for word, as I played them for Mr. Merrick that day.

Two years after *Dolly!* opened, and while it was still packing them in, *Mame* opened at the Winter Garden. It is my favorite show of all. With *Dolly!,* I had to deal with Merrick, who was difficult, and there was a lot of changing and fixing. But *Mame* was one of those unbelievable experiences where nothing had to be changed or added.

I had gone from *Milk and Honey* to *Hello, Dolly!* to *Mame* all in one decade. If nothing else ever happens to me in this business, I thought, it'll be perfectly all right. It was the 1960s, a period of turmoil when, I believe, many people tended to turn to escapism. I was part of that escapism. It was right for me. I have always wanted to entertain.

There was this consciousness rising at the top of my head that said, That's what you're going to be doing for the rest of your life.

• • • • •

BETTY BUCKLEY: When I was eleven, I saw *Pajama Game* in a summer-stock version in Fort Worth, Texas. The choreographer had danced in the Broadway production, and he used the original Bob Fosse choreography. For me it was an epiphany. There was this consciousness rising at the top of my head that said, That's what you're going to be doing for the rest of your life.

Then, about two years later, I was in my bedroom one afternoon listening to the radio and looking out the window at the west Texas plain— a wide field and a windmill—when suddenly I had this awareness that I would become a Broadway leading lady. I felt what the sound of my voice would be like when I grew up; I sensed the qualities I would have as a storyteller in musical theater. It was a clean, clear awareness. That's it, I thought. I'm going to New York City. I'm going to do this.

I made a commitment to that vision, and then I forgot about it. For the next twenty-two years I went about my business of learning and working. I had been studying since I was a little child, performing professionally since I was fifteen. My father was very opposed to my being in show business. But my mother had been a singer and dancer, and she understood. She'd sneak me out of the house to attend classes.

At Texas Christian University I was a journalism major, but I did a lot of theater. During my junior year I was a guest entertainer with the Miss America Pageant. An agent spotted me and arranged for me to audition for the International Famous Agency, which is now ICM.

They asked me what I wanted to do, and I said I had to finish college. After graduation I worked at a Fort Worth newspaper, but they kept calling. Finally they had me attend an industrial show for B. F. Goodrich in Dallas, starring Flip Wilson. They called me up onstage to sing with the band, improvisationally, spontaneously. The buyer was in the audience, and he said, "Put her in the show." So for four different weekends, in four different cities, they kept the same routine. I would sit in the audience, and they'd call me up to sing like I was some local girl.

The agent told me he could get me an industrial show for Gimbel's department store in New York for six weeks, and if I didn't like it, I could go home. So I came to New York. As soon as I got into the Barbizon Hotel, I called him. "We have an audition in fifteen minutes," he said. I was the last girl on the last day to audition for the role of Martha Jefferson in *1776*.

"Who are you?" they asked.

"I'm Betty Lynn Buckley from Fort Worth, Texas."

They kept me for two hours and had me sing this song in all these different keys. I got the part.

After, I played the lead in the London company of *Promises, Promises* for a year, returned to *1776,* and then went out to California, where I got the role of the stepmother in the TV series *Eight Is Enough.* It was a good job, and I was very grateful to have it. But television is really about time and money. We'd shoot twenty-nine one-hour movies a year. It was difficult to grow in that kind of a situation. I kept my cheap little apartment on the Upper West Side, and every six weeks I'd fly back to New York to study with my voice teacher. Though I was always shopping for a house in

Hollywood, I never bought one. I was terrified that once I owned a house, I would be owned by the system, and I'd have to keep working out there to pay for the lifestyle.

There was this young producer on *Eight Is Enough*. He confronted me one day in the Burbank parking lot and said, "You know what your problem is? You've got delusions of grandeur."

"What do you mean?"

"Well, you think you're going to be in the Broadway theater. You'll be lucky if you play American mothers for the rest of your life."

And I thought, Oh no, I won't. Watch me.

After a while I thought to myself, If I have to be in this contract, let me make the money now, and afterward I'll develop my own stuff if it's not too late. It seemed like I'd be there forever. I was in my early thirties, and you know when you're in your early thirties, you think your life is over.

But two weeks after I serenely accepted what I thought was my fate, the show got canceled. And I felt I had been granted a reprieve.

Early in 1982 my agent called: "There's this role—Grizabella, the glamour cat. Get the London album of *Cats,* listen to it." I heard it, and I knew it was my part. On rare occasions, one knows.

I was one of the first to audition. Trevor Nunn thought I was too healthy looking; they wanted a small, wraithlike person. That was in January. The auditions continued for six months.

Toward the end of June, my agent called: "They want to see you back."

"I knew it."

"Go get it," she said.

"I will."

Trevor had me do the number three times. My insides were out. Finally I said, "Trevor, can I talk to you?"

And he said, "Sure."

I said, "You know you've auditioned everybody, the entire American talent pool. There are a few women who could do this role as well as I can, but nobody can do it better. And it's my turn."

He looked at me, really perplexed.

"What do you want?" I asked. "Whatever it is, I can do it. I'm a really good actress. Give me this part. Truly, it's my turn."

He looked at me like, *I don't know what to say.*

And I thought, Uh-oh, maybe I messed up.

Whatever it is, I can do it. I'm a really good actress. Give me this part. Truly, it's my turn.

Then the rehearsal pianist, this woman who had played many, many auditions through the years, gave me the thumbs-up. And as I was walking off, the stage manager said, "All right! Way to go!"

I called my agent from the street. "Are you nuts?" she said. "You probably blew it. I can't believe you said that to an English director. They're different from American directors. When are you going to learn to keep your mouth shut?"

I went to my favorite restaurant, bemoaning my big mouth and feeling really bad about it. Suddenly I was called to the phone. It was my agent: "Are you sitting down?"

I sang the number one song, "Memory," in *Cats* and won the Tony. That same year I played Dixie Scott in the movie *Tender Mercies* and sang "Over You," which was nominated for an Oscar.

I was right. The women at my level, people like Patti LuPone and Bernadette Peters, all had had their shot, their signature moment. Mine was overdue. After all those years of paying dues and learning and dedication, it was my turn.

Eight Is Enough had built my muscles, helped make me so strong, so fierce in my commitment. Without the training of *Eight Is Enough* and without studying voice for thirteen years, I wouldn't have had the strength to undertake the pressure presented by *Cats*.

One day early in the run, as I was listening to the final version of the recording of "Memory," the vision I'd had as a thirteen-year-old came back to me with stunning clarity. I recalled that moment when I looked out onto the west Texas plain and understood what my destiny would be. I was now thirty-five years old; it had taken me twenty-two years to develop into the artist I had known I would become. It was a powerful moment. The awareness I had felt so long ago remanifested itself as if to say, It took you all this time, but here you are.

• • • • •

MANNY AZENBERG: I did not have any great ambition. I think that was the key. My uncle, Wolf Barzel, was an actor—Barzel in Hebrew means the same as Azenberg. When we were kids, my sister and I would go see him on both the English and the Yiddish stages.

I had two pivotal moments. One was seeing John Garfield in *Skipper*

Next to God. To us kids, he was like Brando. Our uncle took us backstage. The dressing room had the Star of David on the door. Garfield's real name was Julie Garfinkel; he was one of our own. The other was seeing *Death of a Salesman* with Lee J. Cobb. I had the inconclusive thought that you could make a living doing this.

I acted in college. Everyone did. I came out of the army when I was close to twenty-five and got a job as the assistant to the company manager of *Legend of Lizzie.* It closed after two performances, but it was exciting.

My wife became pregnant. I delivered music crates, was company manager for the Rye Music Circus, did summer stock, which paid $75 a week, and won $20 or $25 a week in a poker game. I was very careful. Then the baby was born, and I worked off Broadway in *Lend an Ear* and another off-Broadway play that closed in about an hour. I had a stint working for Roy Somlyo and that netted me $121 a week. When I got the job, I came into the apartment and threw the money up in the air. I still wasn't making the equivalent of what I had made in the army.

Then I moved on to be company manager for David Merrick. He was as tough as his reputation. But you learned everything. I must have done sixteen or seventeen shows in three years. I didn't come up off the floor. Robert Redford in *Sunday in New York,* Barbra Streisand in *I Can Get It for You Wholesale,* Tallulah Bankhead in *The Milk Train Doesn't Stop Here Any More,* Albert Finney in *Luther* . . . I was on the road for a year with shows like *Oliver, Stop the World.*

I was thirty-one. I never thought of what a producer did. But when Gene Wolsk decided to do *The Lion in Winter,* I raised a lot of money for him. He graciously said, "You should be a partner." It took us four months to get a theater; they were all occupied. Finally we got the Ambassador on Forty-ninth Street and opened, starring Robert Preston and Rosemary Harris. We did *Mark Twain Tonight!,* starring Hal Holbrook, at the same time. We didn't make much money, but it was auspicious.

I had become friends with Robert Redford when we worked together in *Sunday in New York.* I was making $220 as company manager; he got paid $300. We both had young children and played softball together.

A few years later Redford was in Neil Simon's *Barefoot in the Park.* I became a ringer on the show's softball team. Neil played second base, Redford played first base, and I played shortstop. It wasn't about anyone's career; it was about could you pick up a ground ball. But certainly a lot of seeds got planted. Neil and I became, if not friends, acquaintances. He

I had the inconclusive thought that you could make a living doing this.

invited us to his opening nights. They were Broadway opening nights, not a *schmatte* night. All these stars were killing each other to go in. We'd sit in a corner and say, "Hey, look who's there."

Maybe eight years after the softball games, I came over to Neil's house on East Sixty-second Street. He had just gotten the word that his wife, Joan, had cancer. I walked in the door, and he said, "How would you like to produce my play?"

Clowning, I said, "Ah . . . let me think about it."

He didn't smile at all. He handed me a script and said, "Here, read this and let me know."

I walked home, all the way from East Sixty-second Street to West Ninety-second Street, and I don't know if I touched the ground. Neil Simon had just asked me, the schlepper from the Bronx, to produce *The Sunshine Boys.*

Betty Comden and Adolph Green rehearsing a song for *On the Town,* their first Broadway show, with Leonard Bernstein at the piano and Jerome Robbins looking on (1944).

· · · · ·

BETTY COMDEN: How long have we been together. Must we say? It's more than fifty years. The first Broadway show I saw was *Rosemarie.* I was about nine years old. Adolph saw things like *Showboat,* things I never saw.

ADOLPH GREEN: I did see the original *Showboat* in its second year, 1928.

BETTY COMDEN: Adolph and I first met at NYU.

ADOLPH GREEN: I was wandering around fretfully, trying to get located someplace. Betty seemed very un-show-business. Yet it all jelled somehow.

BETTY COMDEN: We were part of a Greenwich Village nightclub act, the Revuers, which was finally reduced to an act of two. We knew we'd get on Broadway somehow.

ADOLPH GREEN: I had met Leonard Bernstein up at a summer camp where he was a counselor. He came down to the Village to see us perform. Betty was knocked out by him.

BETTY COMDEN: I saw this great-looking guy in the audience. After we finished performing, he went to the piano and played from midnight until six in the morning. We became deep friends and stayed that way until the end of his life.

In 1944 Lenny did *Fancy Free,* a twenty-two-minute ballet with Jerry Robbins. We hung around the rehearsals.

ADOLPH GREEN: And what's more, Lenny's score was dedicated to me.

BETTY COMDEN: The idea came up that Lenny and Jerry should do a whole show based on *Fancy Free* together. Lenny said he knew just the people to write the book and the lyrics. The producers came to see us at the Blue Angel, and we got the job.

ADOLPH GREEN: At that time I was almost starving and Betty was not too well off. We owe a big debt to Leonard, indeed.

BETTY COMDEN: *On the Town* was about three sailors on a one-day leave in New York City.

ADOLPH GREEN: It was either a great idea or a terrible idea, depending on how it worked out.

BETTY COMDEN: It did work out. It was an immediate hit. It opened at the end of 1944 and ran a year and a half.

We wrote in two very good parts for ourselves: Adolph played one of the sailors, and I played a lady anthropologist, Claire de Loon.

Instead of behaving like professionals and going in the stage door, we'd always go in through the lobby so we could see the snake line of people buying tickets. Before, we were nightclub performers, but now we were Broadway writers. We knew our lives would change. All the successes had been special in different ways, but this first one was a miracle. It changed our lives forever.

• • • • •

AL HIRSCHFELD: Sometime around 1926, I went to see a play with Bill Pan, a press agent, and, without thinking, made a sketch of the star on my program. Bill noticed it and thought it was pretty good. "Let me have it," he said. "I'll try to get it published."

My interest was fine arts; I was a painter and sculptor. But to my surprise, this little sketch was accepted by the *Herald Tribune,* and they asked for more. I began doing some sketches for the *World.* And then one day, I got a telegram from the *New York Times* asking for one.

About nineteen years later I was doing a sketch for a play that had a circus background. My daughter Nina had just been born, and I inserted a little poster of "Nina the Wonder Child," a little drawing of a child reading a book. The following week I put just her name in. This went on for two or three weeks, until I thought the joke had worn pretty thin and left it out.

Then mail started coming in from all over the country. Unbeknownst to me, people had discovered this thing. I found it easier to put her back in than to answer all this mail.

It's been more than fifty years, and I'm still doing the Nina thing.

I never—oh no, absolutely never—thought when I did that first drawing that it would reach this point. I'm still unaware of it, whatever the hell that is. You never see yourself as yourself. It's all accident.

• • • • •

RICHARD KILEY: Growing up in Chicago, the idea of being in the theater did not dawn on me until I was in high school and one day, to my horror, I was drafted into playing the Mikado in *The Mikado.* In those days they had footlights, and I discovered that I could deliver a line and, out of the great faceless darkness, get a laugh back in exchange. From that moment, I was hooked.

In those days they had footlights, and I discovered that I could deliver a line and, out of the great faceless darkness, get a laugh back in exchange. From that moment, I was hooked.

Some years later, after a year at Loyola College, a stint in the navy, and some work on radio, I took the train from Chicago to New York with six hundred dollars in my pocket and two suitcases, like Willy Loman. I had to sit up all night. It was rather terrifying. I got off at Grand Central and asked a guy, "Where is Broadway?"

He pointed me in the right direction, and I walked to what was then the actors' typical meeting place, Walgreens drugstore in the old Astor. I wound up living with a family on Eighty-sixth Street in a little room that had once been the maid's quarters.

Since I didn't know anybody, looking for work was very slowgoing, the famous catch-22. Agents would say, "I can't interview you until I see you in something." Producers would say, "I can't accept you unless you're sent by an agent." The saving grace was the Equity Library Theater, which did plays in various libraries around the city. There was no money involved. We worked for the joy of it. We dressed in a coal bin, boys and girls together.

I played Poseidon, the sea god, in *The Trojan Women.* My whole body was painted gold. I had nothing on except a pair of jockey shorts with seaweed. That's how Stephen Draper first saw me. He became the agent I was looking for; I stayed with him for thirty-five years.

I joined the Actors' Workshop, along with many of those who didn't make the cut for the Actors' Studio. It was a wonderful little group, with people like Yul Brynner, Marty Balsam, Ossie Davis, Ruby Dee, and Sidney Lumet, who was just a kid then but very interested in directing. We had a loft on Fourth Street. I was good with carpentry and helped to build a stage.

Still, this was a very rough period. I had gotten married, there was a baby on the way, and we were living in one room on the Lower East Side. I had just about given up when I got a call from my agent. They were looking for an understudy for Anthony Quinn for the touring company of *A Streetcar Named Desire.* Jack Palance had left for a role in the movie *Panic in the Streets.*

Unshaven, I went down to the audition, looking like the bum that Stanley Kowalski really is. I read and sort of threw things around the stage and was rather unruly and saucy with everybody. Then I heard this voice from the depths of the auditorium: "When can you leave for Cleveland?" It was Irene Selznick, David's wife. I understudied Tony Quinn for over a year.

When I came back to New York, live television had begun. Suddenly I was starring in *Playhouse 90, Studio One, The Kraft Television Hour.* It was enormously exciting, but I missed a live audience.

So I was happy to accept a part in *Misalliance* at the City Center. A year or two later the same producer did *Kismet,* and I got the role of the caliph. It was rather daunting to appear on Broadway singing operatic music. I had never sung onstage before. Alfred Drake was marvelous to me, although I understand he objected that I was not a true tenor, which is quite a legitimate gripe. He himself was a baritone, and I came in as a light baritone. They pushed my stuff up so that I was singing in a bright tenor key.

Opening night, I sat in my dressing room in the old Ziegfeld Theater, and through the intercom I heard the overture begin with bars of "Stranger in Paradise." That pretty much sums up how I felt. Talk about an adrenaline rush.

I heard the overture begin with bars of "Stranger in Paradise." That pretty much sums up how I felt.

• • • • •

LESLIE UGGAMS: My mother was a Cotton Club dancer briefly, and my father was a singer. Both my grandfathers were ministers, so they were kind of show business in their own way. But my aunt Eloise was the big influence. She had all these stories of going around the world with *Porgy and Bess.* She was in practically every production. When I was six years old I saw *Porgy and Bess* at the Ziegfeld, with the great Leontyne Price playing Bess. Aunt Eloise was understudy to the Strawberry Woman. That was my first Broadway show, and I couldn't get over it.

I started in the business when I was nine years old, working with Louis Armstrong and Ella Fitzgerald at the Apollo. I'd stand in the wings and watch these incredible performers. As a teenager I was a contestant on the television show *Name That Tune.* They coupled me with a butcher, and we went on to win twenty-five thousand dollars. I was asked what I liked to do. "Sing," I said. They asked me to sing, and I did "He's Got the Whole World in His Hands." Mitch Miller discovered me and put me in his show. I was the only black on national television at that time.

In 1967 I broke into Broadway in *Hallelujah, Baby!* I came into rehearsal knowing the whole script. I thought that was what you were supposed to do. The story was basically about the evolution of black people in show business. There was a black presence in the audience, and I felt I was doing something socially significant.

Opening night, I remember walking out onstage, and the next thing I knew I was taking a bow. It was like I went into a trance. I had had all that experience on television and at the Apollo and so many other places, but nothing like that had ever happened to me before.

Ironically, *Hallelujah, Baby!* won all these Tonys after the show had already closed, including the one for music, the only Tony that Jule Styne ever won. At the award ceremony, we did a number from the show, and then I had to quickly run and get out of my costume and into something glamorous.

All night, I had been asking everybody, "Where's Paul Newman?" He and Joanne Woodward were going to be presenters. They were out campaigning for Senator Eugene McCarthy and were being flown in by a special plane.

I was fluffing up at the mirror when Paul Newman arrived. He passed by and said to me, "I think you look absolutely beautiful." I thought I was going to melt. That was as thrilling to me as winning the Tony. Probably more so.

Ironically, Hallelujah, Baby! won all these Tonys after the show had already closed.

* * * * *

LOUISE LASSER: I had come out of Brandeis University, where I studied political theory and philosophy, but it was all meaningless to me. Then I began studying with Sandy Meisner. I had never auditioned for anything in my life when I went down, dressed in Jackie Kennedy white, very proper, to try out for the Barbra Streisand role in *I Can Get It for You Wholesale.* They needed a fill-in for a short time while Barbra was out.

Sometime in 1960, '61, I had gone with Woody Allen to Bon Soir. Barbra Streisand's name was penciled on the door. This birdlike person, very skinny and awkward, came out on the stage and started to sing. And my world just changed. I cry thinking of it. The sound she made of need—she had so many needs then.

But I didn't know that same girl was the star of *Wholesale,* in a part that was all behavioral: *"Oy gevalt!"* I didn't know how to do what she did. I was still in my Jewish denial period. At Brandeis I always stood on the non-kosher line.

But I got the part—like that, even though I didn't know what I was doing. I had no craft. When rehearsals began Arthur Laurents came in and said, "She's brilliant. She's like Judy Holliday." The night I opened, however, he couldn't believe it—I was that bad. I was terrified, and each time it got worse. I would look out at the audience and think, Why do I hate them?

Barbra would sing "Miss Marlmelstein" and get a standing ovation. I would sing "Miss Marmelstein" and they'd barely know the song was over.

Everyone was kind to me. Elliot Gould tried to comfort me. Woody [Allen], who was writing for *The Show of Shows* at the time, stood in the back for every performance, my rooting section.

Everything was happening to me all at once. While I was in *Wholesale,* I got a part in *No Where to Go But Up,* produced by Kermit Bloomgarden and directed by Sidney Lumet. It was an incredible time. I was doing *Wholesale* at night and going down to Second Avenue during the day to rehearse for *No Where to Go But Up.*

Every day I was three hours late. No matter what I did, my alarm clock would not go off. I put three clocks on the dresser. None of them went off. I would come in saying, "I don't know what happened."

Everyone was starting to get annoyed with me. I had to sing six songs. Some days I could sing the songs, some days I couldn't. Some days I would just sit in the corner and read a philosophy book. I read thirty books that month. That shows how much denial I was in.

For the backers' performance we were supposed to come dressed like Kansas girls. I wore black tights, a black skirt, a black turtleneck, and a black bow in my long hair. They were furious.

Sidney Lumet had this laugh—"Haa, ha!" "What kind of laugh is that?" I asked. "Is that a show business laugh?"

Every day I'd ask Michael Bennett, "Do you think they're going to fire me?"

"No," he'd say. "You're brilliant. Don't you see that you're brilliant?"

We were in Philadelphia when Kermit Bloomgarden called me in. He was a very nice man. "We're going to have to let you go."

"What?" It was like I was being fired from something I was wonderful in. "Why? What did I do?" I was hysterical. "Is it because I was late every day? Is it because I didn't get along with Sidney Lumet?"

"Louise, we'll just talk about it when we get to New York."

"Is it that I complained when I kissed that guy Bert, who hummed when he kissed me, and I found it very distracting?"

"We'll talk about it when we get to New York."

"Is it because I read a book during rehearsal and wasn't paying attention?"

"We'll talk in New York, Louise."

"Just give me a hint of what I did wrong. And maybe you could give me another chance."

"I'm sorry. Someone else is already on the train on the way down."

That killed me. Someone else had been hired before I was told. It was Mary Anne Mobley.

I called Woody. "Get on the next train," he said. "I'll pick you up." He was very fatherly, very kind. For three days I cried. Every time the phone rang, I was sure they were calling to say they had made a mistake. It wasn't until years later that I realized that I'd wanted to get fired.

No Where to Go But Up opened and closed in one week in November of 1962, even though it had incredible people in it: Martin Balsam, Dorothy Loudon, Tom Bosley. But I had my own problems. I didn't work again until I was twenty-six years old. That's how scared I was.

Woody gave me the idea to do comedy. He showed me how; he told me that my humor was not in the jokes but in my attitude. I really started to study and realized I was very comfortable doing physical comedy. I did a year straight of commercials. The first one, for Jell-O cheesecake, won the awards for everything. In 1967 I appeared on Broadway once again in *Henry, Sweet Henry,* and this time, I really was funny.

• • • • •

CHARLES DURNING: I was born into a family of army people in a small town near West Point. My dad died, and I left home at sixteen. I wound up working in a factory in Buffalo. In order to supplement my salary, which wasn't much, I became an usher in a burlesque house.

The second banana in the burlesque house was an alcoholic. Some days he would show up, and some days he wouldn't. The people running things chose to believe I was nineteen years old. One night they said to me, "You're going on."

The top banana gave me a joke to tell. I still remember it: A guy goes to a movie house and buys a ticket. He has a pet duck with him. The cashier says, "You can't bring a duck in here."

"It's a pet."

"I don't care," the cashier says. "It's against the law."

The guy leaves, goes down the alley, opens his pants, and stuffs the duck down in front. Now he's able to get into the theater. He sits down near two women and opens up his fly so the duck can breathe. One of the women turns to her friend and says, "You see what this guy alongside me is doing?"

Her friend says, "Don't worry. You've seen one, you've seen them all."
She says, "Yeah, but this one is eating my popcorn."

I told that joke, and I got a huge laugh. I was hooked.

While I was recovering from a wound during World War II, I became the emcee of this thing called *The Purple Heart Revue,* which was a show performed by recovering wounded soldiers. There I told that joke again many, many times.

I was left with a limp from my wound, which they said would never disappear. My mother said, "Take up dancing." I started hoofing, ballroom dancing. I still had the limp, but it was less pronounced.

Still, dancing didn't pay the rent. So I worked as a comic in nightclubs and sang with a band. I wound up with my own radio show in Newburgh, New York. I listened to Perry Como, Frank Sinatra, the Everly Brothers on the radio. I knew I couldn't be that good.

I took stock of myself. I was an average-looking guy, not a leading-man type. I was not that great a dancer, not that great a singer. While everyone was watching Tyrone Power and Clark Gable in the movies, I was studying Thomas Mitchell and Claude Raines, the character actors. That was for me.

I started dramatic school on the GI Bill. But the powers that be decided I had no talent and told me to take a walk. That was kind of devastating. I joined up with a stock company in Brooklyn, where we did a new play each week in the basement of an abandoned church. In two years I did a hundred plays. Most were light stuff; the most dramatic was *Our Town,* where I played the fourteen-year-old boy. But I was beginning to learn what worked and what didn't.

There was no money. I worked as a cabdriver, dance teacher, night watchman on the Brooklyn docks. Then I did some off-Broadway stuff: Saroyan, Ibsen, Chekhov, Molière, Sheridan, O'Neill, Noël Coward. I was paid ten, twenty dollars a week. One night after a performance in *Two by Saroyan,* I received a note: "I really enjoyed seeing you act." There was a phone number and a request to call. It was signed, "J. Papp, New York Shakespeare Festival."

I didn't know who the hell he was, but I called. He told me he wanted me to read for the Casca part in *Julius Caesar.*

I heard it as "Cassius."

I go in. There's this guy with a big cigar, and he says, "Get up there and read Casca on page . . ."

While everyone was watching Tyrone Power and Clark Gable in the movies, I was studying Thomas Mitchell and Claude Raines, the character actors. That was for me.

I had prepared Cassius; I hadn't even read the whole play. *Who the hell is Casca?* I'm thinking. I read it cold.

He puffed three or four times on his cigar. "How dare you come in here and read Shakespeare without studying it first! If I hadn't seen you act, I wouldn't give you the part. But I'm desperate. We're starting rehearsals immediately."

The pay was twenty dollars a week, with an extra five dollars for understudying Julius Caesar. It was the high school circuit, very early fifties. Peter Boyle was in the crowd scene with me.

Just as I had done in the burlesque house years ago, I would sit around at the New York Shakespeare Festival and watch the performers. I learned to act by watching people who got their start through Joe Papp: Colleen Dewhurst, Julie Harris, James Earl Jones, George C. Scott. Scott did *Richard III* and *Merchant of Venice* and then he was—boom!

I stayed with Joe for twelve, thirteen years. I never left him. He had me play all the Shakespearean clowns. One time I said, "Joe, I want to play more than just the clowns. Why can't I play one of the noblemen?"

"You're here to serve our needs," he said. "We're not here to serve you. And besides, you can't handle the language. But what would you like to do?"

"Troylius and Creeseeda."

"First learn how to pronounce it."

I would get good reviews, bad reviews, so-so reviews. John Simon always wrote how bad I was. But Joe would tell me, "The only people you have to please are the producer and director and yourself. If you think you have to please a critic, you shouldn't be in the business."

When Joe first sent me *That Championship Season,* I didn't like it. "You're not alone," he said. "Nobody down here likes it. It needs work. But we're going to have a reading of it around the table." He did that a lot.

After we finished he said, "There's something in there." Joe's genius was to take a look at a play and make adjustments in scenes, dialogue, organization. He couldn't explain how he did it, but he knew when it was right. It took him five months, and then he got this great cast together.

I didn't do Broadway for years. I knew there were actors who would not go below Fourteenth Street; I was resigned to doing off Broadway. But on September 14, 1972, the New York Shakespeare Festival's production of *That Championship Season* moved from the Public Theater to the Booth, and I was doing Broadway after all.

I was in *That Championship Season* for a year, and then I went out to California to do *The Sting* and didn't come back for seventeen years because I kept getting one movie after another. Still, I didn't like Hollywood. Jason Robards says it best: "If you call yourself an actor, you've got to do stage work." Movies are wonderful for the money, but they're piecework.

You see, it wasn't that I wanted to act. I had to. I gave it up more than once to try something steady. But I always came back. I was obsessed by it. I still am.

• • • • •

MICHEL BELL: I was fifteen years old and had just begun studying voice with a teacher in my school who had offered to give me singing lessons for free at seven each morning. For my first lesson he gave me some art songs by Handel and Haydn, and then he brought out "Old Man River." I didn't like it. I didn't get the dialect, didn't understand what "Lift *dat* bale" meant, for example. We didn't talk that way in our household.

But after my parents explained the dialect and the context the song was sung in, and after a lot of coaxing on my teacher's part, I started singing it in public. One day I performed it in church, and a man walked up to me and said, "Little Bell-boy, you sound like Paul Robeson."

I looked at him and thought, Who is that?

Then I developed a fascination with Paul Robeson, one black man who was valedictorian of his class, Phi Beta Kappa scholar, All-American football player, Columbia Law School graduate, actor, opera singer, master of over nineteen languages, champion of oppressed people. And wherever he went, he was asked to sing that song. It was not of his choosing; people wanted it that way. Through Paul Robeson, "Old Man River" became an anthem.

Now here I was, a teenager in Fresno, California, in the 1960s, and like Paul Robeson, I, too, was always asked to sing that song. I tried to sing it in a nonstereotypical way, I tried to find a place in myself that would make it meaningful. My peers were calling it the "Uncle Tom" song, and I had to deal with that through high school and college while studying opera. Finally I got to the point where I was sick of "Old Man River."

In 1972 I went off in an entirely different direction, and in 1976 I joined the Fifth Dimension. In 1980 I left the Fifth and returned to opera, concertizing. About a dozen years later, I had just arrived in L.A. from

Germany to do a concert when I received a call from my agent. Hal Prince was producing *Showboat,* and he wanted to hear me sing "Old Man River." I was still in jet lag, but I heard my agent say Hal wanted to restore everything that was original in the show. And I thought, How about singing "Old Man River" in the original key of B-flat, as Paul Robeson did? Maybe there weren't many people who wanted to rumble down there. But I had always loved it in B-flat. It gives the song a different color; it suggests a massive command of the river and the wilderness and so on into the distance where life continues.

At the Majestic I sang in the published key of C. Hal Prince and Garth Drabinsky were sitting out in the audience. "That was wonderful, Mic. Thanks for flying out."

"By the way, I can do it in B-flat if you wish."

"What's the reason for that?"

"It's the original key Paul Robeson sang it in."

"Oh. OK, sure. Don't sing the whole thing. Just give us the chorus."

One of the staffers said, "We don't have the sheet music in B-flat."

"But I do," I said. "I have it right here." I had transposed it the night before.

I sang the chorus, and then—maybe it was my imagination—but it seemed like Hal Prince jumped out of his seat and ran down the aisle. In a matter of seconds he was beside me onstage.

"I'm really looking forward to working with you," he said.

Playing the role of Joe the stevedore in *Showboat* has been a good stretch for me. Stepping into the shoes of Joe is like being up there with Paul Robeson, William Warfield, and so many others. The baton is being passed in a relay race, and I'm carrying it now.

In Hal Prince's *Showboat,* "Old Man River" became a metaphor, a Greek chorus, so to speak, moving in and out throughout the play, continually reminding the audience that the river is still there, that the river still flows as life moves on. It's such a major element of the show that it's surprising to learn it was sort of an add-on. As the story goes, Hammerstein visited Kern in his apartment when they were working on *Showboat* and said, "We need another song."

"What do you mean?" Kern said. "We have four hours of songs."

"But we don't have one about the river."

In earlier versions the tempo was much faster. It was designed to hide a scene change. Also, it's not clear if Hammerstein had the song in mind for Joe.

The baton is being passed in a relay race, and I'm carrying it now.

But I found a place in my heart when I sang "Old Man River," a song I did reluctantly as a kid, put away, and then received as a gift so many years later.

• • • • •

PATRICIA NEAL: When I was about ten I saw a woman delivering monologues at the Methodist Church in Knoxville, Tennessee. Well, god, my eyes filled with tears, and I knew that was what I wanted to do. For Christmas they gave me a gift: "You may study drama." When I was about fourteen, I joined the Tennessee Valley Players and got a part in a play. The next summer I appeared in Abington, Virginia, at the Barter Summer Theater, which was started during the Depression, with people bartering food for admission. I spent two years at Northwestern University, and then it was on to Broadway.

Patricia Neal—success on Broadway came to her overnight.

I cut pies and scooped ice cream in Greenwich Village cafés to make a little money. But every spare moment, I was hustling, trying to get a job. After about two months I got the understudy part in *Voice of the Turtle*. One night this agent spotted me and asked, "Would you like to read for Lillian Hellman?"

I got a role in *Another Part of the Forest* for three hundred dollars a week. It was Lillian's first directorial job. Opening night, I almost had a nervous breakdown. My mother was there, driving me crazy. My brother was there. He was about twelve, and he wore boots, which drove my mother crazy. Lillian Hellman's father was there, counting his money out loud while the play was going on. We all got great reviews, except for Lillian, and enjoyed a six-month Broadway run.

It had been quite a year. I'd arrived in New York the fall of 1945. Before the year ended, I had gotten an understudy job. And before the next year ended, I was opening on Broadway in a Lillian Hellman–Kermit Bloomgarden play. Success had come to me overnight. People would stop me on the street. *Life* magazine put me on its cover; *Look* magazine gave me an award as Broadway's brightest newcomer. It was the first year of the Tonys, and I won for best newcomer. They gave me an engraved compact that I still have. It certainly was a thrill, but the best part of the evening was being onstage with the winner for best actress, Helen Hayes.

●　●　●　●　●

CY COLEMAN: My parents were immigrants; my mother owned two tenements in the Bronx before she could sign her name in English. When I was four years old, a tenant skipped on the rent and left a piano behind. They couldn't get it out of the building, so they moved it down to our apartment. I began picking up melodies from the radio and playing them by ear. The muse took me over very early.

The milkman sent his son's piano teacher over. My mother, being a good businesswoman, struck a deal: I'd get three lessons a week and she'd pay for one. I became somewhat of a prodigy, playing classical recitals at Steinway Hall, Carnegie Hall. I went to Music and Art High School and then the New York College of Music.

But I decided not to be a concert pianist. As a teenager I played in bands that accompanied acts up in the Catskills, and it was there that I became infatuated with show business: the shtick, the humor, the whole thing. Jack Robbins, a feisty little publisher, commissioned me to write three Gershwin-like preludes. He liked what I did, but he didn't like my name. "Seymour Kaufman will never do," he said. "We'll call you Cy Coleman."

I began playing for society events, a nineteen-year-old kid from the Bronx in a brand-new tuxedo, listed in the papers with the Vanderbilts and the Astors. I moved into jazz, had a trio that played on NBC and at the top clubs, did a lot of recording.

My first contribution to a Broadway show was to *John Murray Anderson's Almanac,* in 1953. Richard Adler and Jerry Ross did most of the songs, and Jean Kerr provided sketches. The revue kicked off a lot of people: Harry Belafonte, Orson Bean, Billy DeWolfe, Polly Bergen, and Hermione Gingold in her American debut.

I started working with Caroline Lee. Our first big hit was "Witchcraft." We auditioned for *Gypsy,* which we didn't get, but Michael Kidd remembered us next time around and picked us to do the score for *Wildcat.*

I'm a very eclectic composer. I jump from one idiom to another. My classical music background had a profound effect on my score for *On the Twentieth Century,* which is a comic opera. My jazz background came into play in *City of Angels,* although it isn't the kind of jazz you hear in night-clubs, but a pure jazz score with a quartet that sings intricate harmonies. *Barnum, Sweet Charity, Little Me, I Love My Wife,* and my newest, *The Life,* which makes *Sweet Charity* look like Disney—all my shows are different. I try not to repeat myself.

The muse took me over very early.

• • • • •

JUDY KAYE: We had taken the train from Phoenix, Arizona, to visit my father's family. I was a little kid, and I wore a little beret and gloves to go to the theater where I saw my first Broadway show: *Damn Yankees,* with Gwen Verdon. The experience thoroughly electrified me.

Next trip east we saw *Funny Girl,* with Barbra Streisand. I sat in the mezzanine and saw myself up there onstage. A couple of years later, I sang "I'm the Greatest Star" at the Jewish Center in Phoenix, Arizona, and I got a standing ovation.

Although I never thought I'd do it for a living, I went to UCLA, studied voice and theater, and then started going out on calls and getting jobs.

The one thing I was really chicken about was coming to New York. But in 1973 I got a part in the road company of *Grease,* and four years later I appeared on Broadway in that same role.

I auditioned for *On the Twentieth Century.* I didn't get the lead role of Lilly, which I wanted, but the part of Agnes, Lilly's maid, a Zasu Pitts kind of character. On a good night I could get eight laughs with that role. I also got to understudy Madeline Kahn, who played Lilly. Being an understudy is a terrible job; you're depending on somebody's misfortune to get an opportunity to do your job. If they go on a vacation, management usually fills in with another bankable star.

Hal Prince always has a party for the company early in the run. There I was, the lonely understudy, walking around and looking at all the Tony awards and all the pictures, and I thought, I can't believe I'm here. I turned, and Stephen Sondheim was standing nearby. Like a blithering idiot, I stammered something to him, and he simply said, "I know, I know."

I was standing in line at the buffet, getting set to get this really good fried chicken, when Hal put an arm around me and said, "I want to create a role with you, Judy." And I immediately went off to the powder room and cried for about an hour and a half.

When Madeline was not available for rehearsals, I went on for her. Hal told me to lose weight and to find my own character. Instead of directing me into Madeline's performance, Hal freed me. "Fly," he'd say.

He suggested I study some old movie stars. I watched Carole Lombard, who played the role in the film. I also watched Madeline during rehearsals. I thought I would be a little more hard-edged than her.

March 6, 1978, a few weeks after we opened, I spent the morning watching a Carole Lombard film. Then, about one o'clock, I went to my gym, which was on the same street as the St. James Theater. After my workout, I went to call my service. But there was this big line of ladies in their towels, all dripping wet, waiting to use the phone. Well, I'm sure there won't be any messages, I thought, and instead of waiting I walked across the street to a Belgian café, where I had a piece of fish, a lovely salad, and even a glass of white wine—something I would normally never do, but I thought, as I didn't have a note to sing in the entire show, what difference did it make?

Then I strolled over to the theater, opened the stage door, and there was the entire cast draped around the foyer, yelling at me, "You're going on!"

They took me up to Madeline's star dressing room and started trying her clothes on me. Everything was a little short, but it fit. They put the blond wig on me. I'd never seen myself in a blond wig before. I didn't own a pair of eyelashes, because Agnes, the maid, did not wear eyelashes. Luckily, however, I had had the forethought to buy my own shoes.

I was ready. For weeks I had been there sitting there, listening in my fourth-floor dressing room and dreaming about going on. I had also made this deal with myself: *I'm never going on. I will never get to play Lilly. However, if I do, I'll do it as good as I can.* It was a balancing game. It's that way for all understudies.

At the curtain call, I was presented with two dozen long-stemmed yellow roses. Hal's movie version of *A Little Night Music* opened that night, and he had to be there. But everyone else connected with the show was standing in the back. It was a unanimous leaping ovation.

Hal had left instructions that I be brought to his party at the Gingerman. There I was, dressed in a pair of jeans and a lumberjack flannel shirt and a really atrocious green parka, sitting at a table with Hal and Elizabeth Taylor and Len Cariou.

The next day I came back and did the matinee. The audience was made up mostly of women. They're canny. There was a little bit more of the candy-wrapping noise, but it was wonderful; I was the lead. That night, however, I was back to being Agnes, the maid.

About five weeks into the run, I was visiting my agent's office when the phone rang. It was literally Broadway calling, the producer Marty Richards. Madeline was leaving the show, and he offered me the part forever.

The night I took over for good, Imogene Coca, who also starred in the play, and her husband presented me with a bottle of Dom Perignon that they had been given the night they did *The Four Poster*. It was one of those torch-passing experiences. Imogene was the iron butterfly, a delicate lovely creature who hits the wings and then the stage, and the lights go on. She is an indomitable powerhouse.

The forces of Broadway were just happening around me. It was as if I was standing back and watching, taking the advice I got in the telegram Shirley MacLaine sent me the night I took over: "Watch what happens now."

• • • • •

JERRY ZAKS: I was born in Germany after the war, the firstborn son of Holocaust survivors. In that no one expected my mother to ever have a child, I was considered a miracle. She and my father communicated to me, by virtue of their behavior, that I was the chosen one. I was expected to excel, and I did. Being survivors, my parents were suspicious of strangers, particularly non-Jews. I grew up overprotected, fat, myopic, unathletic, soft, with a good smile and a real need to be liked by everyone.

There was no time for frivolity in our household. I worked very hard and got great grades. Still, I indulged in a secret passion. In the course of a day, I would go down into our basement, close the door, and put on a stack of old forty-five rock-and-roll records: Dionne and the Belmonts, the Shirelles, the Everly Brothers, Marvin Gaye. I'd sing along with them, looking at myself in the mirror over the bar. It was sexy, it was cool. It gave me too much joy to be denied. So when people ask why I did *Smokey Joe's Café,* they have no idea . . .

Came the time to apply to college, I heard the name Dartmouth, sent for the brochure, and looked at the pictures. This was 1962—the all-male, old-fashioned Dartmouth. It was everything that I was not. I went up to visit. While there, I had to make a phone call but only had a nickel in my pocket. I asked a passerby for change for a dollar. "How much do you need?" he asked, and he gave me the nickel. That person gave me a nickel! In my experience, no one ever gave you anything. It was a little moment, yet it symbolized something very different from my parents' vision of the world.

I started out premed. By my second year, I was getting more and more miserable about that. But I'd pledged for a fraternity, and since I was a funny fat kid, they asked me to act in an interfraternity play contest. My first time on the stage. We won.

Winter Carnival that year was *Wonderful Town,* performed by the Dartmouth players. It was the first musical I had ever seen. I only went because I had a blind date, and what else can you do Winter Carnival weekend? I was not one of those guys who said, "I'll take my date back to . . ."

At the end of the school year, *Wonderful Town* was revived for the alumni reunion. A bunch of performers had already left campus, so some parts were open. I sang for the faculty director, Warner Bentley. "Where were you the first time?" he asked. Getting a part in that production, I promise you, was as joyous as getting any other acting part I've ever gotten.

Junior year, I dumped premed and committed to an English major, which seemed more responsible than a drama major. I auditioned for the Dartmouth Players, got in, and got the part of the director in *Six Characters in Search of an Author*—beating out the president of the Players, who had once given me shit about the way I pronounced "entertain" in an English class. I don't think he ever forgave me. I acted in as many things as I could. It took over my life, although it was still avocational. I didn't know yet that this was truly about falling in love.

My parents couldn't understand what all this acting meant to me. They were only concerned with whether there was anti-Semitism at Dartmouth. But after one of their visits, my dad took me to see *Do I Hear a Waltz?* the next time I came home.

My parents had been upset when I gave up premed. Then they hoped I'd go into law. I applied to a couple of law schools but ended up in an M.F.A. program at Smith College. That fall I lost forty pounds. For the first time in my life, I was thin.

I came to New York determined to be an actor. It was not an intellectual decision; it was an affair of the heart. My days were all about my acting. I worked out, I worked on my voice, I thought I was the luckiest guy in the world. One thing led to another, until finally I got a part in the national tour company of *Grease*.

There was no one more right for the show than I was. There was no better company. I did the role for ten months on the road, and then on Broadway at the Royale Theater. When I walked out onto Forty-fifth Street, people were at the stage door. It was the top of the world.

I went from play to play, did lots of commercials, and then around 1979 I got to do this wonderful immigrant character in *Tintypes*. We had a very nice director who left us to our own devices. I would go home and create my own scenarios, which included my coming down to front center stage and kissing the ground. I think that was where my directing started.

Around that time a friend of mine was going to play the lead in a farce, *A Soft Touch,* at the Ensemble Studio Theater, and he asked me to direct. On a lark, I did it, and it brought the house down. Then I directed *Sister Mary Ignatius Explains It All for You,* a satirical look at the Catholic Church, which ran for a couple of years off Broadway.

With these two shows, I found I had stumbled into something intoxicating. The feeling of power, the sense that I had the ability to make something happen, was much greater than anything I had ever experienced as

I came to New York determined to be an actor. It was not an intellectual decision; it was an affair of the heart.

an actor. You have to be in the moment as an actor, not watching it, not judging it, but being there. It's an ecstatic place to be, and the really best actors are there all the time. But my ability as an actor was limited by my inability to totally lose myself in a part. I was always watching from the outside and directing myself. Now, as a director, I was able to put it all together.

Nevertheless it is only in recent years that I have become truly proud of what I do. For a long time it was like when I was a kid and played my rock-and-roll records down in the basement with the door closed. There was that reluctance. Ultimately my father grew to love the fact that I was an actor; he would hang around under the marquee just to tell people that his son was in the show. When I played Motel, the tailor, in a revival of *Fiddler on the Roof,* he and my mother would come backstage and speak Yiddish with Zero Mostel. Somehow that legitimized my involvement in the theater for them.

But neither of them was ever able to appreciate the power of art and what it can do. By "art" I mean anything that someone creates that makes the world a little more beautiful. They could never understand how one could be moved by a dance or a painting or a play. It was one of the minor consequences of the Holocaust. The consequence for me was that because of them, there remained that ambivalence. It took awhile for me to understand that people are moved by, affected by, internalize the experience provided by theater.

In the fall of 1985 I began as resident director at Lincoln Center. My first production was the black comedy *House of Blue Leaves,* which, ironically, I had directed as guest artist at Dartmouth the previous summer. We started at the Newhouse and then moved to the Beaumont and then on to Broadway at the Plymouth Theater. It ran and ran. That was my first Broadway play, and it won me a Tony.

What do I remember? They read the names of the nominated directors, and then they announced my name. I was thirty-nine. I loved the fact that I was getting my first Tony before I was forty. I read my speech. Ever since my bar mitzvah, I've never memorized a speech. I'm always terrified of forgetting my lines.

2 | THE WATERFALL AND THE CAMEL WERE STILL THERE

ELAINE STRITCH: Broadway, Manhattan is our town, our town.

BETTY BUCKLEY: I may love working in London, but I'm a Broadway baby. I want it to happen here because this is my home. More than anything else, I want to be on a Broadway stage.

ROY SOMLYO: For purposes of the Tony awards, a Broadway theater is a house with five hundred or more seats. Normally you would say that Broadway, as theater, extends from Forty-first to Fifty-third Streets. But Lincoln Center is up on Sixty-fifth Street. So Broadway is not necessarily geographic; it's not a physical locale. It's an idea.

CAROL CHANNING: To me, Broadway is an audience. That's all I care about. And as the Lunts once told me, after the first two or three months in New York, you're playing to Omaha anyway.

WARD MOREHOUSE III: I was sitting in the revolving restaurant atop the Marriott Marquis not too long ago, and looking down at the Broadway scene familiar to me since my childhood, I saw how much has changed. I could remember a time when Broadway was a ramshackle, dusty area filled with hawkers, street peddlers, and hot dog stands. It still is to some extent, but huge high-rise office buildings and hotels now dwarf the old sites. Still, between the towering skyscrapers, I could make out a few theaters, most of them landmarked, and some of the old hotels, too, like the Knickerbocker on Forty-second Street, which they used to call the Forty-second Street Country Club until it became an office building in 1921 when Prohibition came in. It's part of the cornucopia of legendary Broadway, which includes the Algonquin Hotel, built in 1903, and the old Lambs' Club on Forty-fourth Street.

A theater lobby in the late 1940s, when Broadway shows played every night of the week and the best seats in the house were just three dollars.

MICKEY ALPERT: In the late 1940s, early 1950s, I used to come in on the subway with my parents from Brooklyn. It was a world of glamour, excitement, lights, tons of people all dressed up.

For $1.50 we'd see a movie like *Stage Door Canteen,* followed by six or eight acts of vaudeville with performers like Molly Picon or Jack Carter. Once I saw Georgia Gibbs open for Danny Kaye. We'd have dinner in one of those places they called fancy Chinese restaurants: Ruby Foo's or Old China. But there were many other places: Toffenetti's, a big place on Forty-third Street on the east side of Broadway, the Brass Rail near the Rivoli Theater on Seventh Avenue around Fiftieth Street, Jack Dempsey's, Lindy's.

FREDDIE GERSHON: My mother would take my friend Neil Sedaka and me to New York City, where we'd split one slice of cheesecake at Lindy's. It cost $1.75. Heavy duty. There'd be all these faded black-and-white photographs of mainly Broadway stars on the walls, all of them airbrushed. No one had scars, pimples, wrinkles. The waiters were old Jewish guys who would engage you in conversation like, "You don't want this. It's not that good today. I'll get you something better."

I'd roam the streets, and it was like walking through the pages of a Damon Runyon book. Everyone was a character. Men were super sharpies in zoot suits. Some looked like hoods, some looked like gamblers, and none of them seemed to have a job. I'd hang around in Gray's Drugstore near the Wintergarden Theater and watch the gypsies dressed in their leotards trying on different shades of pancake makeup.

CHARLES DURNING: I had heard all about it, the famous places, the great names. John Barrymore walked these boards, hung out in these places. When I finally got there, I found it a little seedy and shoddy. Yet before long, I began to love the seediness and the ghosts and superstitions. I learned it's OK to say "the Scottish play" but never *Macbeth,* and if you recite, say, a line from *Macbeth,* you have to go outside and turn around three times. It's all tradition, they say.

MERLE DEBUSKEY: To those of us who came back from the war, Broadway was a little surrounded community. The activity there was like a crucible. The heat around was terrific; everyone was concerned with what was going on. If a show opened in New Haven, the word on the street the next morning was, "Do you know what happened? What were the reviews like?" The news would go around.

MARTY JACOBS: Everything was starting up again; prices hadn't skyrocketed yet. Off Broadway was just starting to happen, but nobody took it too seriously.

MANNY AZENBERG: The camaraderie of the Broadway world was wonderful. It was postwar humanism. We were socially and politically aware, left wing. Who could be anything else? You could stay up to two in the morning and pretend you were going to change the world, which is not such a terrible feeling.

There was no such thing as pasta. It was spaghetti, and it cost seventy-five cents. With meatballs, eighty-five cents. You went to joints like Romeo's and Marco Polo's on Forty-eighth Street and had Chianti wine, and people would came over, and you'd talk about how theater could change the course of political society. It was not just trivial entertainment.

HAL HOLBROOK: Theater was mainstream, riding a wave of tradition that was vital and essential to the entire entertainment process in the United States.

We had actors who lived in the theater. That was all they did. We had playwrights who were writing good plays, sometimes astonishing ones. In 1947 and 1948, I came into town and saw *A Streetcar Named Desire* and *Death of a Salesman*. I saw *King Lear* for the first time at the old National Theater. I saw Katherine Cornell, Helen Hayes, Fredric March, Florence Eldridge, the Lunts, Louis Calhern.

MANNY AZENBERG: Olivier, Scofield, Gielguld, Albert Finney, Peter O'Toole, Alan Bates . . .

HARVEY SABINSON: Tennessee Williams, William Inge, Arthur Miller, Kaufman and Hart. There was Irving Berlin, Jule Styne, Cole Porter, Rodgers and Hammerstein, Frank Loesser—great new shows every year.

MERLE DEBUSKEY: You had continuing producers; it was their life. Kermit Bloomgarden would produce a play every year or two.

HARVEY SABINSON: There was a hard-core audience that had to see everything in a season.

FREDDIE GERSHON: Going to the theater was an event. It was very carriage-trade.

MORTON GOTTLEIB: I loved the glamour; I don't mean just the dressing up, but the whole feel of how lucky you were to see a Broadway show.

FRED EBB: As a kid, I'd save money for standing room, which was fifty-five cents. Or I'd show up and ask the concessionaire if he needed help checking coats or selling Orangeade during the intermission. Different kids got the jobs every night. That's how I got to see *The Glass Menagerie*.

MARTIN RICHARDS: In my early years I'd second-act everything. I'd sneak in with the crowds after intermission and find an empty seat. I can't tell you about first acts, but it seems I remember second acts that go back a hundred years.

MAURY YESTON: I was no more than nine when I saw my first Broadway play: *No Time for Sergeants,* starring Andy Griffith. There was a moment when Andy is cleaning the latrines. The sergeant comes in to check on him and says, "'Ten-shun!" Andy responds, "'Ten-shun!" and clicks his heels, and all the toilet seats pop up at once. That was it. I was smitten.

FREDDIE GERSHON: The first Broadway show I saw was *South Pacific,*

It was 1949; tickets were seventy-five cents.

with Ezio Pinza and Mary Martin at the Majestic Theater. It was 1949; tickets were seventy-five cents.

Afterward I could sing every song. I would run to the piano to play them. Thereafter, whenever a new show would come into town, my mother would take me. She would buy the cheapest seats in the last row of the last balcony. My uncle gave us his binoculars from World War II. They were five pounds and came in a huge case, and we schlepped them to every show. I saw the hits, *Pajama Game, Damn Yankees, Can-Can, Kiss Me Kate,* and the failures, *Miss Liberty, Jenny.* I didn't know it at the time, but I was immersed in the heyday of American musical theater.

FRED GOLDEN: After the curtains went up, the managers and press agents would come out and walk through Shubert Alley to Sardi's and have a drink at the bar. I could do all of my business that way.

I was one of the few admen that the union permitted into the box office. "Oh, a lot of tickets are still on the rack for next Tuesday night," I'd say to myself, and make a note to schedule a little advertising.

HARVEY SABINSON: Press agents used to congregate at the Blue Ribbon Restaurant on Forty-fourth Street. We'd swap stories and lies. There was a collegial feeling. You'd walk around the theater district and talk to this manager and that manager.

I typed my own press releases with carbon paper, made six copies, and sent them out. I didn't have a secretary, I didn't have a mimeograph machine, and I never had a day off. But I had a good time.

While I was working on *Finian's Rainbow,* a friend of mine was handling a show called *Up in Central Park.* We staged a rowing race between the girls of both casts. The gimmick was that the Parks Department would refuse to give us a permit, we would all get arrested, and that would give us newspaper space. Only, the police refused to arrest us.

A page from the *Fanny* playbill in the spring of 1955 reveals the richness of Broadway offerings in the postwar years.

YOUR INTERMISSION INTERVIEW

How many of these hits have you seen?

If your score is 12 or more you are a star; 11, you are featured; 10, you're a bit player; less than 10, you need more rehearsals at the box office.

MUSICAL

☐ THE BOY FRIEND	Royale	A New Musical Comedy of the 1920s
☐ CAN-CAN	Shubert	New Cole Porter-Abe Burrows Musical
☐ FANNY	Majestic	EZIO PINZA / WALTER SLEZAK
☐ THE PAJAMA GAME	St. James	JOHN RAITT / JANIS PAIGE / EDDIE FOY, JR.
☐ PLAIN AND FANCY	Winter Garden	A New Musical Comedy
☐ SILK STOCKINGS	Imperial	HILDEGARDE NEFF / DON AMECHE
☐ 3 FOR TONIGHT	Plymouth	MARGE & GOWER CHAMPION / HARRY BELAFONTE

COMEDY

☐ ANNIVERSARY WALTZ	Booth	MacDONALD CAREY
☐ BUS STOP	Music Box	By William Inge
☐ COMEDY IN MUSIC	Golden	VICTOR BORGE
☐ LUNATICS AND LOVERS	Broadhurst	Sidney Kingsley's Gay and Impudent Farce

DRAMA

☐ ANASTASIA	Lyceum	VIVECA LINDFORS / EUGENIE LEONTOVICH
☐ INHERIT THE WIND	National	PAUL MUNI
☐ THE DESPERATE HOURS	Barrymore	KARL MALDEN / NANCY COLEMAN / PAUL NEWMAN

We fared better with our scheme for *Subways Are for Sleeping*. Out of town, it looked like it would bomb. Opening night, I went into David Merrick's office. "Why aren't you watching the show?" he asked. He had a rough temper.

"David," I said, "you don't pay me enough to watch this show twice."

He had a Manhattan phone book on his lap. "You know," he said, "there's another Howard Taubman here."

"How about Walter Kerr?" I said.

We looked up this one, that one, and ended up with seven people who had the same names as seven New York critics.

FRED GOLDEN: Harvey and I took the seven guys—one of them came from Utah, South Dakota, one of those places—for dinner at Sardi's and then to see the show. We asked each of them for a good quote. They said, "Write whatever you want."

I worked from eleven o'clock at night to five in the morning putting together the ad with all these invented quotes by guys with the same names as the New York critics. No one in my office knew what was going on. The *Times* wouldn't run the ad, but it made the *Tribune*. They always ran second and were glad to get the money. It was picked up all over the world and gave the show enormous publicity. Merrick loved every minute of it.

MERLE DEBUSKEY: There were so many outlets in the postwar years— eleven or twelve newspapers in New York City. In terms of magazines, *Look, Life, Liberty, Collier's*. There was radio, but television had not yet made its encroachment, and the media was very open to theater; they considered it important. The *New York Times* had six reporters and seven columns a week devoted to the theater. There were columnists like Kilgallen and Sobol on the *Journal American*, Winchell on the *Mirror*, Ed Sullivan and Danton Walker on the *News*, Lyons and Wilson on the *Post*. The *Tribune* had a guy named Hal Gardner, but he wasn't the same type as those.

You would supply the columnists with a lot of gossip that had nothing to do with your own client and star the one that was about your client. That was the payoff. A columnist would decide what he wanted to use. And if he thought you had done well that day, he would print your item.

HARVEY SABINSON: When you visited the papers with your story and photos, there were no security guards all over the place, no ascerbic, skeptical, pain-in-the-ass editors. The guys were glad to see you. They became your friends.

SHIRLEY HERZ: Your hot and first news would go out to Walter Winchell. All the press agents would hang out at Hanson's Drugstore on Fifty-first and Broadway at three or four in the morning, waiting to give him their items. He would make notations: "It's bullshit." "Have checked with the FBI—it's OK." When he would send something back, they knew it was safe to pass it on.

MERLE DEBUSKEY: Leonard Lyons, Walter Winchell, Dorothy Kilgallen— they hated each other. It was really bloody. If you serviced one, you could be dead with the others.

I knew Lenny Lyons well. Somebody once described him like a shamus of a very high class shul. I had an "in" with Winchell and his girl Friday, Rose Bigman.

I'd call: "Rose, it's Merle."

"Oh, how are you?"

I'd pitch an idea to her. If she thought it was in the general area, she'd have me send it over.

The first time I met Winchell he said, "Are you the same one who was the great lacrosse player?" How he knew I was an All-American lacrosse player, I don't know. He never explained himself.

All the press agents sent their hot news first to Walter Winchell, pictured here at the radio mike in 1953.

Winchell could be nasty, but Kilgallen could be villainous. I stayed away from her. She would go out of her way to hurt people. *Little Me* with Sid Caesar was coming in with great advance interest. Yet in previews, day after day, Kilgallen attacked us. We didn't have the foggiest idea why. We hired a column press agent named Mike Hall, who was in tight with her. He came back and reported that there was a theater party the night she came to see the play, and she wound up having to sit in the balcony.

MICKEY ALPERT: When I began working for Max Eisen out of the Sardi Building in 1961, there were still seven newspapers in New York City. My job was to bring them daily press releases. First I'd go to the *Times*. Sam Zolotow was a legend there. Everybody tried like crazy to get their stuff into his daily theater column. You could walk into your office and say, "Did you hear the world blew up yesterday?" And someone would say, "Was it in Zolotow's column?" If you said no, the guy would say, "Then how would I know?"

From the *Times* I'd walk over to 240 West Forty-first Street, to the *Herald Tribune*. Then I'd take the subway downtown to the *Post* on West Street, and from there I'd walk over to the *World Telegram and Sun* on Barclay Street, where the guy would always greet me with, "Why do you come here every day? Whatever you give me, I throw it in the garbage." Next I'd take a cab to the *Journal* at 210 South Street, and from there I'd take a cab up to the *News* on Forty-second Street. From there I could walk over to the *Mirror* on Forty-fifth Street.

The columnists could not make or break a show, but they were very important in terms of mentioning your client's name. Leonard Lyons was in a class by himself. If he didn't use material you sent him, he would send it back. A lawyer by education, Lyons was a celebrity lover. He'd start his day around noon at Sardi's. Then he'd go to 21, the Four Seasons, looking for people. Those were his lunchtime rounds. He would go down to the *Post* on West Street and begin to put his column together and then go to his fabulous apartment on Central Park West.

About six o'clock he'd come out again, go to the screening of a movie, the premiere of a play. And then the rounds again: back to Sardi's, Arthur's, and P. J. Clark's, which was the last stop for him and Earl Wilson. They used to write until three, four in the morning.

VINCENT SARDI, JR.: All the columnists came to Sardi's. Not only was it Leonard Lyons's home base, Walter Winchell visited us a few times a week.

The columnists could not make or break a show, but they were very important in terms of mentioning your client's name.

He was known for his Stork Club connection, but after he broke with Sherman Billingsley, he became more of a regular. He used to plug "Mama and Papa Sardi's little fooderia" in his column and on his radio show.

MERLE DEBUSKEY: When shows tried out out-of-town, the press agent went along: Detroit, Boston, Philadelphia, New Haven. Whatever happened there, you either kept quiet or inflated. That helped your box office on Broadway.

MARTY JACOBS: These cities had legitimate theaters downtown, with experienced stage crews. Sometimes there'd be a company touring while the show was still playing in New York. They might take one of the stars along as an attraction, or they might let the road company do one or two performances in New York so they could advertise "Direct from Broadway."

We lived out of the Pullman cars. We would bring our own liquor along. Some of the towns were dry. There are stories of stage managers going crazy trying to get actors out of jail to make the show.

LINDA LAVIN: Out-of-town was hands-off to critics: "Don't come until we're ready." It could be weeks, it could be months. Every day there were new pages, new scripts, new songs. Help from New York would come in to re-create, restructure the play. That's how Neil Simon got his name Doc. These people never got credit for their work. It was a professional courtesy.

FREDDIE GERSHON: Abe Burrows would walk into a rehearsal in New Haven when a show was in trouble, stand in the back, and give notes for nothing.

SHIRLEY HERZ: You'd go out on the road with a show and never know when you were going to get back. Pre-Broadway tours were always being extended. A two-week engagement could become four. It was like a plane circling to land at Kennedy. All the New York theaters were booked; you'd be waiting for someone to fail so you could come in.

HARVEY SABINSON: When a play finally got to Broadway, the opening night was a glamorous event. People dressed; many were in black tie.

DOUGLAS WATT: Sometimes there would be two or three openings in one night.

MERLE DEBUSKEY: Opening night was for critics who had to file for the next day's early edition, editors, columnists, and magazine people. Feature writers, weeklies—people who didn't have deadlines—came second night. Relations between media and theater people were very organized and understood, quid pro quo.

The press agent, with the consent of the producer, was responsible for seating. If I had a show opening at the Barrymore Theater, I would call the press agent who'd had the last show there, ask for his seating chart and whether there were any problems.

PETER STONE: Feuer and Martin, quintessential musical producers, would seat their opening-night audience like they were arranging a dinner party. They wouldn't let anyone in who had seen it before. They wouldn't let backers sit in the middle. They wouldn't let lawyers and agents sit downstairs. They wanted as close to a real audience as they could get.

MERLE DEBUSKEY: Opening night for *Mary, Mary* by Jean Kerr, Walter Kerr's wife, we looked at the list and saw Ed Sullivan was to be seated on the aisle in front of Earl Wilson. Since Sullivan was twice as big as Wilson, we thought the sensible thing to do was to switch them. As the lights began to go down, Sullivan rose up out of the seat, took his wife by the arm, and in a fury dashed up the aisle and out of the theater. He didn't like being seated behind Wilson. But that was the only instance during that period that we had problems.

There was a pecking order. You didn't want to sit Winchell near Kilgallen. You had to be sure that Brooks Atkinson from the *Times* and Walter Kerr from the *Tribune* were well situated.

DOUGLAS WATT: Walter Kerr always brought a notebook along. He'd take notes copiously until his wife, Jean, would remind him to look up at the stage. It's a pity the *Herald Tribune* is no longer there to counterbalance the *Times,* which has always felt it's on Mount Olympus.

When the *Times* hired Stanley Kaufman, they got him tickets for a pre-opening-night performance so he could have more time to write his review. For some reason he was not equipped to go back and write a review the same night. David Merrick got wind of it and canceled the performance, claiming there was a rat in the generator. He gave everyone their money back. So Kaufman had to go to opening night. But that started the business of allowing the press to come to previews.

Before then, the curtain would come down and you'd dash up the aisle, almost knocking some elderly couple over on your way out, rush to your typewriter, and write a review in thirty or forty minutes. You couldn't wait to write it. At three in the morning you might wake up and think of an adjective you should have used. But having time to mull it over, you could never display the same enthusiasm as fully.

MERLE DEBUSKEY: After the show, people used to assemble at Sardi's. It's around the corner from the *Times,* and when the second edition, with Brooks Atkinson, came out, the papers would be dropped off. The place could either be filled with excitement or empty out in a flash. I can't tell you how quickly a restaurant can empty out.

VINCENT SARDI, JR.: When the producer or press agent told us not to let the papers in, we'd get the message. It's not a good review.

Sardi's had begun in a brownstone at 146 West Forty-fourth Street in 1921. We lived over the restaurant and took in boarders. All the old hotels were full of theater people back then. There was no radio, no television,

Sardi's in 1947. Even then it had been a Broadway hangout for more than twenty years.

no movies. It was all live theater, whether drama, vaudeville, burlesque, nightclub acts. Theater people, directors, actors, musicians—they all lived here. That's what the neighborhood was like, and Sardi's was a neighborhood restaurant. My parents were Italian, but they never called Sardi's an Italian restaurant because that connoted tomatoes and spaghetti.

In 1927, when they moved to the current site at 234 West Forty-fourth Street, it was still Prohibition. Ninety percent of the restaurants in the area were speakeasies. Dad never ran a speakeasy, but those he knew were able to get some liquor in a cup.

It was a comfortable atmosphere, friendly. Dad was here all the time. Mother did all the buying. Nobody had charge accounts back then, so there was a lot of holding the tab until people eventually paid.

MERLE DEBUSKEY: The Sardi family was theater oriented. If you were broke they took care of you and not a word was said. They did a lot of that.

VINCENT SARDI, JR.: There was a crowd that went to all the openings; they had their own tables. That's how the opening-night tradition got started. When Shirley Booth came in after *Come Back, Little Sheba,* the restaurant was full, and she got a standing ovation. That's how that tradition got started.

V. MAX KLIMAVICIUS: I was told that Alec Guinness used to sit at what is now table number one and read. The lamp is still there. The front area on the left became the preferred place to sit, simply because it's the easiest place for the maître d' to control.

Some of the caricatures have disappeared along the way. Today, as soon as they are signed, we make two copies: one goes on the wall and one goes to the subject.

VINCENT SARDI, JR.: After Jessica Tandy's success as Blanche Dubois in *Streetcar,* we had a caricature made of her. She signed it, "Now I know that I have arrived."

MERLE DEBUSKEY: The Russian Tea Room attracted theater people; they congregated in the first booths opposite the bar before the restaurant proper. Harold Clurman was the guru of that corner. The Algonquin was another high-class place where the literati used to hang out. Thornton Wilder seemed to always be at the blue-mirrored bar. When the English came over—Olivier, Gielgud—they would stay there. It was quiet. You didn't go there to be seen.

There were also the less fashionable places, little restaurants and bars dotting the whole area. On an empty night you'd go over to Patsy's down on Forty-fifth or Harry's on Forty-sixth Street, where you could hang out the night eating a big bowl of bean soup. Lindy's had another crowd, not so much legit theater people as nightclub types. There were jazz joints on Fifty-second Street and nightclubs all around the place. The scene was such that you could stay up till midmorning.

NORMAN BEIM: A lot of us starving actors hung out at the Horn and Hardart at Forty-sixth Street. We'd make tomato soup out of ketchup and hot water, or lemonade from lemons, sugar, and water. I lived on eighteen dollars a week, including my room, which was six dollars. In the morning I'd load trucks or do odd jobs. In the afternoon I'd make the rounds: 1776 Broadway, 1650 Broadway, the Brill Building, the Paramount Building. If I was lucky I was sent out on auditions.

I auditioned for a role in *A Respectful Prostitute* for a summer production. They asked, "Are you Equity?" I said, "Of course." Then I ran over to Equity, located in an old brownstone on Forty-seventh Street near Sixth Avenue. I dashed up several flights of stairs, past a picture of Edwin Booth in the hallway, and paid my dues with borrowed money. At last I was a professional actor.

LINDA LAVIN: The first show I auditioned for was *A Family Affair.* There was an audition just about every day if you could sing. I was the only chorus member who could walk and talk at the same time, so I ended up with four different speaking parts. In those days you got five dollars extra for every speaking part.

ARTHUR SEELEN: After the war the American Theater wing gave courses to reinstruct professional actors. That was where I met Hal Holbrook. One day Hal told me he wouldn't be making the next session because he was opening in this little thing at some small theater. A few days later I was looking through the *Times,* and there was an extraordinary review of *Mark Twain Tonight!* I know this guy, I thought, he can't be famous.

But I got to know many famous theater people after I bought the Drama Book Shop. Every actor who has ever studied at the Neighborhood Playhouse, the Actors Studio, anywhere, has bought books here. One hot summer day, Marlene Dietrich came into the store in a white silk dress and wide-brimmed hat. "I'm very anxious to get a copy of *Witness for the Prosecution,* and I believe it's out of print," she said. "Import it. Do whatever is possible. I don't care what it costs."

ROZANNE SEELEN: It took us just one day to find a paperback copy.

The theater was cooking and you were there.

Cost: twenty-five cents. We called her up, and she came right down. It was hard to tell what got her more excited, the price or the fast service.

ARTHUR SEELEN: Laurence Olivier asked us to send up a copy of a play. One of my young people brought it into his hotel. They thought he was a bill collector and kept him waiting. When they finally let him up to the room, Olivier was packing. A few bottles of champagne were on the dresser. "Shall we pack these or drink them?" he asked the kid.

FOSTER HIRSCH: When I arrived from California in the mid-sixties, Broadway was a little bit dilapidated, but every theater was open. It was the last gasp of the old Broadway, when plays were produced. Some were very modest sorts of things—mild comedies, mild murder mysteries. In 1965 the top orchestra price was $6.90.

MANNY AZENBERG: "Fertile" would be the understatement for that period. The theater was cooking and you were there. Theater was the queen of battle. Film wasn't important and television was low-rent. Theater was art; the rest was shlock.

The waterfall and the Camel billboard blowing smoke rings—unmistakable symbols of the Great White Way.

HOWARD KISSEL: In the 1950s, when I was growing up in Milwaukee, Broadway was still a national institution, and I had a clear sense of New York as the center of the American theatrical universe. First-class touring companies came to us. I saw my first Broadway play at the Pabst Theater when I was a high school freshman: *The Lark,* starring Julie Harris, who had done the role on Broadway. It was a great play, a perfect play for an adolescent, and a transforming experience. I had seen amateur plays before, but I knew that this was special. The two hours I was in the theater, I felt I was living life on an exalted plane. I couldn't wait to go back.

During the four years I was in high school, I saw *The Visit* with the Lunts, *The Diary of Anne Frank* with much of the original cast, Constance Bennett in *Auntie Mame,* Geraldine Page and Rip Torn in *Sweet Bird of Youth,* and Miriam Hopkins in *Look Homeward Angel.*

When I came to New York as part of my high school's junior class tour, the waterfall and the Camel were still there. And so was the sense of endless bustle and excitement. We stayed at what was then the Manhattan, now the Milford Plaza, on Forty-fifth and Eighth. We took our meals at the *New York Times* cafeteria. To see the lights of Broadway was like a dream come true. My father worked on a newspaper in Milwaukee, and he was able to get me sixth-row center seats for *West Side Story.* It was astounding.

I was an odd child. While my friends were listening to early rock, I was saving up to buy original cast albums. I had bought the record to *West Side Story* shortly after it came out, and I loved it. But to see it was beyond belief. The next night we sat up in the balcony and saw *The Music Man.* It still had its original cast.

In its heyday Broadway was a world as vibrant, if not more vibrant, than the so-called real world. It had been going on for a long time. We didn't know this was a golden age; we thought it was normal. But it was something extraordinary.

The postwar euphoria somehow expressed itself in the theater. Which is not such a strange phenomenon. If you go back over the centuries, you have great periods of theater when a nation is at its zenith. When is the great period of Greek drama? The Age of Pericles. When is the great period of English drama? After the defeat of the Spanish Armada, when Elizabeth I had come to the height of her power. When is the great period of French drama? The seventeenth century, under Louis XIV. It seems to me there is some kind of correlation. It has to do with the buoyancy of a nation aware that it is at the peak of its power.

3 | IT WAS AN EXCITING TIME TO BE IN THE THEATER

ROBERT WHITEHEAD: It was after the war. Nobody was hiring me, and so I thought of a way to hire myself. I read in the *New York Times* that a new version of *Medea* by the modern poet Robinson Jeffers had been dropped by the Theater Guild. If the Guild had been interested, I thought, it must be something worthwhile. I guessed they had become fearful of producing it. If I had been twenty-five years older, I would have been fearful, too.

I picked up a copy at the Drama Book Shop. This *Medea* is very modern, very strong, and very American in feeling. All of that appealed to me. Jeffers stayed exactly with Euripides, yet he wrote the play in relation to our times. His Medea is a schizophrenic character; she never commits herself to killing her children. It's like this idea comes to her of destroying Jason by destroying her own sons. She can't bear the idea, yet she can't get rid of it. It keeps coming back to her, like a recurring theme of a symphony. Until finally she does it. This is a more horrific *Medea*.

Jeffers made the work a social calamity. He wrote it soon after the war, and the aura of the nuclear age hung over the play. He attached the story to the fate of the world. Jeffers's Medea was a force of nature, a danger that you shouldn't play with because if you do, it will destroy you totally.

I thought if I could get a very great actress in the middle of this, it would excite an audience. I got Judith Anderson to play Medea. And then I got John Gielgud to play Jason and direct.

Judith Anderson was extraordinary; she had a huge talent. She was an animal-like figure on stage. But at all times we had nothing but disagreements. Our relationship was horrible. I think she felt I was a kind of young upstart. I wanted to do the play in certain ways that were probably too modern in feeling for her. She was right, I'm sure.

OPPOSITE PAGE

A scene from Robert Whitehead's second production of *Medea*, starring Zoe Caldwell as Medea (left) and Dame Judith Anderson as the nurse (1982).

After it played in New York, I wanted to put *Medea* on in London. I asked Judith if she would do it. "Not if you're the producer," she said. That burned me up so much that I went off to London and did it with somebody else. It was a mistake; it didn't work. I was so angry, I thought I would never speak to Judith again.

Thirty years passed. One day I got a call from the Robinson Jeffers Foundation asking me if I would come out to Carmel, California, where Jeffers had lived, and do *Medea* in their open-air theater. They said my wife, Zoe Caldwell, is the one woman in the world who can play the title role. Zoe read the script. "I think I can play that lady," she said.

I went out to meet with the people from the foundation. "You really must go up and see Judith Anderson, who is living in Santa Barbara," they said.

"Why do you say I must see Judith Anderson?" I asked.

"Because she's the one who told us to call you, and she's the one who said you are married to the only woman in the world who can play Medea."

Judith was now about eighty-five. She stepped out of her house. "You stopped me from doing the one thing I wanted to do in my life," she said to me.

"What are you talking about?"

"The London production of *Medea*."

"I begged you to do it. But you said you wouldn't if I produced it."

"Why should I? You treated me so terribly."

I thought to myself, This is the exact conversation we had thirty years ago. Finally I said, "Let's forget all of that. Let's not discuss it."

Then she said, "I want to play the nurse."

"I couldn't do it with you, Judith, I couldn't."

"Whom are you going to get who is better?"

"I couldn't direct it with you."

"Oh, my god, don't tell me you're going to direct?" Then she quickly added, "I still want to play the nurse."

We tried out at the University of Tennessee at Knoxville, then went on to Kennedy Center in Washington, D.C., and finally brought the production to New York. Judith was marvelous, and this time we had a great relationship. She was helpful; she wanted to live again through Zoe. She stayed away and came in at the right moments. We had an absolute love affair, and I saw her year after year until she died. I spoke at her funeral.

At the time Zoe and I did *Medea,* our sons were about the same age as the two boys in the play. As director, I was evoking my feeling for our children, and Zoe had a strange seeking depth of emotion in Medea's catastrophe. When she got into that aspect, she had something more deeply moving than Judith. I set this production back in the Bronze Age, a more primitive time. And I put that staircase dead center stage. It's easier to stage the play with the staircase off to the side. But I couldn't resist having that staircase dead-on.

Eugene O'Neill is one of our American playwrights whose plays have the kind of lasting power that *Medea* has. After his death in 1953, his widow, Carlotta Monterey, asked me to go up to Yale and read *Long Day's Journey into Night*. She had it impounded in the Yale Library. "The play will never be done in my lifetime," she said, "but you must read it."

It was not a clean script. I sat all day in the Yale Library. Then I came back and told her, "You've got to do that play right away. It's an extraordinary American work that should be done immediately."

"Eugene expressly said it should not be done until twenty-five years after his death. And I will live up to his wishes." She went on and on.

"It's crazy," I said. "It should be done now. I wish you'd let me go to work on it."

Carlotta was beautiful, but she was not easy. She was manipulative, determined to bring O'Neill back. She gave *Long Day's Journey into Night* to the Circle in the Square people in Greenwich Village, who had already done a production of *The Iceman Cometh*. I was in England when I read about it, and I was burned up.

We met in her apartment after I came back. I told her she was a traitor. "Never mind," she said, "I have a present for you." She went upstairs and took a manuscript out of a safe. "This play is for you," she said.

"I want the other one," I said.

"Be satisfied with this."

It was *A Touch of the Poet.* I did it with Helen Hayes, Eric Portman, Kim Stanley, and Betty Field. Eric was a drinker, he was a mess sexually, but he was brilliant, perfect for the part. Eric was a wild black Irishman. He had something inside his guts, and it always came out. Where he got it from and why is impossible to explain.

I did a lot of things with Helen. They all were successful because she was successful. She was a terrific pro, tough-minded, terribly bright—

there are very few people who get to that size as an actress who aren't bright. But she was not sweetness and light.

During the production there were historic fights backstage. Helen accused Eric of drinking and me of producing the play without enough intelligence to keep it together. Kim Stanley was another big, impossible talent. Only Betty Field, a lovely actress, tried to keep out of it. We played for quite a while, but the atmosphere backstage was so bad that I closed the show early. I was never happier to close a show. It was like getting in the line of fire whenever you walked backstage.

PHILIP LANGNER: My parents believed serious American drama began with Eugene O'Neill. Their organization, the Theater Guild, was his producer during the 1920s, 1930s, and 1940s, mounting such works as *Mourning Becomes Electra; Ah, Wilderness!; Days without End; The Iceman Cometh; A Moon for the Misbegotten.* The most expensive, my father told me, cost the horrifying sum of thirteen thousand dollars. But they neither produced nor ever saw *Long Day's Journey into Night* because of the stipulation O'Neill made in his will. They felt Carlotta betrayed him.

O'Neill was always very kind to me. He was lean and muscular, a strange, absentminded kind of person who would wander about our house in a world of his own, so concentrated on what he was thinking that you could speak to him and he'd never hear you. When I was in my early twenties, he invited me to his Park Avenue apartment for tea. He and Carlotta spent the entire afternoon telling me how terrible life was. "You must have a hard time of it, my son," they said. "Don't you agree that things are really grim?" Before I left, they presented me with Spengler's *Decline of the West.* When I finally got away, I had the sense of having spent some hours inside a dark Eugene O'Neill play.

Carlotta was such a dominating personality, and Eugene was so pitiful, so shaky, so physically weak. They were living up in Marblehead, Massachusetts, when he came down to the city one day and called my mother, asking if he could borrow some money. She gave him five thousand dollars. A few days later Carlotta burst into our apartment, absolutely furious. She got ahold of my mother. "I'm giving you the money back," she said, and there and then wrote a check.

My father, Lawrence Langner, together with five partners, had founded the Theater Guild in 1919. He was a patent attorney who came to this country from Wales around 1910, and he continued his law practice

I had the sense of having spent some hours inside a dark Eugene O'Neill play.

throughout his professional life. He used to joke that he needed to earn the money in order to lose it in the theater. That was probably true. When they had a flop or needed money, each of the partners would put his hand in his pocket and bring out five hundred dollars. In the 1930s, the Theater Guild did thirteen flops in a row.

My mother was the actress Armina Marshall. She appeared with George Abbott in one play; he was an important actor before he became a director. When I was very young I saw my mother in a play where somebody locked her in a bathroom onstage, and I started to cry tempestuously because I thought it was the real thing.

I was born with a silver spoon in my mouth, a theatrical silver spoon. We lived on West Twelfth Street in Greenwich Village and were part of the exciting theater scene of the times. As a child, I met hundreds of famous people, although I had no idea of their importance. One who made a big impression on me was Anna May Wong, the Chinese actress from California who wore very exotic flowing silk clothes. She was typical of the glamorous artists who peopled that world.

My father had an office in a building just to the west of the Theater Guild Theater. His office and the balcony of the theater were connected by a big sliding fire door. I would cross over from the office to the balcony and watch what was going on below. It was quite an introduction to the theater. In 1935 they brought me to see *Porgy and Bess,* which the Guild produced. They planned on taking me home before the last scene, which they thought would be too sad for me. But they forgot, and I didn't find it that sad. The whole point was lost on me.

According to my parents, before the Theater Guild, American theater was totally commercial: comedies, vaudeville, revues, and soap opera–type melodramas. It was the Guild that began bringing over serious plays from Europe by people like Bernard Shaw, August Strindberg, Franz Werfel. It was the Guild that brought Alfred Lunt and Lynn Fontanne together for the first time, in 1924 in *The Guardsman,* by Ferenc Molnár. It was the Guild that raised America's theater consciousness.

The Guild brought Richard Rodgers and Lorenz Hart together in *Garrick Gaieties* in 1925. It was a little tiny thing they did in an afternoon at the Guild Theater, but it included such songs as "Manhattan" and "Mountain Greenery." Rodgers and Hart had written in college together, but this was their first Broadway production. At that time Rodgers was just one day away from

OPPOSITE PAGE

Lawrence Langner (right), one of the founders of the Theater Guild, with Laurence Olivier and June Havoc.

taking a job in a ladies' underwear company. That's what his folks wanted to him to do—get involved in a serious business.

Katharine Hepburn's first work for the Guild was in a Philip Barry play in 1935. They had spent a great deal of money on it. But when they were in Boston, she decided she hated the play and didn't like herself in it. She asked my parents not to bring it in. They agreed. That was a real twist: agreeing to not do a play. Ever after that, Katharine remained their loyal star. She never had a contract, just a handshake. When Equity insisted she have a contract, she would work for minimum until the show paid back.

Walter Huston also worked without a contract. My father suggested they draw one up when Huston was cast in William Saroyan's *Love's Old Sweet Song*. "Oh no," Huston said. "You can break a contract, but you can't break your word."

That play was a favorite of my father's, even though it was a flop. It came on the heels of Saroyan's big hit *The Time of Your Life,* which the Guild produced as well. Until *A Streetcar Named Desire, The Time of Your Life* was the only play to receive both the Pulitzer Prize and the Critics' Circle Award.

I remember Saroyan as being somewhat demented in a nice sort of way. During rehearsals he'd sit around eating pears and apples that he'd peel with a dangerous-looking pocketknife. He had all these cousins, an Armenian Mafia, who began coming in from the West Coast. "This is my cousin Joe," he'd say. "We've got to give him a part in the play."

"You can't just give someone a part," my father would protest.

"I'll write something for him." Saroyan was constantly adding new parts. His plays had that crazy-quilt quality.

Gene Kelly, who played Harry, was not an Armenian relative, but he had danced in a little revue in my parents' summer theater in Westport, Connecticut. After George Abbott and Richard Rodgers saw him in *The Time of Your Life,* they picked him for the lead in *Pal Joey,* and from there Gene went on to his great career in Hollywood. William Bendix as the policeman and Celeste Holm in her Broadway debut, as Mary Ell—they also went on to great success as a result of appearing in *The Time of Your Life.*

CELESTE HOLM: We used to eat lunch at Walgreens, and then we would go and look for jobs. Walking up Forty-fourth Street, I ran into Richard Whorf, who was in the Lunts' National Company. He said they were casting for *The Taming of the Shrew,* and I'd be perfect for Bianca. "Fine," I said, "but how do I get past the woman at the door?"

Card

Celeste Holm began her Broadway career in the Theater Guild's production of *The Time of Your Life.*

"Just say I sent you," he said.

The woman at the door sent me upstairs, where a bunch of college girls were waiting. They all wore saddle shoes, cashmere sweaters, strings of pearls, and glasses, and they were all carrying their Shakespeares. I was wearing a black dress, black hat, pearl button earrings.

The door opened, and there was Lynn Fontanne. She had the most incredible skin. It looked as if there were a light coming from the inside. Black eyes, black hair, gray dress, and terribly English. "I'm terribly sorry," she said. "I only have time for one more. I'll see . . . you!

"I don't want you to waste your time by asking you to do something that you don't want to do," she said. "Let me tell you exactly what I want."

I did what she wanted, and she said, "You're very good indeed. Can you come back tomorrow?"

The following day Sydney Greenstreet, who was part of the Lunt Company, was there. Alfred Lunt was pacing up and down. Lynn said, "Sit down, darling, I want you to hear this girl."

I read. He jumped up and said, "You're wonderful. Where have you been?"

I said, "School, stock."

That night the telephone rang: "This is Lynn Fontanne, and I'm terribly sorry. But I've given your name to Theresa Helburn, who is an executive of the Theater Guild. You'll hear from her."

The following week I got a call to come in and see Miss Helburn.

She had blue hair. She looked like a Pekingese with her flat face. "Oh, my dear," she said, "you're much too young. This woman has to be at least thirty."

"Can I read?"

"Of course."

I went into the ladies' room and did my hair up the way my mother did hers, and I washed off all my makeup, because makeup is specific.

I was in the waiting room reading *The Time of Your Life* along with every well-known ingenue in town. They all knew each other, which made me feel like a real outsider.

Then Miss Helburn came out. "Come on, children."

We went downstairs and onto the stage. There was an upright piano there. I sat behind it and was able to see everyone, although they couldn't see me. They were all fine; they were all charming. After they finished Miss Helburn asked, "Is that all?"

I stood up. "I'm still here."

She said, "You look entirely different."

"I washed my face. May I read?"

I read. There was a dead silence. "I understand there is another part. I can be shorter if I take off my shoes," I said.

A voice from the third row called out, "What's the matter with this part? Don't you want it?"

Miss Helburn came scuffling over to me. "This is, uh, uh, William Saroyan."

"How do you do," I said.

Miss Helburn said, "Can you leave for Boston tonight?"

And I said, "You bet."

All night long the train was saying, "You're working for the Theater Guild. You're working for the Theater Guild." Beside me a man was snoring. I don't think I slept a wink. The next morning I was bumping bottoms with him. He turned out to be the head of the Guild, Mr. Langner.

"Oh, Miss Holm, may I take you to the theater?"

I wanted to go to the hotel first. But I went to the theater. I never saw so many scared actors in my life. Julie Haydon came in, a dear person. She was one of those strange creatures who act even when they're offstage. Somebody said she was always looking for gum under the seat.

"You should be playing my part," she said.

Mr. Langner asked me to read again, but Eddie Dowling, the codirector, said "What are you trying to do, kill an actor? You don't ask an actor to audition in front of a company that has been rehearsing for four weeks and playing for one. It's against the law."

So Mr. Langner said, "Come to my hotel around four o'clock this afternoon."

Well, I thought, I had been chased around a couple of desks, so I went to the Ritz. I had nothing to worry about, though. He couldn't have been nicer. I read, and he liked it. He sent me to the wardrobe master, who gave me a hundred dollars to buy myself a dress since I was replacing a woman who was a lot bigger than me. I went to Filene's Basement and bought a gray dress. I thought it looked like something Lynn Fontanne would wear. I also got gloves and shoes and came back with forty-nine dollars in change.

The Time of Your Life ran twenty-six weeks. William Bendix was a dear bear. Gene Kelly was charming. The part and the tapestry were fascinating. It remains one of my favorite plays.

ELAINE STEINBECK: About three or four us who worked for the Guild would sit in this big office, and the door to the office led onto the stage of the Theater Guild Theater, which is now the Virginia. I'd open it, and there would be Celeste Holm and Gene Kelly and all these people doing

She was one of those strange creatures who act even when they're offstage.

The Time of Your Life, or Walter Huston singing "But it's a long, long time from May to December," or Kate Hepburn rehearsing for *The Philadelphia Story,* which was such a great success both for her and the Guild. I'd see Jessica Tandy, who had just come from England with her child, had gotten out from under the Blitz. She was playing the ingenue to Paul Muni, who was a big star; Alfred Drake was playing the juvenile.

It was an exciting time to be in the theater, to work for the Theater Guild, to see plays by Robert Sherwood, Sidney Howard, S. N. Behrman, and Maxwell Anderson being produced. And this Texas girl had it right there at her fingertips. I had always wanted to act. I went to school with Lady Bird Johnson, and she still tells me what a good actress I was. But when I came up to New York it was very hard to get acting jobs, so I went into production. And, as it turned out, I was a witness to Broadway history.

During that time they had me stage-manage Paul Robeson's *Othello,* with Uta Hagen and Jose Ferrer. Then I was switched to *Oklahoma!* because they knew I came from Texas and was so passionate about the show. I wasn't the whole cheese. I was just a young woman, and *then* they would never let a young woman run an entire show.

Nine months of the year, I worked in New York City for the Guild, and three months at the Langners' Westport Country Playhouse.

PHILIP LANGNER: My parents had purchased their summer place in Westport, Connecticut, in 1929. A few years later, they bought an old barn and tannery that they turned into a theater. Their plan was to pre-pare a repertory of plays, performed by a repertory group, and bring the plays to New York the following season. Many great performers were first noticed at Westport: Patricia Neal, Montgomery Clift, Zachary Scott. Ethel Barrymore, Eva Le Gallienne, and Helen Hayes appeared there. Thornton Wilder took parts in his own plays—*Our Town* and *The Skin of Our Teeth,* which my mother appeared in as well.

It was at the Westport Country Playhouse that Dick Rodgers came to see *Green Grow the Lilacs,* which became *Oklahoma!,* one of the three musi-cals based on plays the Guild had produced, the other two being *Porgy and Bess,* from *Porgy,* and *Carousel,* from *Liliom.*

All along my father and my mother had only one aim, and that was to do good plays and get good notices. They did not look to the theater to espouse a particular point of view. Those who did—Elmer Rice, Clifford

Odets, and other young Turks—had left the Guild years before and started the Group Theater.

CHARLES STROUSE: In his time, there were few playwrights as famous as Clifford Odets. He was part of that political schism in American life, one of the great left-wing types, the fiery young playwright who wrote *Waiting for Lefty, Awake and Sing!,* and *Golden Boy,* which was produced by the Group Theater in 1937 and which was probably his biggest hit of all.

But by the time Lee Adams and I caught him, it was at the end. We were making a black musical out of *Golden Boy,* starring Sammy Davis, Jr. This was after Odets had gone out to Hollywood, and to us, he strongly conveyed a feeling of having sold out to the bitch goddess of success. He reminisced a lot, but he also bragged about flying out to Vegas in Frank Sinatra's plane and about sixteen-year-old starlets. He dropped names.

We were in Vegas. He told us he had a terrible problem with gambling, that we shouldn't let him near the tables. Nevertheless, around midnight, we would have to pull him away and say, "Get ye to the typewriter, because we've got to meet Sammy." I'm an early riser, and at six-thirty the next morning, I'd pass by the casino and see an unshaven Clifford. "I was going to quit," he'd say, "but I was ahead."

The first week of rehearsals for *Golden Boy,* Odets died.

PHILIP LANGNER: The Group Theater disbanded in 1940, but the Theater Guild thrived through the 1950s. We did *Picnic, Sunrise at Campobello,* several Sean O'Casey plays, and the musical *Bells Are Ringing,* with Judy Holliday.

In the spring of 1994 the Theater Guild celebrated its seventy-fifth anniversary at the Players Club. During the evening I mused about the impact the Guild has had on American theater, how it introduced both serious drama and the book musical to the American public, how it mounted the original productions of some of the greatest plays of our time and showcased some of the immortals of American theater. But more than twenty years had passed since the Guild had last produced a Broadway play. The risks had become much too great. If we could still be doing plays for thirteen thousand dollars, I'd be doing ten a year. But nowadays endowment funds are needed for serious drama. We had turned to touring plays and performances on cruise lines.

And then in the spring of 1996, we brought *State Fair* to Broadway. It was the production Jamie Hammerstein had been doing at the University of North Carolina in Winston-Salem, and somehow it seemed appropriate. The

Clifford Odets, one of the fiery playwrights of the Group Theater, after he had forsaken Broadway for Hollywood.

Theater Guild had done the first three Rodgers and Hammerstein musicals, *Oklahoma!, Carousel,* and *Allegro.* And *State Fair* was a show I had always loved.

There was a poignancy to the fact that it was Jamie and me, and Mary Rodgers was involved, too—the second generation of the Rodgers and Hammerstein–Theater Guild connection. We shared an empathy as the children of those people.

JAMES HAMMERSTEIN: *State Fair* is an audience show with a very simple story and simple characters. We never planned to bring it to New York, and then when we did, we expected to get killed because it was old-fashioned, not high tech at all. We couldn't afford spectacle. That would cost six million; we were a two-million-dollar show.

SUSAN L. SCHULMAN: Elaine Steinbeck paid for the painted scrim as a gesture to the Theater Guild, to Philip Langner.

It seemed everybody connected with *State Fair* needed it for different reasons. The Theater Guild needed it to get back on the map. John Davidson had gone on to television but always hoped to come back to Broadway. Kathryn Crosby had always wanted to be on Broadway. Although Andrea McArdle had had an enormous amount of early attention, she had never gotten back to the peak she had in *Annie.* Although Donna McKechnie had always worked, she never regained the kind of attention she had gotten in *A Chorus Line.*

PHILIP LANGNER: For six months we worked on doing and redoing it. I've never seen a play able to be worked on for so long a period of time. Finally there was nothing anyone could think of to make it better.

FOSTER HIRSCH: There were people who acted as if it was some kind of an insult for *State Fair* to be shown on Broadway. I imagine because it's innocent. We don't have innocent shows anymore. Even the musicals have to have a hard, corrosive edge.

PHILIP LANGNER: It got rave reviews everywhere, even in difficult cities like San Francisco. Chicago, Boston, Philadelphia, Washington. Then we came to New York and one critic on the *New York Times* hated it. It was a terrible slam.

Some plays get terrible slams and they survive, but for us it was the end. There were also the two "mod" musicals arriving in the same month: *Bring in 'Da Noise, Bring in 'Da Funk* and *Rent.* People wanted to see them and they didn't want to see ours with the same amount of passion. If it had been a previous season, with different competition, we "could have been a contender."

We don't have innocent shows anymore. Even the musicals have to have a hard, corrosive edge.

4 | THAT SENSE OF TRUTH

PHILIP LANGNER: For all the illustrious playwrights on its roster, the Theater Guild did not end up as the producer for two of the major post-war American playwrights: Tennessee Williams and Arthur Miller.

Tennessee actually was with us at the very beginning. In 1940 my parents invited him to spend the summer in a cottage on our Westport property. It was pretty rare for us to have a summerlong guest, but my parents believed Tennessee was the most promising young playwright they had come across in years. They wanted him to have solitude and quiet to work on his first full-length play, *The Battle of Angels.* At that time everybody brought their first plays to the Guild.

When my father introduced him, I thought how funny his name was. "He's a shoe salesman," my father said, and I thought that was very funny, too. But that's what Tennessee did in Saint Louis.

ELAINE STEINBECK: Opening night of *The Battle of Angels* in New Haven was chaotic. After, there was a big meeting. Everyone spoke up with suggestions about how to change the play. Tennessee just sat quietly and listened. When it was all over he said, "I put it down that-a-way, and that's the only way I know how to put it down." We moved on to Boston, and *The Battle of Angels* closed.

PHILIP LANGNER: After that, Tennessee was so very upset with my parents, he never let them do another one of his plays.

ELAINE STEINBECK: Once Tennessee heard me recount the story of that opening-night fiasco in New Haven, and he wrote a postscript that he made me promise to add every time I tell it: "After that, Tennessee went to see many plays all over the place and watched the audiences and how they reacted. And then he wrote *The Glass Menagerie* and *A Streetcar Named Desire.*"

IRVING SCHNEIDER: I began working with Irene Selznick after the war. Our first play was *Heartsong,* by Arthur Laurents. It wasn't very good, but

OPPOSITE PAGE

A scene from the original Broadway production of *A Streetcar Named Desire,* which starred Jessica Tandy (left), Kim Hunter, and Marlon Brando (1947).

Tennessee Williams leans against a ladder during a rehearsal of *Summer and Smoke* with producer and director, Margo Jones (right), and actors Margaret Phillips and Tod Andrews (1948).

we went over it hammer and tongs. Hovering around the production was an agent named Audrey Wood. We didn't know she was keeping an eagle eye on us for a purpose. Not much later Tennessee Williams completed *A Streetcar Named Desire,* and Audrey offered it to Irene. We were hysterical with joy. I became the production manager.

We got Elia Kazan to direct, and the cast fell into place quite naturally. We saw Kim Hunter in an English film. I had never heard of her but she seemed to answer all the specifications for Stella. We were lucky there. Jessica Tandy had done an evening of three one-act Tennessee Williams plays out in California, one of which became the basis for *Streetcar.* Kazan and Irene were able to see her as Blanche, a comparable role. Karl Malden was a perfect balance and certainly got his share of praise.

But when Marlon Brando threw open the door and came into the office, the whole staff went mad. Actually he was younger than the script called for, but one could tell very early on that he had a special dynamism. He didn't come in to read, just to talk; Kazan much preferred having conversations with actors. After, he sent Brando up to Provincetown to read for Tennessee, but en route Marlon disappeared for two days before he finally showed up. Nobody ever found out where he had been.

PRICE BERKLEY: In 1947 *The Eagle Has Two Heads* was trying out at the Playhouse Theater in Wilmington, Delaware. The flamboyant Tallulah Bankhead was the star of this play by the renowned French playwright Jean Cocteau. A relatively unknown actor by the name of Marlon Brando was playing the role of Stanislas, a revolutionary poet. At one performance, when Miss Bankhead was in the midst of a monologue, Mr. Brando kept distracting her by his continuous mumbling. The very next day Bankhead had him fired. When the play opened in New York at the Plymouth he had been replaced by Helmut Dantine.

The Eagle did not fare well on Broadway. It closed on April 12, 1947, after twenty-nine performances. However, before the end of the year—to be exact, on December 3, 1947—Mr. Brando opened at the Ethel Barrymore Theater in the role of Stanley Kowalski, a role with which he would become identified throughout his entire career.

KIM HUNTER: Marlon had that sense of truth. As Karl Malden said, "Marlon can make wrong choices, bad choices, but the one thing he cannot be is false."

We had all kinds of mishaps and adventures during the run. There was a trio up onstage playing the music during the play. It would not have worked to have them in the pit. One night the music didn't come through. It was very important, especially in the scene where I came down the stairs. Marlon and I talked about it afterward. We both felt naked; we almost forgot what the scene was about without the music.

Once when Marlon threw the radio out the window and I grabbed at him, his T-shirt tore. Somehow it looked right, so he kept it that way. Another time he came down the stairs and carried me into the bedroom, which was behind a screen. We got onto the bed, only the lights didn't come down. "Oh Christ," Marlon said, "how far do we have to go for realism?"

One time in the rape scene neither the lights nor the curtain came down. Nothing was happening. So Marlon picked Jessie up and carried her over to the closet. "What are you going to do?" she said to him. "Hang me on a hook and rape me there?" Jessie had some problems with Marlon every now and then.

IRVING SCHNEIDER: Jessica always behaved like a professional; Marlon sometimes did and sometimes did not. He got bored, would play tricks backstage, practical jokes. We had to live with that. He kept a motorcycle outside the theater and took one spill during the run. We got off easy.

KIM HUNTER: We had a marvelous property master, Moe Jacobs. Every night his wife cooked a chicken for the birthday dinner scene—except for one night when she may have been sick or something and Moe picked up a chicken from some deli. The scene called for Marlon to stuff himself, make a pig out of himself, and usually that was no problem. But this time the chicken was pink, nearly raw. Nevertheless Marlon stuffed himself with it and finished out the scene. But he came off furious. "I'd rather eat dog shit than that," he said. Next night, someone put dog shit from one of those joke stores on his plate. He managed around it, but for about a week afterward, that dog shit wound up all over the stage.

We tried our best to keep *Streetcar* fresh, as if it were always the first time we were going out there. But by the time we got together to do the film, Kazan said, "All right, now let's get back to Tennessee's original play."

IRVING SCHNEIDER: All during rehearsals and even on the road, we really didn't know *Streetcar* would be a smash hit. It was rather earthy and different. We didn't realize what we had. Throughout the entire run I would stand outside and marvel. I never got over it.

I see the point I want to make, and I make it. And if there's a joke along the way, I make that, too.

KIM HUNTER: After *A Streetcar Named Desire* opened in New Haven, Irene Selznik hosted a party for Tennessee Williams and the cast. She also invited Thornton Wilder, who was teaching at Yale at the time. And of course everyone waited to hear what Thornton had to say about the play. He said it was marvelous in most respects, except he thought the character of Blanche was just too complex.

And Tennessee said, "But people are complex, Thorn."

Irene attempted to change the subject. "It's so rare to have two marvelous writers in the same room at the same time. How wonderful it would be to hear how each of you work."

Thornton started. And it was all logical. He explained how he came up with his idea. He described how he did his research. He went into detail about how he made up an overall outline and outlines for all his characters. Eventually, he said, he got around to writing dialogue. His method was very orderly.

All the time Wilder was talking, Tennessee was squinching down in the couch, getting redder and redder in the face. Then it was his turn.

"Well," he said. "I get a couple of people together, and I get them talking. And eventually I see the point I want to make, and I make it. And if there's a joke along the way, I make that, too."'

MAUREEN STAPLETON: Tennessee Williams was a delicious man, always the gentleman. I not only love his writing, but I love the fact that he gave me a lot of work. All in all, I was in six of his plays. My first big role was Serafina in *The Rose Tattoo,* opposite Eli Wallach.

Tennessee was away in Italy when I added this wonderful bit, kissing the statue of the Virgin. It only took a second. Then Tennessee came back, and one night he came to the theater, and afterward we went out to dinner together. All during the meal I kept waiting for him to mention this magic moment I had found. But he didn't say anything. Finally, as we were going out the door, he nonchalantly turned and said, "Hey, Maureen, what are you doing slobbering all over the Virgin?"

"Tenn," I said, a little taken aback, "I thought it was a wonderful touch."

"Don't do it, honey. Just blow out the candle and get out."

PHILIP LANGNER: At one time Arthur Miller had been one of Terry Helburn's protégés. But sadly for us, he went to Kermit Bloomgarden to produce his plays.

FLORA ROBERTS: My first job out of college was working for Kermit Bloomgarden, who had just started as a producer and had yet to have a hit. The office was on the corner of Forty-sixth Street and Broadway, above the Gaiety Delicatessen. I was involved with the story and casting departments and read plays in a small back office that was used by other people as well. But mostly I sat behind a little gate and worked as switchboard operator, receptionist, and secretary. Part of my job was to gather the theater review page of every newspaper each morning and put them across the gate. When Kermit Bloomgarden came in, he'd pick them up along with the key to the men's room, and read them in the john.

Whenever I read new plays I would put my hand over the name of the playwright so as not to be frightened by the author. One day I read a play called *Death of a Salesman*. The author was unfamiliar to me. But it was so painfully moving, and except for Eugene O'Neill and the best early Tennessee Williams, as good a play as I had ever read. I knew only a few people had seen it, maybe Elia Kazan and a few others. So it was a real thrill for me to have the chance to write it up for Kermit Bloomgarden.

Kermit decided to produce it, and even though it had no stars and an unknown playwright, I gave him the five hundred dollars I had saved up to that point. Ultimately it cost sixty thousand dollars to put on. It was five thousand here, ten thousand there, and five hundred from me.

Theater parties had started the season before, with *Kiss Me Kate*. All the theater-party agents seemed to be big women with large bosoms who wore black Persian lamb coats. They were very emotional over fixing dates for "their girls," which was how they called the women in their organizations.

Mrs. Hershkowitz was the great theater-party agent. When she heard about the new play we were doing she said to me, "Kermit Bloomgarden is a liar and a thief. You're still a nice girl. Tell me the truth, darling, is this a good play?"

"Mrs. Hershkowitz," I said, "this is so good a play that I invested five hundred dollars in it. I don't want you to buy theater-party tickets, because you get wholesale prices. This play is going to be a great hit, and you'll cut into my profits."

"Aha," she said, "you're learning to be a liar and a thief."

Then she took a look at the manuscript title. "My girls won't buy *Death*."

We actually had a meeting over whether we should call the play *Death of a Salesman*. "This is about the *death* of a salesman," Arthur Miller said. And that's how it stayed.

The original Broadway production of *Death of a Salesman* starred, from left to right, Mildred Dunnock, Lee J. Cobb, Arthur Kennedy, and Cameron Mitchell (1949).

The play opened in Philadelphia on a Saturday night. The set wasn't ready, so we opened late. We had no advance sales, but Paul Muni was starring in *They Knew What They Wanted* across the street, so we got the overflow.

There were a lot of young dating couples in the audience. We sat up in the balcony. It was very, very quiet. Nobody knew what to expect. Then it began. And as the play unfolded, everyone in the audience moved forward in their seats. The woman sitting next to me started to cry. I remembered how during rehearsals people would always be crying, and Kazan would say, "Please, keep quiet. I'm trying to listen to the actors."

When the play ended there was no applause whatsoever, only deathly silence. The actors came out for the first curtain call, and still there was total silence. It was only when the curtain came up again that everyone started applauding.

I walked out of the theater into the lobby. There in the corner was Mrs. Hershkowitz, who had come down to Philly. Her face was covered with mascara. Obviously she had been crying. I went up to her. "Mrs. Hershkowitz," I asked, "is this is a good play?"

"Oh yes," she said. "It is a good play. But maybe you could call it *Life of a Salesman?*"

HAL HOLBROOK: When I saw the original production of *Death of a Salesman* in 1949, it was like a blow right in the solar plexus; I couldn't talk afterward. It had the power of a great big freight train. For years afterward, when I thought of Willy Loman the image of Lee J. Cobb, this big, brooding, round-shouldered guy, was in my brain.

CLIVE BARNES: I saw Paul Muni play Willy Loman eight times in England. It was remarkable, a universal play. Interestingly enough, in England Lee J. Cobb starred in *All My Sons*.

DOUGLAS WATT: I still can't forget Lee J. Cobb. He was immense. Whenever I see somebody else play Willy Loman, I can't entirely accept him.

HAL HOLBROOK: I had never played Willy Loman, never saw myself playing him. And then, early in 1996, I had the opportunity to do it on national tour. I started thinking of my grandfather who brought me up in South Weymouth, Massachusetts, the same territory Willy Loman covered. My grandfather was a very successful salesman who had traveling salesmen come through the house all the time. Neither he nor any of his colleagues looked like the Willy Loman of Lee J. Cobb. They had

wing-tipped shoes, usually a little mustache, neatly combed hair. They suggested how much of a salesman is about appearance. It was out of these salesmen I had seen as a kid, as well as hundreds of other people I have met in my life, that I created my own kind of Willy Loman.

PAUL LIBIN: I was a young man growing up in Chicago when I saw *Death of a Salesman* in a touring company with Thomas Mitchell, and I've had a passion for it ever since. That was when I said to myself, "I want to be an actor." The play went right to my heart.

After the play I saw Thomas Mitchell walking down the stage-door alley of the Erlanger Theater with his hat tucked down over his head, and I was stunned. "My god," I said, "Willy Loman is alive!"

I was on a double date with my friend Sheldon Mitchell, who had borrowed his father's car. On the way home he and his girlfriend were talking in the front seat of the car, and all I kept thinking was, How can they talk about something other than the play?

I thought about the stories my dad used to tell. He delivered milk with a horse and wagon. One day all the milkmen were called in and lined up. The foreman said, "Which one of you guys has a driver's license?" Three out of the twenty-four did. He said, "Come with me." Half hour later, he came back. "You guys are fired," he said to the other twenty-one men. He didn't even have the courtesy to tell them they were fired for not having a driver's license. My father was one of the twenty-one.

Arthur Miller tapped into something so true about American culture, about the ruthlessness of capitalism, about how people delude themselves into thinking they're part of the American dream. There are lines in that play that give me the chills even today. Like when the owner of the firm tells Willy he has a tape recorder at home, and when he and his family go out on Sunday nights and can't listen to Jack Benny, they just turn the tape recorder on, and when they get home, they listen to him and have a good laugh. And Willy is kissing his ass, saying how wonderful that is, how wonderful. Or later, when Willy tells his neighbor Charlie, "Your son, he didn't even say he was going to the Supreme Court to argue a case." And Charlie says, "He doesn't have to."

But the most heart-wrenching part of the play for me is when Willy and Biff and Happy are in that bar, and the sons are picking up these girls, and one of the girls makes mention of Willy sitting all by himself and says, "Who's that man looking at us?" And Happy says, "Oh, he's just a guy." This all sank into me, ripped me apart. My kids know what a passion this play is for me. I always tell them, "When you go for an interview and a pencil falls on the floor, don't pick it up. They have office boys for that."

HAL HOLBROOK: On national tour in 1996, we discovered dimensions that did not rise to the surface all those years ago. If anything, *Death of a Salesman* is an even more powerful work today. We see a dysfunctional family that is trying to hold together. In 1949 we weren't even talking about dysfunctional families. When we did a couple of morning performances for two thousand high schoolers in Nashville, the kids were riveted. You could feel the depth of their silence during the scene when the two sons are upstairs and Willy comes down to have his milk. The sons are talking about how they have possessions but still are lonely. They've come home to their parents, they don't know where they're going, they're lost. It's a scene that taps right into today.

What is the first thing Willy Loman does? He gives his son a punching bag. He attacks his neighbor because he doesn't know who Red Grange is. If you don't know sports, you're illiterate. That, too, is a dimension of the play that is so topical. We've replaced the Statue of Liberty with a pair of sneakers. It's all power, bang. Every time somebody shoots a basket or throws a football, they jump up. Macho sports permeate the play, making the irony darker than it ever was.

PAUL LIBIN: In 1957 I was working for Joe Mielziner as a production assistant. We wanted to do *The Crucible* off Broadway. The Broadway production had been acclaimed, but it didn't flourish.

Arthur Miller wanted to approve the theater. We found a fifty-by-fifty-foot space at the Hotel Martinique on Thirty-second Street and Broadway. I asked the owner if I could bring the playwright down to see it.

"We don't have an arrangement yet," he said, but he agreed.

Arthur Miller and Marilyn Monroe had recently married. She was always with him. I knew if I could get her to come down with him, this guy would wet his pants.

"We'll be down around eleven o'clock," Miller said. I understood "we" meant he and Marilyn Monroe.

They enter the Martinique and walk the twenty-five feet across the lobby. By then the buzz is all over. I take them into the office and close the door. Through the glass pane I can see twenty, thirty people straining to look inside. The owner comes in. He's heard Marilyn Monroe is there, and he's shaking. Arthur looks over the space while I tell the owner how we want to do it, and he says, "OK."

We built the theater. It was all makeshift. I bought canvas chairs from a summer-stock music tent. I figured, If the play is successful, we'll buy theater seats later on. I kept having this nightmare that the lights in the ceiling would fall down and a hundred people would be decapitated. We finally hired an engineer to check them out.

We realized that if Arthur and Marilyn came opening night, everyone would watch them and not the play. "It's a two-hundred-seat theater," I told him. "Wherever you sit, all eyes will be on you and your wife." They didn't come.

This production of *The Crucible* was directed by Ward Baker. He and I and a couple of others produced it for $17,500, and when we opened we had a $4,500 reserve. It ran about a year and a half and was a nice success.

I've since been involved in over two hundred plays, but that production of *The Crucible* remains a very special one. We always felt the original Broadway production had not succeeded because it came out at the height of the McCarthy period, when people were afraid to go and see things that were identified with causes, particularly a play that was an allegory about the McCarthy witch-hunts. But by 1957 the climate had changed. McCarthy was finished.

KIM HUNTER: The blacklist was like the Salem witch-hunt, the reason people like Sam Wannamaker and Charlie Chaplin left the country altogether. Elia Kazan disappointed a lot of people by going before the House Un-American Activities Committee and naming names. For that reason, Lillian Hellman didn't hire him to direct *The Children's Hour*. She did it herself.

Because of the blacklist, I didn't work in film for five years. I couldn't work in television; they would threaten the sponsor. Theater was different, because each producer was on his own. He didn't have to cater to General Foods.

PHILIP LANGNER: The Theater Guild ran *The United States Steel Hour* for sixteen years. We went into television in the early 1950s, and there was a whole list of actors the sponsor would not allow to be used. Many wonderful people were kept out. But the theater never had that problem. On the contrary, there was an attempt to help keep people working.

MERLE DEBUSKEY: One of the great things about the theater is that independent producers have courage. Unlike what happened in Hollywood and on television, people who were blacklisted could perform on Broadway.

KIM HUNTER: I had signed petitions in favor of civil rights and against the hanging of people in Georgia. I had appeared in a Lillian Hellman play. I had worked with a director who was named before the House Un-American Activities Committee. Then I got a letter asking if I would be a sponsor of this organization of people from the arts and sciences who were seeking to find a way out of the Cold War. It had a list of four hundred sponsors, including Albert Einstein and Eleanor Roosevelt. I never went to any meetings because I was in rehearsal. Nevertheless the organization was labeled red as a firecracker, pro-Communist. And the word got out: "Don't hire her."

I received a letter that said for two hundred dollars I could find out why I was being blacklisted. Some people made money out of this. At one point I called the FBI and told them to check me out and then tell me what my problem with my country is. They said, "You don't have a problem with your country. Your problem is with your unions."

MADELINE GILFORD: A lot of people who were subpoenaed in 1955 were window dressing. I was one. We weren't subpoenaed because we were stars, but because we were active in the union on bread-and-butter issues.

KIM HUNTER: I worked in Sidney Kingsley's gorgeous play *Darkness at Noon.* But Sidney damn near ruined it. He was so terrified people would think the play was pro- and not anti-Communist, he made everything black and white, which was not the way he had written it.

BOB EMMETT: In those days of the Group Theater, nobody knew who was a Communist and who was not.

KIM HUNTER: And it didn't matter. It never was against the law to be a Communist.

MADELINE GILFORD: When my husband, Jack, was offered the role of Dussel, the dentist in *The Diary of Anne Frank,* it came just in time. We were practically starving from the impact of the blacklist.

MERLE DEBUSKEY: Kermit Bloomgarden read *The Diary of Anne Frank,* and he felt it should be a play somehow. Meyer Levin developed a script, but Kermit discarded it. He asked Lillian Hellman to write one.

MADELINE GILFORD: Hellman thought the Levin script was too sentimental; she felt it should be written by non-Jews.

MERLE DEBUSKEY: Lillian declined to write the script but suggested a

A lot of people who were subpoenaed in 1955 were window dressing.

couple of screenwriters, Frances Goodrich and Albert Hackett. Garson Kanin came on board as director.

They cast an odd batch of people. Susan Strasberg was Anne. She had only been in a couple of things off Broadway. Joseph Schildkraut was the father. He had been a great matinee idol in the 1920s but had not been onstage in a million years. Gusti Huber, a perfect WASP, was the Jewish mother of the other family, with Lou Jacobi as her husband. What a couple! But perhaps the oddest was Jack Gilford, the comic, as Dussel, the dentist. It was his first serious dramatic role.

MADELINE GILFORD: In Philadelphia it seemed like the play was a flop. *The Diary of Anne Frank* embarrassed the bourgeois Jews of Philadelphia. The characters in *Diary* were human, not heroic, and the audience didn't like the truth of a fourteen-year-old girl and her family. Theirs was a *shashtill* (quiet, don't say anything) mentality.

After the play ended, there was no applause. Jack and Lou Jacobi got to their dressing rooms and Lou said, "I told you they hated it." On the train ride back to New York, Garson's wife, Ruth Gordon, tried to be gracious. But no one ate, no one laughed.

MERLE DEBUSKEY: We opened October 5, 1955, at the Cort Theater. Garson Kanin and I went backstage to Schildkraut's dressing room. He was very nervous. "Remember, Peppy, less is more," Garson said. Schildkraut tended to be a ham.

He became dyspeptic because of all the attention paid to Susan. Originally his name was the only one above the title. Then, for crass reasons, we decided to elevate Susan's name above the title as well. He was very unhappy.

We came up with the idea of getting him to climb up to the top of a ladder outside the theater and have Susan behind him. He would hold her hand, the idea being that the grand man was leading the youngster to stardom. I presented the concept to him as the great man of the theater taking this young child to a place where he has been. "You, Peppy, are bringing her up," I said. "What a magnanimous gesture for you to allow her costar billing. It's going to be all over the place. Think how your reputation will be enhanced." And he bought it.

MADELINE GILFORD: What happened in Philadelphia happened in New York over and over again. The play would end, and there would be no applause. But what we finally realized is that it wasn't that the audience

There would be an initial silence. Then one person would clap, and then another, and ultimately it built into a crescendo.

didn't like the play. They were stunned by it. There would be an initial silence. Then one person would clap, and then another, and ultimately it built into a crescendo.

Anne Frank was an enormous success. Jack stayed in it for two years. He was lucky the part came along. During the years of the blacklist, many marriages broke up. Jack and I kept saying, "We can't get divorced because we can't afford it, and no one wants the kids." We wondered how long it would go on. I said five or ten years. Jack said fifteen. Some people said forever.

MERLE DEBUSKEY: Back in 1953 Jack Gilford, along with some others who were blacklisted, including Howard Da Silva, Morris Carnovsky, and Ruby Dee, put on *The World of Sholem Aleichem* written by Arnold Perl. They wanted to demonstrate that the blacklist need not kill you as an artist.

I signed on as press agent. We couldn't afford a theater, but we were able to get a room with a stage at the Barbizon Plaza Hotel for seventeen odd dates when it wasn't booked for something else. When we finally got it on, *The World of Sholem Aleichem* was not a regular theater attraction; it couldn't play eight times a week.

The press were scared to death of it. Even those who wanted to do something were afraid. Although, oddly enough, we got a lot of help from the *Daily News* and the *Journal American*. And we had all the smaller papers: the *Forward,* the *Freiheit*.

But the people of the left, the progressives, were ready to support it. That's where some of the money came from. And also from the people who knew and loved *Sholem Aleichem*. They were the audience.

And then, to everyone's surprise, this thing became a smash hit; you couldn't get in. We didn't know what to do with it. Through Aline Bernstein, a great woman who did the costumes, I was able to get a meeting with Brooks Atkinson. He didn't talk to very many people.

Atkinson came to see the show and was absolutely enthralled. In a short space in one of his Sunday pieces, he glorified what we were doing. After the summer we reopened with more dates. This time everyone came to review. This time we got raves everywhere. I was besieged with house-seat requests, but at least half of them said, "Please don't tell anyone I'm coming." They were still afraid of the blacklist.

The World of Sholem Aleichem ran at least a year. After, we formed a production company and put on *Tevye and His Daughters,* by the same Arnold Perl. It became the basis of the book for *Fiddler on the Roof.*

The secretary of our production company was a young playwright, a black woman named Lorraine Hansberry. At that time there were no plays about blacks in contemporary society written by a black woman. Then Lorraine wrote *A Raisin in the Sun*, and I was its press agent.

We were able to raise money because of what the play was about. People believed in it. We were able to get a star, Sidney Poitier. But we were unable to get a theater in New York. No one would give us one. We opened to raves in New Haven. That got us a booking in Philadelphia. We got raves there as well. But still no theater in New York to move on to.

But now people were interested. They were coming around to see what was going on. I can still see this guy walking in backstage at the Walnut Theater in Philadelphia. It was Jack Small, general manager of the Shubert organization. "How much time do I have?" he asked.

I told him a few weeks. He said, "Let me make a phone call." About fifteen minutes later he came back. "Listen, you can have the Barrymore Theater but not for six weeks." Something else was playing there, I think *A Majority of One*. "Go on to Chicago," he said, "and play the Shubert there. We'll guarantee you against loss."

Chicago was where *A Raisin in the Sun* was set. It was also Lorraine's home. The play was a big hit there. Then we came to New York, and we had to start all over again. Those of us who'd been around long enough knew very well that there's no way of knowing when the mule is going to kick. We couldn't advertise because we didn't know what theater we'd be in. We didn't have a huge advance sale.

We opened at the Ethel Barrymore Theater. For someone like me, who lived and worked in the theater, it was a monumental moment. Before *Raisin in the Sun*, the only blacks onstage were domestics or not real people. What excitement this play caused, what it meant to the black arts community! This was right in the middle of the civil rights movement. *Ebony* did a piece on it, and it was the first time they ever did anything for a Broadway play. They were Chicago based, very proud of Lorraine and the play.

BILLIE ALLEN: My first role on Broadway was the daughter, Beneatha. I auditioned about thirteen times, and each time I wore a bulky sweater over tight pants and six-inch heels. They didn't know I was pregnant until I finally told them.

"Oh, we were going to ask you to lose weight," they said.

We opened at the Ethel Barrymore Theater. For someone like me, who lived and worked in the theater, it was a monumental moment.

I was hired as stand-in for Diana Sands. And after I had my child I went into the play. It was a wonderful experience to work with Sidney Poitier, Claudia McNeil, Louis Gossett. Backstage was a core of people. Ossie Davis, the understudy to Sidney Poitier, was busy writing *Purlie.* We could hear his laughter coming from the dressing room as he thought up jokes while his wife, Ruby Dee, was onstage playing the wife, Ruth. Lonnie Elder III, who was one of the moving men, was backstage, too, working on *Ceremonies in Dark Old Men.* Douglas Turner Ward was there. While the play was going on, the Negro Ensemble was being formed. And a very intense Lorraine Hansberry was around as well. She was only in her thirties, so young and beautiful. Her death at a very young age was one of the most tragic losses.

Acting in a play by a black woman about a real family that she knew, we felt we were part of something that had not been done before. Sometimes the audience was more black than white, and we could always tell. We felt their response. They were not just observing a play, they were in there with us.

A Raisin in the Sun saw the Broadway stage give voice to the black experience. There had been serious black plays written before, but they didn't get produced on Broadway. After, there was a coming out, a cornucopia of works like *Ain't Supposed to Die a Natural Death, The River Niger, For Colored Girls, Blues for Mr. Charlie* . . . and of course *Purlie,* which came from some deep, deep well. When you lifted the bucket, you had gold.

LUTHER HENDERSON: Doing the dance music for *Purlie,* I was struck by the whole idea of the Preacher Man. It's not a minstrel, it's not burlesque, it's an authentic black folk story brought to the proscenium arch.

MERLE DEBUSKEY: Ossie Davis had written the comedy *Purlie Victorious* nearly a decade before *Purlie* opened with Cleavon Little and Melba Moore. While Ossie was assistant stage manager for *The World of Sholem Aleichem,* we encouraged him to write a libretto based on his play. And so out of our little company, which developed from *The World of Sholem Aleichem,* came all these wonderful shows.

I had quit working on Broadway to be the press agent for *The World of Sholem Aleichem.* No one else would touch it. But I didn't like the blacklist. Also I had very little to lose since I was nobody.

TONY WALTON: Jerome Robbins had named names during the McCarthy era. Jack Gilford's wife, Madeline, was one. Zero Mostel was another.

CHARLES DURNING: Zero Mostel didn't work for ten years. He told me he went from making a thousand to a hundred dollars a week. "What kind of secrets was I giving away," he'd ask, "acting secrets?"

TONY WALTON: Zero Mostel and Jack Gilford were cast for *A Funny Thing Happened on the Way to the Forum*. George Abbott had become the director, and I was doing the set and costumes. We were floundering out of town, an absolute disaster. When we opened in Washington, George Abbott gave an interview saying, "I think we could save the sucker if we threw out all the songs."

Steve Sondheim made a big pitch to Hal Prince to bring Jerry Robbins back in. Robbins had been the original director but had backed out before rehearsals because he had a gigantic success with his *Ballets U.S.A.* at the Spoleto Festival in Italy and needed to shepherd its company on the resulting world tour. Hal phoned Zero to ask whether he would be prepared to work with Jerry Robbins.

"Are you asking me to eat with him?"

"I'm just asking you to work with him."

"Of course I'll work with him," Zero said. "We of the left do not blacklist."

As it turned out, Robbins was absolutely amazing. It was as if you had given him a pocket handkerchief and said, "Do something magical with this." Whatever we had that was lying around, even bits of costume that had been cast away, he took and used and turned into amazing and imaginative bits of comic business.

The original opening number had been a light, lovely soft-shoe called "Love Is in the Air." George Abbott was very keen on it because it was something he could hum, and he felt the opening number *should* be something you could hum. But Robbins said the opening number has to let the audience know what it's in for. The existing song led them to expect something elegant and light, whereas the show is actually broad low comedy and slapstick.

So Jerry nudged Steve Sondheim into writing "Comedy Tonight." Some of the lyrics were lines virtually right out of Jerry Robbins's mouth. Steve wrote it in sort of a white heat. The song went into the show on the first preview in New York, in the spring of 1962. It literally changed *Forum* into an overnight smash.

But when Jerry first came in, we were all terrified. He was already a daunting figure. This was—after all—well after *West Side Story*. We stood on the stage of the National Theater in Washington. Jerry Robbins ran the gauntlet, shaking everyone's hands. When he finally got to Zero, everyone held their breath. The tension was palpable.

Then Zero boomed out, "Hiya, loose lips."

And everybody burst out laughing—including Jerry.

ANNE KAUFMAN SCHNEIDER: For someone who was known for being funny, my father, George S. Kaufman, was in reality a very serious person, although he never took himself seriously. He was what you would now call a workaholic, also a hypochondriac, cool and aloof, and not a real Broadway person in the sense of being one of the guys who hung out. But he loved the theater.

I was five years old when he took me to see my first Broadway show, *Babes in Toyland.* I don't remember it much, but awhile ago I saw *Tintypes,* and when a song from *Babes in Toyland* was sung, great gushes of tears suddenly flowed out of my eyes and rolled down my face. The curtain came down, and this lady sitting next to me said, "Oh, was there something special that I missed?"

Soon after *Babes in Toyland,* my mother took me to see the first Kaufman and Hart collaboration, *Once in a Lifetime.* Apparently my father was quite nervous about my being there. "How did you like it?" he asked when I was taken backstage after the show.

"Great," I said, and added quickly, "Can I please meet the man who made the train noise?"

Moss Hart was only twenty-five when he met George S. Kaufman, and he quickly fell under his spell. My father had exquisite manners; his shoes and shirts and suits were all made to order. Moss followed in his footsteps, even outdid him in extravagance, shopping at Cartier's and places like that.

Moss started off much poorer than my father, and the money that came to him from *Once in a Lifetime* was a revelation. He got into a taxi, drove out to Bensonhurst in Brooklyn, picked up his brother Bernie, his mother, and his father, and said, "We're moving."

And they said, "What about our furniture and dishes?"

"Leave everything."

They drove over the Brooklyn Bridge into Manhattan, and he got them an apartment in the Ansonia that was quite grand.

No one had ever heard of Moss when he submitted a play to Sam Harris. My husband's half-brother, who worked for Sam, read it and gave it to my father. Kaufman and Hart went on to write seven plays together.

They absolutely adored one another. My father once described their collaboration like a marriage without sex.

Their plays, like *You Can't Take It with You,* have longevity, mass appeal, and hilarious humor, although the humor emerges from the content of the play rather than a clownish aspect. They are very American, yet they are very successful in England.

Around 1946 Alexander Wolcott came to Moss's house in the country, and in the guest book, he wrote, "I will think of this as being one of the most unpleasant weekends I've ever had. I don't know what went wrong."

Moss said to my father, "Can you imagine? What if something had happened and he had to stay longer than three days?"

My father said, "That's our next play."

And indeed it was: *The Man Who Came to Dinner.*

Moss Hart (center) and George S. Kaufman (right) with the inspiration for *The Man Who Came to Dinner:* Alexander Wolcott.

KITTY CARLISLE HART: I had gotten the part of the opera singer in the Marx Brothers' movie *A Night at the Opera* that George was directing. We were making the movie in Hollywood when Moss and Cole Porter came out looking for a leading lady for their new musical, *Jubilee*. George introduced me, and Moss said they'd like me to audition. So that evening I went to their hotel, where Cole played the score, and I sang one of the songs. P.S. I didn't get the job. And soon after, my movie career was over, and I was back in New York.

I'd see Moss off and on, because the theater was smaller then. People didn't live out of town the way they do now. I thought he was divine. Every once in a while he would say, "We'd like you to head up the first company of *The Man Who Came to Dinner.*"

And I would say, "Oh, I'm making too much money performing in nightclubs. I can't afford to do that now."

It wasn't until eight years after our original meeting that Moss and I finally wed.

ANNE KAUFMAN SCHNEIDER: The last thing Kaufman and Hart wrote together was *George Washington Slept Here*. Moss felt the need to prove to himself that he could work without George. My father did not have such needs. He liked collaborating.

BARRY NELSON: After seeing me in a movie called *A Guy Named Joe*, Moss Hart wanted me for the first play he would do without George S. Kaufman. It was *Light Up the Sky*, for which he was both playwright and director. He was able to get me a leave of absence from MGM. My first look at Broadway was awe inspiring: the lights, the marquees, the names. But even more exciting was the prospect of working with Moss Hart.

There was quite a lot of excitement about the play and its volatile cast, which included Sam Levene, Virginia Field, and others with a great deal of talent and temperament to match, so much so that some of them were considered unemployable. But that's what the play was about: a tryout at the Ritz Theater in Boston and the troubles that came from a temperamental cast. Moss Hart actually had the boldness to assemble a bunch of people like that to sort of play themselves.

Sam Levene gave Moss a hard time. He was always telling everyone in the cast what to do, until one moment during rehearsal when Sam was giving out directions and there was some yelling going on. Moss stood up. "I am the director, and I want you to know that, Sam," he said. There was great silence. It had been years since anybody had spoken to Sam that way. Later Moss told me, "I had to wait for the right time to say what I said. It's a thing that can only be done once. If you keep it up, they'll think you're a nag."

All the performers had pieces of business that they overdid. As the rehearsals went on they overdid more and more, trying to outshine one another. They stole from every play they had ever been in. I decided the only way for me to get through the experience was to underplay them all.

KITTY CARLISLE HART: Moss always said that an audience decides in the first fifteen minutes after the curtain rises whether it likes the play or not. With *Light Up the Sky,* we could tell right away it was catching fire. Opening night in New York, when the curtain came down, Moss took me by the hand down the side aisle to the front of the theater so we could look back at an approving audience.

BARRY NELSON: *Light Up the Sky* ran about eight months, which was very good in those days. And I got very good reviews, which led to my receiving a lot of scripts with leading-man roles. Aside from Robert Preston and Gig Young, there weren't too many actors doing light comedy.

I appeared in *The Moon Is Blue* with Barbara Bel Geddes, a good technician whose timing was impeccable, and Donald Cook, who was considered the best farceur at the time. He was an imperious fellow. All three of us initially turned it down because Otto Preminger had signed on as director. He had the reputation of always yelling at his actors. But the producers called a meeting with the cast and assured us Preminger would not be a problem. Reluctantly we all agreed to do it. Otto did not shout, and it was a tremendous hit, running for three years.

There was no censorship problem with the play, but a huge controversy ensued over the movie because the word *virgin* was used. Years later the play was considered so tepid, they didn't even do it in summer theater.

After that, I did *Mary, Mary,* with Barbara Bel Geddes again, and Michael Rennie. When *Cactus Flower* was out of town in Washington, I came in as a replacement for the male lead. Abe Burrows had directed him to sit on a bench all the time, nodding his head. "I'll do it if I can choreog-raph just my part without anything else changing," I said. They agreed, and I took the role—not knowing anyone in the cast, which included a very strong Lauren Bacall and Brenda Vaccaro, who made a big explosion and went on to Hollywood.

Moss always said that an audience decides in the first fifteen minutes after the curtain rises whether it likes the play or not.

Comedies like *Cactus Flower* and *Mary, Mary* would have a tough time today. People don't listen to dialogue; they want action, spectacle.

ANNE KAUFMAN SCHNEIDER: Kaufman and Hart shared a work ethic. That was true of all their crowd: Lillian Hellman, Edna Ferber, George and Ira Gershwin. They all helped each other for the pleasure of doing the best they could for a friend.

ELAINE STEINBECK: George S. Kaufman wrote to John Steinbeck and told him he was interested in doing *Of Mice and Men* as a play. John wrote back that he was willing to try but didn't have the money to come to New York. Kaufman sent him the money. They worked together in New York and Bucks County, got along wonderfully. The play was a big hit.

Now we skip a time. After John and I were married, we were having supper after the theater one evening when John said, "Oh, my god, look who's at that table." It was George Kaufman with a group of people. "I treasure him as a friend," John said, "but he won't speak to me."

"Why?" I asked.

"Well, Elaine, he never understood. I came east to work on the play. And then I went home to California. I didn't come back for the opening because I didn't have the money. Only, I never had the opportunity to tell him that."

"Well," I said, "let's just stop at his table on the way out."

We did that. John just stopped and stood there. And George got up and threw his arms around John, and they embraced. From then on we saw George very often up until the time he died.

ANNE KAUFMAN SCHNEIDER: Both George S. Kaufman and Moss Hart died in 1961. My father was seventy-one, Moss was fifty-five. Kitty and I have handled their plays together ever since.

BARRY NELSON: Looking back over my career, I think I spent far too much time worrying about how things were going to come out, fussing about the bad weather, the drabness backstage, the routines. I should have appreciated more the great adventure of working with the best directors, actors, and writers. Imagine, I started out on Broadway working with Moss Hart.

5 | SOMETHING WONDERFUL

FOSTER HIRSCH: Americans have been so wonderful in creating musicals. You can go back to the early decades of the century—the likes of Sigmund Romberg, Jerome Kern, George Gershwin, Richard Rodgers and Lorenz Hart, Cole Porter. Although the books were primitive, maybe hopeless, you had Al Jolson singing Irving Berlin, George Gershwin.

JOHN LAHR: Even though there is poverty in America, we are a culture of abundance. And the images and myths of abundance are enacted in the Broadway musical. The notion of putting your name in lights, of going in a nobody and coming out a star—the whole mythology of American individualism is built into the musical.

MAURY YESTON: The greatness of the American theater is that we find optimism in the most unlikely places. This oppressed Jew in czarist Russia who hasn't got so much as a pot to pee in sings, "If I were a rich man." Cinderella, who is left home when the others go off to the ball, sings, "My own little corner of the world." This widowed schoolteacher in a faroff land looks at these two kids who are in love, and though she's got nothing, she sings, "Hello, young lovers."

JOHN LAHR: The optimism of America is a very strange thing to anyone outside the culture. The reason the English don't do American musicals very well is that they don't believe that everything is coming up roses, that something's coming, something good, if you can wait.

FOSTER HIRSCH: We have produced more great musicals than any other country, and mostly they've been written by Jewish people.

CY COLEMAN: When Jerome Kern was asked what kind of score he planned to write for a musical about the Italian Marco Polo set in China, narrated by an Irishman, he said, "The same good old Jewish score I always write."

GEOFFREY HOLDER: Harold Arlen told me that after his father heard

Louis Armstrong sing the blues, he was convinced Louis Armstrong had to be Jewish. Harold's father was a cantor, and he heard the minor keys in Louis's song, those colors, those tones.

MAURY YESTON: Interestingly enough, many Broadway composers have an immediate relative who is a cantor: Irving Berlin's father, George Gershwin's father, Kurt Weill's father. I hesitate to put myself in the category of those gods on Mount Olympus, but my grandfather was a cantor, too.

What does it mean? Every Saturday morning and on Rosh Hashanah and Yom Kippur, a young boy is taken to this big room where there's a man who gets into a costume. He wraps himself in a tallith, puts something on his head, stands in the middle of a platform, and unaccompanied, sings his heart out at the top of his lungs. He is joined by a huge chorus of other people, and the entire scenario is taken as ordinary. Think of what this does to a three-, four-, five-year-old.

Now, you take this person and you put him in a theater with Merman on the stage, and it feels like home to him. I think it's no accident that so many of these composers had Orthodox, cantorial singing in their backgrounds. It's mother's milk to them. I don't think Cole Porter was kidding when he said to Richard Rodgers, "You know, I think I discovered the secret of great songwriting in America."

And Rodgers asked, "What is it?"

"Yiddish melody."

MARY ELLIN BARRETT: I can't explain my father's ear, his gift for melody and words. Irving Berlin had some kind of inner radar that picked up the moods, the feelings in the air. Whatever it was, love, or loss, or feelings about this country, he was able to capture it. A person who heard one of his songs would immediately identify with it.

My father composed on the piano. Usually in the evening, we'd hear these peculiar disconnected sounds behind the closed doors. Eventually those piano-tuner sounds would become hits in a show.

His first show was *Watch Your Step,* in 1914. It featured Irene and Vernon Castle and a two-part number, "Simple Melody." Thirty-six years later he would repeat that pattern with "You're Just in Love" in *Call Me Madam.*

Irving Berlin had many peaks in his life, but I think the highest one was July 4, 1942, opening night of *This Is the Army,* a new version of *Yip Yip Yaphank,* which my father had originally written in 1918, during World

War I. He had been working on it all spring. I was fifteen then and it was the first opening night I was allowed to attend. I remember the crowds lining the street outside the theater. Not only were the usual opening-night celebrities in attendance, but generals and other military brass were there as well.

There was a sense of anticipation in the audience, a buzz in the theater that something wonderful was about to unfold. Then the curtain rose on a bleacher with about three hundred young men singing the opening chorus. It went on, scene by scene, a spectacular and funny revue with two beautiful ballads, "I Left My Heart at the Stage Door Canteen" and "I'm Getting Tired So I Can Sleep."

During the intermission I watched my mother being friendly and greeting everybody, but I knew how apprehensive she really was, because in the next act my father would be performing. He had not performed in public for a very long time.

It was late, close to eleven o'clock, when the curtains parted. And there was Irving Berlin sitting sleepily on his cot. He stood up, opened his mouth to sing, and the house exploded. The audience stood up and cheered and cheered while my father just stood there waiting to begin singing his song.

For me it was an extraordinary moment. I had known my father was a famous personality, but it was not until that night that the public and private person came together for me. I understood all these people weren't just cheering for *This Is the Army*. They were cheering for Irving Berlin and what he meant to them, both as a songwriter and as an American.

After ten minutes or so the applause finally ceased, and he sang "Oh, How I Hate to Get Up in the Morning." It was one of the first of his songs I learned, and I can truly say it was his theme song. He really hated to get up in the morning. So did my mother. We even had an alarm clock that played that song.

My father did not have the strongest or the greatest voice, but it was always true. He hit the note on the note. Nobody can sing "Oh, How I Hate to Get Up in the Morning" the way he can, and that night he sang it through, and when he stopped, the cheering began all over again.

This Is the Army had a sell-out Broadway run for over three months and then it went overseas to Great Britain, to Italy right up behind the Fifth Army, to the South Pacific. It toured until late 1945 and made a good deal

My father did not have the strongest or the greatest voice, but it was always true.

of money for the Emergency Army Relief. My father was not a heavy talker, but you knew he felt this enormous gratitude to America. "God Bless America" represents that with the simple line "land that I love."

Annie Get Your Gun, his first postwar show and one his biggest successes, did not get rave reviews. Ward Morehouse said the score was just OK. But it was an instant hit with the public, and one by one its songs came onto the Hit Parade.

Miss Liberty came next and got reviews that my father had never seen before: "too much corn, not up to his standards." But with *Call Me Madam,* everyone said Mr. Berlin is back in town. I had been to Boston and saw the audience break up over "You're Just in Love," which had been added overnight in New Haven. My father was sixty-two then, totally exhausted, and so pleased to be back in town with another hit.

JOHN LAHR: American musicals are the epitome of corporate art making. It's always been that way. What has changed is who leads the discussion. Initially it was the comedians. That's when it was truly musical comedy. In the 1940s, the comedians were succeeded by the Rodgers and Hammersteins. They created a situation where the story and songs were so integral, no cavorting clown could mess it up.

JAMES HAMMERSTEIN: When Richard Rodgers linked up with Oscar Hammerstein II, the combination was stupendous. My father was a perfectionist. Richard Rodgers was more than a composer; he comes close to being the best musical dramatist ever going.

The switch from Larry Hart to Oscar Hammerstein II was a major step for Dick Rodgers. Hart came from the world of revues, my father from the world of operetta. With Hart you changed the story to allow for your best songs. With Hammerstein you changed your songs so they worked best for the story. It's night and day, totally different ways of looking at theater.

The Hammerstein story began with my great-grandfather Oscar I, who came to this country from Germany during the Civil War. He was an opera impresario who built opera houses and theaters. But he also had a vaudeville house, the Hammerstein-Victoria, which made enough money to support his opera houses.

Oscar I was everything my father, Oscar II, wasn't. If he didn't like you he would hit you in the jaw. For many years he engaged in a war with the Metropolitan Opera, which was funded by the Astors and the Vanderbilts.

Oscar's opera was financed only by Oscar. At one time it was suggested that he become the head of the Metropolitan board, but the idea of a Jew in that position was very dubious back then. They ended up buying him out for a considerable sum of money.

One of his sons, my grandfather Willie, booked people like Al Jolson and W. C. Fields. He came up with the comic routine of throwing a pie in someone's face. They dimmed the lights on Broadway when he died.

They did that when my father died as well.

THEODORE BIKEL: Oscar Hammerstein II was an aristocrat in bearing and attitude. He always struck me as a New England Brahmin, but also as a very gentle man.

JAMES HAMMERSTEIN: Dad was terribly well balanced. We lived a very normal family life in Bucks County, Pennsylvania. Moss Hart and George S. Kaufman would come by, but not very often. Dad didn't like to stay up late.

When I was stage manager for *The Flower Drum Song,* I asked my father to come and wait for the reviews. "No, I'm going home to bed," he said.

"It's opening night," I said. "How can you do that?"

"The newspapers will say the same thing tomorrow as tonight."

As far as I know, that's the way Dad was with all his shows. He was famous for what they called the Hammerstein shuffle, coming to a party so early that he would be leaving as the other guests arrived.

He worked like a truck driver. Every morning at eight-thirty, he'd go into his study and work till lunch. He'd take a half-hour nap, and then go back into his study and not come out again until four.

Rodgers and Hammerstein hardly ever worked together in the flesh. Dick was in New York or Connecticut, Dad in Pennsylvania. They communicated by phone.

When Rodgers switched from Hart to Hammerstein, people asked, "What's the big deal?" The big deal is when you're completely successful doing one thing, why should you experiment? With Larry Hart, Dick had to sit in the same room with him to make him work. With my father, Dick was working with the most disciplined person in the theater, with someone who could write lyrics in that subjunctive vein: "Only Make Believe," "People Will Say We're in Love," "If I Loved You."

MARY RODGERS: Larry Hart was an alcoholic, and he became increasingly unreliable. Daddy had to lock Larry in the room, play him a tune, have him do the lyric, and *then* let him out. With Oscar it was totally

James Hammerstein, son of Oscar Hammerstein II. "When Richard Rodgers linked up with Oscar Hammerstein, the combination was stupendous."

opposite. The lyrics always came first. He and my father would discuss a scene very thoroughly, who the characters were, what the song was about, and who would sing it. And then Oscar would go off to write it, very slowly. My father was pretty fast, but also he had all this information ahead of time. So when they said he wrote "Bali Ha'i" in the length of time it takes to play it at the piano, it's true—but not really.

ERIC STERN: Growing up I was very much into pooh-poohing Hammerstein. I thought Rodgers and Hart were much better. Hammerstein seemed sort of dull and rosy eyed and slightly sexist. When I walked into the 1994 revival of *Carousel,* I was a nonbeliever. But by the time the show was up and running, I was deeply in love with the piece. I had come to see that Hammerstein's art was not showy and not congratulatory, that it spoke about things that mattered to him. He represents the core of what we do well in this American art form.

The powers behind *Oklahoma!*: director Rouben Mamoulian, lyricist Oscar Hammerstein II, the Theater Guild's Theresa Helburn, and composer Richard Rodgers (1945).

MARY RODGERS: When he began working with Oscar, my father started to take piano lessons again. He reintroduced himself to the classics that he loved: Brahms, Mendelssohn, Schumann. And the result is the most gorgeous expansion of melody, like "Lonely Room" in *Oklahoma!* or the bench scene with "If I Loved You" in *Carousel*. There was a thing about his music—"Some Enchanted Evening," for example—the melodic choice to go up instead of down. You'd think, How weird, and then, How perfect.

Until much later in his life, when he worked at his office, my father wrote at home, and I grew up hearing all these songs. I would pass by the living room, and there would be melodies in the air. Over the years we've all developed these incredible batlike ears for Daddy's music. We can hear two bars of something across a very crowded room and know right away that it's one of his songs.

Stephen Sondheim was about nineteen when he asked if I could get my father to give him an interview. I set it up. But Steve was disappointed. "It was awful," he said. "He couldn't tell me anything." My father was not an intellectual writer. He had gone to Juilliard, and he knew plenty. But he didn't sit down and figure out intellectually where a song should go or how it should be constructed. Composing was just something that came so easily to him. He didn't have a trunk, like other composers. He always said a trunk contained stuff that belonged in a trunk. If he needed a song, he could always write one.

JAMES HAMMERSTEIN: The golden age of American musical theater started with *Oklahoma!* My feeling is that everyone was trying to write *Oklahoma!*, from Victor Herbert on. And when Rodgers and Hammerstein finally did, they didn't so much invent anything as throw out a lot of baggage. It became a kind of a guide to what you don't have to do anymore. There was no star turn at eleven o'clock and no Jewish comic (the peddler in *Oklahoma!* is Persian, not Jewish; they actually had Persian peddlers in Oklahoma). It was a musical where you could believe everything.

HARVEY SABINSON: *Oklahoma!* integrated the book, score, and choreography as if they were done by one person. Once that came along, everything else tried to be like it.

ELAINE STEINBECK: I had been working for the Theater Guild on a play called *Green Grow the Lilacs* by Lynn Riggs, which was about the settlers in Oklahoma. It was originally produced by the Guild in the 1930–1931 season. They thought it had the potential to be a good musical, and when

Mary Rodgers, daughter of Richard Rodgers. "Over the years we've developed these incredible batlike ears for Daddy's music. We can hear two bars of something across a crowded room and know right away that it's one of his songs."

A scene from Rodgers and Hammerstein's first collaboration: *Oklahoma!*, which changed the whole idea of American musical theater (1943).

it was playing in the Langners' Westport Country Playhouse, they invited Dick Rodgers, who lived in Westport, over to see it.

Rodgers thought it had a lot of potential. "But it's not for Larry," he said. "It's not his material. Let me think of somebody else I can collaborate with." Hart was sick then and drinking a lot.

PHILIP LANGNER: Even after Rodgers and Hammerstein had gotten together and agreed to work on the project, it took two years to raise the money. The Theater Guild was a bit low, and a lot of people they went to turned it down. One of the biggest objections from investors was that the play was too clean. It had no striptease, no suggestive jokes, none of what was in the successful musicals of that era. Philip Barry had a royalty account with the Guild for his plays, and when they suggested he take ten thousand dollars and put it in, he declined. Later on he pinned two telegrams up on his wall. One was to Barry from the Guild: "Would you like to invest in a wonderful new play?"

The other was to the Guild from Barry: "Forget it."

Oklahoma! would have made him a good eight hundred thousand dollars.

At one time they thought of calling the play *Down on the Strip*. When *Oklahoma!* was suggested, some people thought it was too static. The decision to settle on *Oklahoma!* had a lot to do with my family's connection to Oklahoma. My mother's parents met on a stagecoach in Oklahoma. Her father was the driver and her mother a passenger on her way out west.

CELESTE HOLM: One day I read in the *New York Times* that Richard Rodgers and Oscar Hammerstein were working together for the first time, doing a musical based on *Green Grow the Lilacs*. It was during the war, and I was working in the Stage Door Canteen in the basement of the Forty-fourth Street Theater, waiting on tables and dancing with these naive kids from all over the country in their new uniforms who were scared to death, not knowing what they were getting into.

I called up my grandmother and found out what the original play was about, and it seemed to me that this could be the most perfect show for right now. Young people were going out to fight and perhaps to die for this country. What better time to be reminded of the unself-conscious courage of those folks who settled the West?

I called my friend Elaine Steinbeck at the Theater Guild. "When is the next audition for Rodgers and Hammerstein?" I asked. "I want to sing for them."

"Next Thursday. St. James Theater. Bring your music and know your keys."

I tripped and fell flat on my face; my belt busted and my music skated out in front of me. A voice from the audience said, "That was pretty funny. Could you do it again?"

I arrived in the pouring rain. I hadn't read the script. I didn't know what part I was trying out for. I also didn't notice there were three steps leading to the stage. I tripped and fell flat on my face; my belt busted and my music skated out in front of me. A voice from the audience said, "That was pretty funny. Could you do it again?"

ELAINE STEINBECK: Celeste has made up more stories. But I did lean over to Dick and Oscar and say, "Guess who's going to audition for you next? Celeste Holm."

They said, "She can't sing."

And I said, "I don't know whether she can or not. But please listen to her."

CELESTE HOLM: The voice from the orchestra continued, "My name is Richard Rodgers. What are you going to sing?"

I answered, "My name is Celeste Holm. 'Who is Sylvia?'"

My singing teacher from Australia had told me not to sing a Richard Rodgers song because if you didn't dot the quarter notes, he'd feel you'd ruined his song and wouldn't pay any attention to you. She also advised that I not sing a song by a rival composer, either. "Darling, sing something you've known since you were twelve," she said.

I sang all three choruses of "Who Is Sylvia?"—better than I'd ever sung in my life, because I wasn't nervous. After you've fallen flat on your face, what's to be nervous about?

After I finished, Richard Rodgers said, "Can you sing as if you never had a lesson?"

"What is that like?"

"I want a bold, unedited farm-girl voice."

"I can call a hog."

"I dare you."

So on the stage of the St. James Theater I said, "Sueeeeeeeeeeeeeeeeee!"

ELAINE STEINBECK: We had some great Ado Annies over the years, but Celeste owns that part.

CELESTE HOLM: Opening night in New Haven, Lawrence Langner came into my dressing room. "Celeste," he said, "I hate to bother you on an opening night, but just remember the Chaplinesque quality of your part. The fact that Ado Annie can't say no is a great tragedy to her. That's the spine of the part." And he walked out.

Miss Helburn came in. "We're counting on you for the comedy, Celeste. Lift every scene that you're in. Good luck."

And then Mrs. Langner came in. She kissed me on the cheek and said, "I suppose I shouldn't say this, but I think you're absolutely wrong for the part. Good luck."

Fortunately at that moment, the overture began. I thought of the first time I heard "I Can't Say No." Oscar had sung it for me. Now I went out there and did it and stopped the show cold.

It's a terrible thing to say, but I've never ever seen anyone else do Ado Annie as well as me. It would have been nice to have gotten the movie part, but Dick was mad at me at that time.

KITTY CARLISLE HART: I was twenty-two years old, living in Hollywood, and not allowed to go out except with the de Mille girls, Margaret and Agnes. Agnes—who was brilliant, hardworking, and very concerned about her career as a choreographer—came to me one day: "I don't know what I'm going to do. I'm at the end of my rope. I have this play. I wonder if you will read it."

It was a musical version of *Green Grow the Lilacs.* I read it and told her it was wonderful and the chance of a lifetime for her. "By all means try and get this."

ELAINE STEINBECK: There was a terrible row over Agnes de Mille. It was very awkward at first. She was very demanding and lording it over everyone.

MARY RODGERS: She had a very sharp tongue and did not suffer fools gladly. One of the things that irritated the hell out of her was that choreographers didn't get royalties. And she was furious at R & H for that, particularly my father. She was always poor, never had any money.

JOHN RAITT: But her contribution to *Oklahoma!* was enormous. It was out of the operatic vein where the ballet continued the story.

MARY RODGERS: Warts and all, Agnes was an entrancingly brilliant woman. Even though she cared about her dancers to the exclusion of everything else, my father loved her talent.

ELAINE STEINBECK: She auditioned all the ballet people. Of course they were good ballet dancers, but they didn't look like chorus girls. Dick Rodgers couldn't get used to that.

MARY RODGERS: I'm sure my father wondered what Agnes was doing when she hired Bambi Linn, who was a tiny sixteen-year-old at the time, with heavy legs. Agnes went for unusual casting; she looked for real people.

ELAINE STEINBECK: We rehearsed in the Theater Guild Theater, which is now the Virginia. It was dark at the time, so we rehearsed all the dialogue and songs upstairs while Agnes rehearsed the dancing downstairs. Every day the director, Rouben Mamoulian, and Agnes would confer. One Sunday when the Hammersteins and Langners had gone to the country, Rouben told me to go very quietly downstairs and tell Agnes to bring her group up so that we could integrate a number with the dialogue.

I said, "Oh, boy."

I knew that Dick and Dorothy Rodgers were in town. I called them and told them to come to the theater, sit in the back, and not let anybody know they were there.

They started melding the dance with the story with "Many a New Day." It was a high, high moment. "We really have something here," Dick said. We were a whole different kind of show.

While we were on the road in Boston, Terry Helburn said we need a wonderful ending, and it should be about the land. That Saturday, Dick and Oscar went home and wrote "Oklahoma." Sunday, Rouben put it in, and Monday night, the chorus rushed down to the footlights and sang, "You're doing fine, Oklahoma, Oklahoma, O-K-L-A-H-O-M-A, Oklahoma!" right into the laps of the audience. And we realized we had something. Oh, boy, did we have something.

PHILIP LANGNER: There was something tremendously exciting about seeing everyone laugh and yell and scream around you. You thought, god, there's something wonderful going on here. *Oklahoma!* was so different from any of the other musicals that were running at the time. Except for *Showboat*, none had the poetry, mood, or Americana that characterized *Oklahoma!*

Out of town, the reviews were great, although when Walter Winchell's right-hand woman went up to see it in New Haven, she wired, "No legs. No sex. No chance."

ELAINE STEINBECK: Coming into New York, we weren't confident. You're never confident. You're always scared to death, particularly with something so new. We opened March 31, 1943. It was a rainy night. How could I forget it?

DOUGLAS WATT: The curtain opened, and Alfred Drake walked out onstage singing "Oh, What a Beautiful Morning." Then there was "Surrey with the Fringe on the Top," "Everything's Up-to-Date in Kansas City," "People Will Say We're in Love"—it was a succession of great songs, one after another.

Oklahoma!
was so different from
any of the other
musicals that were
running at the time.

JOHN RAITT: People were used to coming ten or fifteen minutes late to a musical because they expected nothing much to happen at the beginning of a show. If they did that with *Oklahoma!* they missed some of the greatest songs ever written.

JAMES HAMMERSTEIN: The show is very seductive, slowly seductive. There's no number that stops the show, but by the second act there's a purple haze over the audience.

PHILIP LANGNER: We had wondered how New Yorkers would respond to the fact that for nearly forty-five minutes not a single chorus girl appeared on the stage. But as one beautiful song followed another, the audience took the play to its heart. After the ballet there was a tremendous outburst of applause. It had been many years since a Theater Guild play had received such an ovation from its opening-night audience.

DOUGLAS WATT: When it was over, we all stood on the sidewalk outside the theater. We were stunned. People didn't want to talk. No one had expected anything like that.

ELAINE STEINBECK: We were not prepared for what we got. We were knocked for a loop.

MARY RODGERS: The morning after *Oklahoma!* opened, I walked into my parents' bedroom, where my mother always had her breakfast in bed, and Daddy at a chair beside her. This morning the whole bed was covered with newspapers. All the reviews were raves. My parents told me that I could go riding. It was very expensive, but this was an event.

With *Oklahoma!* my father really hit it. He was forty-one at the time. Before that he was just one more songwriter and not all that rich.

DOUGLAS WATT: Little had been expected of *Oklahoma!* It was Rodgers and Hammerstein's first collaboration. Prior to it, Hammerstein had had a series of failures. Actually, his last real hit had been *Showboat,* in 1927.

ELAINE STEINBECK: Oscar took out a whole page in *Variety.* He listed every flop he had had and said, "I did it before, and I can do it again."

The rush for tickets became so fantastic. That whole first year, the box office was always jammed. Tickets were impossible to get. It was such a very big hit. Mayor Fiorello La Guardia kept calling for tickets whenever distinguished visitors came to New York. Eleanor Roosevelt came; all kinds of generals came. The Duke and Duchess of Windsor were in the first-row balcony of every Saturday matinee.

PHILIP LANGNER: In 1944 at the Democratic National Convention in

Chicago, where Roosevelt and Truman were nominated, the keynote speech was made by Governor Kerr of Oklahoma. Before he began, the orchestra played "Oklahoma." "Oh What a Beautiful Morning" was used as an optimistic theme song for the upcoming campaign.

CELESTE HOLM: *Oklahoma!* ran for five years. For the year and three months that I was in it, people in uniform were always in the audience. Since then people have come up to me and told me it was the last show they saw before they went overseas and how proud it made them feel to be an American. It was so wonderful to have been a part of people's lives at that time.

JOHN RAITT: I was under contract at MGM when my agent called one day: "You're going to meet Mrs. Langner of the Theater Guild. Wait for her outside her hairdresser's in Beverly Hills. She'll interview you in a cab on her way to the Twentieth Century Fox studio." So there I was, waiting outside a beauty parlor till Mrs. Langner came out.

We got into a cab and she said, "Would you come to New York City and audition for the role of Curly in *Oklahoma!*? We're looking for a replacement for Alfred Drake."

"That would be very exciting," I said.

We got out of the cab. "Maybe you'll be hearing from me," Mrs. Langner said.

About two weeks later I got a registered letter offering to pay my way to New York—and back if they didn't like me. I decided to go. I sold the car and gave up the apartment. The wife and I took a lower berth in the train, and in about four and a half days we were in New York.

I was met at Penn Station by an agent who whisked me to the St. James Theater. The word had gotten out that this young fellow was being brought all the way to New York by the Guild, and about fifty people were there, including Rodgers and Hammerstein, waiting to see if he could sing or not. I hadn't sung since I left for New York, and I warmed up by singing the "Figaro" aria from *The Barber of Seville,* in English of course, while my wife accompanied me. Then I sang all the songs from *Oklahoma!* There followed a deathly silence. I found out later I almost didn't get to play Curly because I couldn't fit into Alfred Drake's costume.

They shipped me off to Chicago to replace Harry Stockwell, Dean Stockwell's dad, who was shipped to New York to replace Alfred Drake. I played Curly there for ten months and then went on to play the Theater

Guild's subscription cities. It seems so funny now when I recall that my first impression of *Oklahoma!* was that it was a bit racy. I had come from a very protected church family.

But I'll go out with my daughter Bonnie now. She'll bring me on-stage, I'll sing "Oklahoma," the kids will join in with me, singing the "yows" and everything, and every time, the place comes down.

"You people probably know me better as Bonnie Raitt's father," I told the audience for the rock musical *Tommy* at the St. James Theater the night of March 31, 1993. Fifty years, exactly, after *Oklahoma!*'s opening night and in the place where it all began, I sang "Oklahoma" once again. That year fourteen hundred productions of the show were being performed throughout the United States. *Oklahoma!* is the greatest folk musical ever written. It's so American; it endures.

PHILIP LANGNER: Soon after the success of *Oklahoma!* my father and Terry Helburn began thinking of working on another musical with Rodgers and Hammerstein. They came up with the idea of *Liliom,* by the French playwright Ferenc Molnár, which the Guild had produced in their third season, 1921. Molnár was skeptical until he saw *Oklahoma!* After that he said that if his play were treated as charmingly and tastefully, he would be agreeable.

But it took nine months to convince Rodgers and Hammerstein, who were afraid it was too foreign, until Rodgers came up with the idea of a New England locale.

JOHN RAITT: Although I had no way of knowing it at the time, when Rodgers and Hammerstein auditioned me for *Oklahoma!* they said I might be a good bet for the lead in their forthcoming work. The Theater Guild flew me to New York to meet with Rouben Mamoulian. He had directed not only *Oklahoma!* but also *Porgy and Bess,* and he had been in the Moscow Arts Company. I stood in awe of him because of these accomplishments. After we talked for a while, he said, "How do you feel about playing the part of Billy Bigelow in *Carousel?*"

"I'm not sure I have the qualifications as an actor," I said.

And he said, "Johnny, you look like the guy and you don't have to worry about the singing. Let's you and I work out the rest."

After the second day of rehearsal, they handed me some paper that was folded up like an accordion. Unfolded, it was about fifteen feet of sheet music. I subsequently learned that Rodgers and Hammerstein got the idea for "Soliloquy" when I sang the "Figaro" aria at my *Oklahoma!* audition.

Oklahoma!
is the greatest
folk musical ever
written. It's so
American; it endures.

Our first orchestra rehearsal was at the Taft Hotel in New Haven, in a room big enough to hold a forty-piece orchestra. Normally, if the orchestra members like something, they just tap their stands. But after our first run-through, they gave me a standing ovation. The "Soliloquy" is a challenging number, but it was no problem for me because I was one of the few Broadway performers who could approach it as a concert singer. But when I came to the line "What the hell? What if *he* is a *girl?*" Rouben said, "Don't sing it, Johnny. Just say it. It tells the story better."

I never stopped the show with "Soliloquy"; it wasn't that kind of number. It wasn't situated in the show for that purpose. But in all the annals of Broadway musicals, there's nothing like it. It became my signature.

PHILIP LANGNER: At one of the last rehearsals, a white-haired gentleman was sitting in the rear of the theater weeping. Not many knew who he was, but of course my father knew Molnár very well. "I'm afraid they have made *Carousel* far too sad," he said. "I doubt whether anyone will pay six dollars for a ticket to have their heart completely broken."

JOHN RAITT: When *Carousel* opened on April 19, 1945, the critics were there with hatchets. "How dare they do a musical like this, where a guy kills himself in the second act? It can't be as good as *Oklahoma!*"

During the tryouts in Boston, Dick had hurt his back. Now he was wheeled into the Majestic on a stretcher and tucked into one of those boxes. I came about ten minutes late. We were very cocky in those days. We knew what we had. We gave the show that night just for Dick Rodgers.

MARY RODGERS: My father was lying behind some heavy velour curtains. Because the curtains deadened the sound, he couldn't hear the applause, and he thought he had written a flop, while all over the theater, people were crying, including me. I was fourteen years old, and it was the first opening night I was allowed to attend.

JOHN RAITT: We never expected "If I Loved You" to become a hit song. You've got to put that *d* on there, which most people don't. It's a song that projects what would happen "*if* I loved you." And unless you see the show, you can't understand that Billy is protecting himself with that little "if." But it has become a classic nevertheless. It's probably the best example of the wedding of music, lyric, and dialogue that I know of.

I've always thought if a play works, then it should be enhanced by the addition of music. And I believe *Carousel* is a better play than *Liliom*. Eva Le Gallienne came to see me backstage. She had played in the original *Liliom*. "You're the greatest of the Lilioms," she said.

"No, I'm not," I told her. "I'm not playing Liliom. I'm playing Billy Bigelow. He's much more palatable than Liliom because he can sing."

I could never get a part as right and as strong for me as Billy Bigelow, nor have a more memorable experience during a run. The first time I ever set foot on the boards in New York was opening night of *Carousel*. VJ Day came not too long after, and the lights on Broadway were turned on again. And night after night I heard that glorious score, great song after great song. The music was Oscar's and Dick's favorite. And of course it will always be mine.

OPPOSITE PAGE

The original Anna and the King of Siam: Gertrude Lawrence and Yul Brynner (1951).

PHILIP LANGNER: When Dick and Oscar decided to do *South Pacific* with Leland Hayward and Josh Logan instead of the Theater Guild, there was a lot of sadness and anguish. All their joint work until then—*Oklahoma!, Carousel,* and *Allegro*—had been done with us. It was not that they were betraying the Guild. It was that Michener's *Tales of the South Pacific* was owned by Hayward and Logan.

TED CHAPIN: Who but Rodgers and Hammerstein could come up with the idea of a British woman and the King of Siam dancing a polka? *The King and I* has been on for an hour, and the audience is on to the attraction between the pair. But Anna and the king are not, not until that moment. "Shall We Dance" is an example of Richard Rodgers's genius, of how he could write music that took you emotionally where you needed to be.

SUSAN L. SCHULMAN: The story is that when Gertrude Lawrence and Yul Brynner were creating the characters, they were kind of floundering until Yul said, "We have to play it as potential lovers. Otherwise the play is just about two cultures, and who cares?" The sexual undercurrent added an electrifying element.

RONNIE LEE: Unfortunately I never got to see Gertrude Lawrence and Yul Brynner in the "Shall We Dance" number because I was backstage at that time, doing my homework. *The King and I* was three months into production when I took on the role of the crown prince. I saw Gertrude Lawrence from the vantage point of a thirteen-year-old kid . How could I know she was this huge international star?

MORTON GOTTLIEB: Offstage, she was one of the least good-looking stars there was, which is why she only made three movies. But onstage, with the lighting and costumes, Gertrude Lawrence was a presence.

MARY RODGERS: She sang flat all the time, which drove my father crazy.

RONNIE LEE: One day Miss Lawrence invited me, the boy who played Anna's son, and the assistant stage manager, Ruth Mitchell, to her East

Side townhouse. We were served lunch in this stately dining room. Then a chauffeured car took us to the theater where a matinee performance of *Antony and Cleopatra* starring Laurence Olivier and Vivian Leigh was playing. After the performance she shepherded us backstage. We took the elevator to a dressing room. She knocked on the door. "Miss Lawrence to see Mr. Olivier," the dresser said. We entered.

"Oh, darling, darling, darling," Laurence Olivier said.

And Gertrude Lawrence said, "It was thrilling. I know you must be exhausted. We'll leave you."

We went up another flight of stairs and knocked on another dressing-room door. A dresser came to the door. "Miss Lawrence to see Miss Leigh," she said. We entered.

"Oh, darling, I'm thoroughly exhausted," said Vivian Leigh.

And Gertrude Lawrence said, "I know, I know, I know. It was thrilling."

I took it all in nonchalantly. When you're thirteen years old, you don't know from a Gertrude Lawrence, a Laurence Olivier, a Vivian Leigh.

MORTON GOTTLIEB: During the run of *The King and I,* Gertrude developed cancer and subsequently died. Her husband, Dick Aldrich, and I produced her funeral as if it were an opening-night event. Critics sat where their opening-night seats would be. Rodgers and Hammerstein spoke and played her songs.

TED CHAPIN: The idea for *The King and I* came from Gertrude Lawrence. She planned it to be a vehicle for her. But then Yul Brynner took the show and made it his own. The image of him with his arms up in the air came from his curtain call. It had nothing to do with the play; it was a celebration of Yul Brynner, and it worked. He went on to star in the movie, returned to the role in the Broadway revival of May 1977, with Constance Towers as Anna, and continued touring as the king until his death in 1985.

MARY RODGERS: By the time I spent any time with Yul, he was so king-like—he had just become a king. No one really knows the true story of Yul's origins. For all I know, he was born in Hoboken.

RICHARD KILEY: Every time you would speak to him, Yul would give you a different story about where he was born. One time he was a Romanian gypsy; another time he was a Russian prince. When I first saw him he was in a road company of *Lute Song* and hadn't yet affected the shaved head. But he already had a mysterious Oriental aura.

By the time I spent any time with Yul, he was so kinglike—he had just become a king.

RONNIE LEE: In the final scene of *The King and I,* Yul Brynner would lie on the deathbed, and I would kneel beside him. The bed was toward stage left, I was to the left of the bed, and the traveler, the curtain that goes in one direction, would be moving stage right to open stage left. As that was happening, Yul would whisper dirty jokes to me. I was supposed to be weeping, but instead I would be shaking with hysterical laughter.

One of his favorites was about the gods Thor and Mercury up in heaven, where Mercury is telling Thor about his sexual exploits on earth. This motivates Thor to go to earth, where he meets a young woman. After they make love sixteen times, he goes back to Mercury and tells him how fabulous it was.

Mercury asks, "Does she know who you are?"

"No."

"You really should tell her."

Thor goes back down to earth, sees the girl, and tells her, "I am Thor."

"You're Thor?" the girl says. "I can hardly sit."

Yul Brynner was still in his king's costume when he posed with press agent Susan L. Schulman at the twenty-fifth anniversary of the Tony Awards (1971).

SUSAN L. SCHULMAN: In 1971, for the twenty-fifth anniversary of the Tony awards, all those great performers you had seen over the years did their socko-boffo numbers. Richard Kiley did "The Impossible Dream," Robert Preston did "Trouble in River City," Nanette Fabray did "Papa Won't You Dance with Me?", Vivian Blaine did "Adelaide's Lament," and on and on.

But when Yul Brynner, who at this point had not done *The King and I* for years, came on with Patricia Morrison and began "Shall We Dance," it seemed that each person in the house burst into tears. All the top stars were there, but it was Yul Brynner who knocked everybody's socks off. Many people have said that if you had to pick the single most magical moment of the theater, that would be it.

CY FEUER: Our connection with Rodgers and Hammerstein came by way of John Steinbeck. One day my partner, Ernie Martin, came to me and said, "Why don't we do a musical based on the Steinbeck characters in *Cannery Row?*" It's a very colorful setting and story. There's Doc, a marine biologist, a kind of dropout from society who runs a marine laboratory supplying specimens to biology classes and so forth. He wears a beard (in those days, guys never wore beards), and he lives on Cannery Row in Monterey with this bunch of bums. We go to John and tell him our idea, and we lay out a story line.

At the end of the summer, we have a story. We set it in a brothel with a Madam Fauna (she wasn't Flora, she was Fauna) and a vagrant girl coming through.

We wanted Frank Loesser to do the music, but he was busy with other things. We wanted John to do the book, but he told us, "Listen, I can't write a book for a musical. Why don't we do the following? I'll write a novel based on this. You guys own the dramatic rights and do whatever you want with it." So he wrote *Sweet Thursday,* the sequel to *Cannery Row.*

And now here we had this thing and we had nobody. Someone said, "Why don't you go to Dick and Oscar?"

So I said to Dick and Oscar, "Look, you've been in the sweetness and light business. You're always writing shows with little girls running around the stage with bows on their asses. We're in a gritty business. Why don't you come down to our level? Get into this. It has John's literary stamp on it."

They come back and say, "We'll do it. Only, you guys are out. We produce our own shows. We don't need producers. But you own fifty percent of the show."

We say, "Terrific! We're rich. We own fifty percent of the next Rodgers and Hammerstein show."

And then they do a thing called *Pipe Dream*. A big flop. The shortest run of any Rodgers and Hammerstein musical. You know why? They changed it back into Rodgers and Hammerstein. For one thing, they got rid of Henry Fonda, whom we had gotten to play Doc. We had sent him for singing lessons. He said, "Feuer and Martin had me taking singing lessons for a year. They followed me around on the road with a singing teacher. At the end of the year, I couldn't sing for shit."

Dick Rodgers said, "I'm not gonna have Henry Fonda singing my music, for Chrissake."

A few years later I was out in California trying to develop some of our properties. I ran into Oscar, who was out there with Dick doing *State Fair*. Oscar said to me, "You know the reason *Pipe Dream* was a flop was you."

I said, "What do you mean? You guys screwed it up."

"Yes, but fundamentally, it's your flop. You talked us into giving up sweetness and light. And we're really sweetness and light guys."

THEODORE BIKEL: I was making a film in Holland when my agent called and suggested I audition for *The Sound of Music*. He thought that I was an ideal choice for Captain von Trapp. I was already familiar with Rodgers and Hammerstein, having seen *Oklahoma!* and *South Pacific* when they toured in London. I was young, and you know, fools rush in. I was not in awe of Rodgers and Hammerstein.

The R & H office flew me to New York to look at me and listen to me. I sang a couple of things from *Guys and Dolls.* I had brought along my guitar and played some of the songs, which probably sold them as much as anything else.

I understand that after I had done my audition, Mary Martin leaned forward and said to Richard Rodgers, "We don't have to look any further, do we?"

I didn't get to America until I was thirty years old, after having performed in Israel and then on London's West End. But I was born in Vienna, and therefore *The Sound of Music* had personal echoes for me, although the Austrian aristocrat that I played, Captain von Trapp, was able to make choices I could not. The story was candy coated; they pulled punches in those days. The Nazis in the play were not as nearly villainous as I remembered them to be. But this was long before we had musicals like *Evita* and *Les Mis,* which have an edge to them.

FRANK GOODMAN: Oscar was in the hospital when the show was trying out. It wasn't until the second week of the run he flew up to Boston for a matinee performance. There he decided the Nazi-type song that Kurt Kaszner sang was too downbeat, and they threw it out.

THEODORE BIKEL: One night when we were appearing in Boston, Richard Rodgers took me to dinner in a Chinese restaurant. Muzak was playing, and every three minutes or so, one of his tunes came on, and each time he got up and took a bow.

But he was not lighthearted about the show. It was eleven days before opening night, and both he and Hammerstein felt something was still lacking. "We have this young leading man, and we have to write something for him that will utilize what he can do," they said. They retired to a hotel room at the Ritz Carlton in Boston, where they proceeded to write me a song that I would sing eight times a week for the next two years thereafter.

When I heard "Edelweiss" for the first time, I thought, Ah, at last I have something that I can get my teeth into. It had that folk feeling, it used my guitar to the best advantage, and it integrated itself into the action very well. But frankly, the nostalgia was not heartfelt. I never had much nostalgic feeling toward Austria. It was not a country that behaved terribly well to the Jews.

The song has great meaning for me, nevertheless, because it is the last song that Oscar Hammerstein wrote. He was sick at the time, and I find it meaningful that the last word he wrote creatively was "forever."

RICHARD KILEY: The first musical Rodgers did after Hammerstein died was *No Strings,* starring Diahann Carroll and myself. Dick and I had a couple of run-ins because I had a tendency to bend the notes a little bit, and he didn't like that at all.

I had first met him years before, when I auditioned for a part in the chorus of the original company of *South Pacific.* There were about a hundred guys on the stage of the Majestic Theater that day, and all of them seemed to know Rodgers and Hammerstein personally. They stepped up one at a time, handed down their music, and sang in these glorious voices. I waited and waited for my turn. Finally the guy immediately before me got up and sang "The Song of the Open Road." That was the song I had prepared; it was kind of a rousing number that I thought I could do well. But this guy sang it like Placido Domingo.

I have a choice, I thought. When they call my name, I can look around like I don't know who that is and just sneak out. Instead I stepped up,

handed down my music, and said in very shaky voice: "You've just heard the definitive version of that song. Here is the comic version." My knees were knocking. I couldn't find the pitch. I sang off-key. It was the most god-awful experience.

About fifteen years later, after I had done *Kismet,* after I had won the Tony for *Redhead,* Dick Rodgers asked to see me. It was at the Majestic again, and there was the great man sitting on the stage doodling on a pad under a work light.

"We're putting together this musical," he said to me. "It takes place in Paris, and it's about a black girl and a white expatriate writer. Would you be interested in playing the leading man?"

Of course I would be. He asked what key was I comfortable in. I said F. He played some of the songs for me; I sang a bit. We had a very pleasant exchange about the role and how he was writing the songs at that time. As I was leaving he said, "I'm a big fan of yours. It's really nice meeting you at last."

I said, "We've met before, Mr. Rodgers."

"When?"

I told him about my ill-fated *South Pacific* tryout.

"Jesus Christ," he said, "was that you? Oscar and I would often say to each other, 'Whatever happened to that poor son of a bitch?'"

LEE ROY REAMS: I got to audition for Richard Rodgers for the role of Will Parker in the 1969 Lincoln Center revival of *Oklahoma!* I was told not to sing a Richard Rodgers song because he didn't like singers doing his material unless they were coached by him or his people. So I decided to sing the Leonard Bernstein number from *On the Town.* Stupid mistake. I'm auditioning for *Oklahoma!* singing "New York, New York . . ."

He yelled, "Stop it! What are you doing, coming in here and singing a song like that? You're auditioning for a comedy character. Don't you have a comedy song you can do?"

I just froze. And then I said, "No, Mr. Rodgers, I don't."

"Then what are you doing here?"

I said, "I can sing 'Kansas City.' I know that."

"Then why don't you sing it? You'll sing it in the show."

"I will," I said, and sang two choruses of "Kansas City."

He said, "Can you dance for me?"

I did my dance routine. He called me to the front and said, "Is there anything you can't do?"

Mary Martin and Richard Rodgers listen to a playback during the recording session for the original Broadway production of *The Sound of Music* (1959).

"No, sir, there isn't."

Richard Rodgers! At that time in my life, he looked very old to me. Half of his face was missing because of the cancer surgery, and he walked very slowly. But still, Richard Rodgers!

He was always dressed in a tie and a business suit, shiny shoes. Always formal, immaculately groomed. A thorough professional, a man of few words. When he spoke, he got right to the point.

Remarkably, he did three shows after that revival: *Rex, Two by Two,* with Danny Kaye, and *I Remember Mama.* Here was this legend who certainly did not have to be concerned about work. But he was consumed by his love for it. That's what kept him alive.

MARY RODGERS: The truth is my father was not interested in music in the abstract. He almost never wrote music that wasn't for the theater. *Victory at Sea* is one of the few exceptions. What he loved was the whole world of theater, the camaraderie, the out-of-town tryouts, the greasy spoon restaurants. He loved staying up till two in the morning trying to figure out what to do with a show. He loved going to see his shows over and over, standing anonymously in the back of the theater. He bought the whole package.

6 | WE WERE THE ESSENCE OF NEW YORK

ALVIN COLT: Cy Feuer and Ernie Martin. They were into everything. They were Damon Runyon characters themselves.

FRED GOLDEN: Ernie was the hard-nosed guy, always with the cigar. He was very fussy, loved to stretch out on the sofa, smoke a cigar, and make you feel like a little fella. That was his method. Cy was the one to throw oil on troubled water and keep things nice and light and friendly. They were great, great theater people.

CY FEUER: Ernie Martin was a California kid. Graduated from UCLA, started as a pageboy at CBS. Worked his way up to be head of comedy programming, came to New York. That's when he saw a Broadway show for the first time.

I was a Brooklyn kid. Stationed at Wright Field in Dayton, Ohio, during the war. Transferred to New York before I was shipped out. That's when I saw a Boadway show for the first time.

Now it's after the war. We're both in Hollywood. It's the golden age of the musical, and we're young, running and jumping. We come to New York, go to Broadway, and see this cockamamy little stage. A great Broadway musical comedy looks like a pipsqueak. "Jesus," we say, "that's nothing. That's where we ought to go." All the talent was going out to Hollywood in those days, and the competition was pretty tough. We said, "Guys like us can't get a movie on. Let's go in the other direction, where there's so much less competition, and take on this junky little Broadway."

Our first show was *Where's Charley?* It started out to be *An American in Paris* before *An American in Paris* was ever made. Ernie was a friend of Ira Gershwin's. They had met at the Santa Anita track. Ernie was a good hand-icapper, and he also had that great drive. He could walk into any situation and sell it. "Listen, what about *An American in Paris* as a Broadway musical?" Ernie asked Ira. And Ira said, "Great, why not?"

Ernie told me, "Listen, I got an idea. I told it to Ira. He likes it." We got all excited about it.

Ernie came to New York and saw Ray Bolger in *Three to Make Ready.* Bolger was what we called a rube dancer, but he wore white tie and tails and made it look high class. Ernie told Ray Bolger, "I want to make a show for you. I got *An American in Paris.*" Ray was fun, an up guy, and he was fascinated by Ernie.

AL HIRSCHFELD: After I drew him, Ray Bolger claimed he copied my drawings in his dancing. I'm not constricted by gravity; I can make 'em fly. All I did was push a little bit further what Ray already did.

CY FEUER: We got Bolger. Now we started trying to get ourselves in position. We went to Harold Reinhart, the number-one show business attorney at the time. Ernie said, "How about giving us some advice? And later on, if anything develops, you got yourself some good clients."

Harold said, "Great."

The interesting thing is, getting a lawyer turned out to be the big thing. Because trying to arrange this *American in Paris* and clear the rights turned out to be complicated. I got a call one day from Harold. He said, "Listen, you know what show would be great for Bolger? *Charley's Aunt,* by Brandon Thomas. My clients have been trying to get that property for a musical for years."

They had been unsuccessful because Thomas's heirs were living on the fifty thousand pounds a year they got from stock and amateur productions. They worried about injuring the property by making it into a musical. Harold said, "I got an idea that with Bolger they might be interested."

One of us had to go to England to see these people, and we were both working. I said to Ernie, "OK. I'm quitting my job, but you got to give me some radio shows to do so I can keep eating."

And what we did was this. We got a copy of *Charley's Aunt,* which was a farce in four acts. The story is about Jack and Charley, two students at Oxford, living in these digs with a butler. Their two Victorian ladies, whose uncle is about to whisk them off to Scotland, are coming to visit them. It's Jack and Charley's last chance to get to them. The chaperone is supposed to be Charley's aunt, who is coming that afternoon from Brazil. But the train is late, and Charley's aunt doesn't show up.

After I drew him, Ray Bolger claimed he copied my drawings in his dancing.

Cy Feuer and Ernie Martin—they were Damon Runyon characters themselves.

Meanwhile, Lord Fancourt Babberley, a zany guy who lives across the hall, comes in dressed in a drag costume. He says, "This is the costume I'm wearing for the Varsity Show."

They say, "You're going to be Charley's aunt." Babberley stays in the costume for the entire show, camps all over the place, and at the very end reveals himself. That's the whole thing. Now we said, "Because we've got Bolger, we want dancing. He's a dancing star. We got to get him out of that dress." So we cut out the part of Babberley, who was the leading man. Charley becomes the guy with the costume for the Varsity Show. He shows it to Jack, and Jack says, "You're going to play your own aunt."

What I did was take the Samuel French copy of the play and write a play with all the dialogue but without Lord Babberley. I made certain adjustments and got on the plane and went to England. Harold arranged for a barrister out there, and we met with the estate. They said, "With Bolger playing this, we'll go for it. But it's got to be done with this outline and no other way."

Now we had to get somebody who knew something about show business. We had to raise the money, which we thought we'd manage. We knew how to ask a guy to give us five thousand dollars. But how do you put on a show? Where do you rehearse? What do you do?

So we went to George Abbott. We walked in and said, "Look, here's what we got." And we laid it all out. He looked the outline over. "It's a piece of cake," he said, and he signed on. The minute he signed on, we had a show. And off we went into the wild blue yonder.

Frank Loesser was supposed to be the lyricist, and the music was supposed to be by Harold Arlen. While we were preparing, Harold's house in California burned down. He called and said, "I can't go to New York. My wife's terribly upset. I'm going to have to pull out."

Frank said, "Let me do it all by myself." He had done things in the army, like "Praise the Lord and Pass the Ammunition" and "Private Roger Young." I had to call Ray Bolger and tell him, "Look, I'm switching on you from Harold to Frank."

I didn't know what was going to be. What did I know? We were all a bunch of neophytes. We were digging a ditch, working side by side. Frank was good, I thought. His stuff sounded good to me, but I didn't know about anybody else.

With words and music by Frank Loesser, *Where's Charley?* opened in Philadelphia. Ray Bolger knocked himself out. He collapsed with physical exhaustion, and we closed after one performance. Here we had moved our families to New York and everything, and we thought it had died.

We opened in New York and got terrible notices. There were seven newspapers in the city at that time, and only the *World Telegram* gave us a good review. The *Times*'s headline was "Bolger's Here, but Where's Charley?" Luckily we had some advances on the basis of Bolger.

None of the critics even mentioned the score. But Frank came in one day with a telegram from Dick Rodgers. It said, "Bravo! What a score!"

There was a recording strike then, and we never had a cast recording. That's why the score, except for the one song that stepped out, "Once in Love with Amy," has hardly been heard. Not too many people know the other songs, like "The New Ashmoleon Marching Society and Student Conservatory Band," which has lines like "The New Ashmoleon could have licked Napoleon / with all those deadly instruments at hand."

Ernie and I had moved into the same apartment with my wife and two sons and Ernie's wife. It was a sublet way uptown, 102d Street and Park Avenue. We figured between the two of us we could make the rent. It was all very family-like. Ray Bolger, who was also our coproducer (that's how we got him), used to come up all the time. He became very friendly with Bobby, our seven-year-old son.

In those days they made acetate records as demos of the score. Bobby had his own machine and would play these demos a hundred times. When we took him to the first matinee, he knew the entire score by heart.

In the second act, Ray came on to do "Once in Love with Amy" and blew the lyric. He stopped the orchestra. "Hold it, hold it, hold it. I forgot the lyric. Does anybody here know the lyric?"

Bobby stands up from his seat, second row center. "Yes, Ray," he says, "I know the lyric."

With the spotlight in his eyes, Ray can't see who's talking. He says, "Will you sing it with me?" Bobby says, "Sure," and starts singing, "Once in love with Amy . . ." The audience is fascinated with this kid, and Ray has lost them. He's got to get them back.

He says, "Why don't you all sing it with me?" and he starts a singalong. Somehow he gets the audience back and finishes the show. But he came off burning. "What the hell is this? What the hell's going on down there?"

I went backstage and I said, "Ray, it was Bobby."

And finally he said, "You know, maybe there's something to that. I had a feeling when I was out there. Maybe I ought to try it."

Well, he started experimenting, and he wound up stepping out of the show completely, kidding with the audience, using them as a chorus, doing everything but the kitchen sink with "Once in Love with Amy." And that became the hit of the show.

At the end of six months, we were selling out on the basis of Ray Bolger jumping around the stage, fooling around with "Once in Love with Amy." Opening night, the song ran three and a half minutes. Closing night, it ran twenty-five minutes. As it turned out, we played the St. James for a couple of years, had 792 performances, went on the road, and then they made a movie.

• • • • •

Ernie and I had come to New York for *Charley*. And we stayed.

One day Ernie called me and said, "I have in my hand the greatest title for a Broadway show you ever heard."

I said, "What is it?"

He said, "*Guys and Dolls*." Ernie was holding a collection of Damon Runyon stories. There isn't one called "Guys and Dolls," but it's a phrase Runyon frequently used. The anthologist picked it up for the title of his anthology.

We got very excited. A Damon Runyon musical. That would be our second show. Many, many Runyon movies had been made, but maybe only two of them worked. And both of us happened to be great Damon Runyon fans. So we went to Robbie Lantz, who represented the estate, and said, "We'd like to make a deal to do a musical."

He said, "Why don't you pick out a story and I'll let you know if it's available."

And we said, "No, we don't want to do that, because we're running now, and we're excited. We want to make a deal with you that says we will make a musical to be called *Guys and Dolls* based upon *X* to be filled in later." And we made that deal.

We sat down and started to read. A lot of the stuff we read through, the picture rights were gone. We didn't want anything without clear picture rights. Then we came upon "The Idyll of Sarah Brown," the story of the missionary and the gambler. She's a flop as a missionary on Broadway, and he gets taken with her. He gets all his crapshooter friends together and says, "Against all your markers, I'll put up cash, and your marker is you gotta go to a prayer meeting." He wins the bet, and they show at the prayer meeting, and the mission is saved. We based it upon that, and off we went.

When we told Frank Loesser it was Damon Runyon, he jumped. And then we started to figure out the writers. We went through quite a few people and finally wound up with Jo Swerling. He was a very well-known screenwriter, did a lot of Frank Capra movies, a very nice man. Jo had a place in Malibu, and I went down there and we worked on this thing.

One day Ernie came down. He didn't work creatively on a day-to-day basis like I did, but every now and then he would come up with an oblique thought that was just right. Now he said, "Listen, we're doing a show about a gambler and there's no debt. How can you do a show about a gambler without a debt?"

Jo said, "I don't know what you're talking about. We're trying to construct this act here, and you're talking about bets." But Ernie insisted we needed something with a bet.

Finally I said, "I remember there was a show called *Sailor Beware*." It was about the navy. The fleet was coming into San Diego or somewhere, and there was a beautiful dame at the dance hall there. Her last name was Jackson, and she was known to the fleet as Stonewall Jackson because no one could make her. There was a great ladies' man on the ship, and they said, "This is the guy who's gonna knock off Jackson." They made book on it. The plots of these musicals were very stupid.

Two of the men who made *Guys and Dolls* happen: composer and lyricist, Frank Loesser (left) and writer, Abe Burrows.

I said, "What about stealing this Stonewall Jackson thing? We could have Sky make a bet that he could knock off this missionary."

We went to see Oscar Hammerstein. He and Richard Rodgers had admired the score of *Where's Charley?,* and we had become friends. They treated us like a couple of bright boys. We said, "Oscar, this is what we're playing around with."

He said, "Look, you can make the bet, but don't make it about knocking her off. Don't do that; it's not right. Make the bet about something else."

So Ernie and I said, "Let's make it that he can't get her to go to Havana with him."

We went back to Jo and said, "This is what we want to do. We think it will spice the story up."

Jo said, "I won't have anything to do with that. You're stealing it from that other show."

I said, "What's wrong with stealing it? What the hell? It's not copyrighted."

He said, "I won't do it. It's below my standards."

And we said to ourselves, "Jesus, we want to do this. We want this bet. It has a Runyon feel here that we're not getting with Jo." We said to Jo, "We want to do the bet."

And he said, "If you do the bet, I'm withdrawing."

It was done without much hostility, I must say. We go to his agent and we make a deal for his withdrawal in which he has a percentage. He wanted to keep top billing because he had written a whole book.

We had raised nearly all the money. Now we said, "No sense keeping this money in the bank. It could take us six months, a year. We feel funny about keeping it." But a lot of the backers said, "Hold on to it." We had an account and let interest accrue to the account and all that.

Now we had to find a new writer. Frank was good friends with a well-known radio comedy writer, Abe Burrows. He wrote *Duffy's Tavern,* a radio show about this blue-collar tavern. It always began with Ed Gardner calling Duffy, the owner, reporting what was happening. I still remember the first joke. Gardner says, "Duffy, the opening is going great. The place is full of flowers. Everybody sent flowers. There's a big horseshoe wreath with a satin ribbon across it from the waiters' union. It says, 'Best wishes to Duffy's Tavern, which is unfair to organized labor.'" That was typical of Abe's humor. It always had a sociological base to it.

HARVEY SABINSON: One of my favorite Abe Burrows stories is about the time Abe went to a fat farm to lose weight. Cy called him a few weeks later and asked if there was anything he could do for him. "Yeah," Abe said. "Send me a file with a cake in it."

CY FEUER: Abe had written all these songs with lines like "Some folks remember their mothers, and others their girlfriends behind, But I am walking down Memory Lane without a goddamned thing on my mind." Together with Frank, he wrote "I'm in Love with the Girl with the Three Blue Eyes." But he had never written a show.

Now we said, "Look, come on and do this." And he agreed.

Abe wouldn't read Jo Swerling's stuff. He didn't want to be influenced by it. I had a structure of scenes that I laid out for him. He started to write. At the end of writing the first act, we went to George S. Kaufman, who knew Abe from the show *Information, Please,* on radio. He read it, and he said, "I'll sign on to direct. But we must be very careful, because we're on to something here."

He said to me, "You're out. Three people make a committee. And, besides, we don't need you." He was the great collaborator, a great influence. He made a tremendous contribution to the second act.

I understand Jo Swerling read the new script and threw it across the room, saying, "This is garbage." But he insisted on keeping first billing. And to this day, the billing is *Guys and Dolls,* by Swerling and Burrows, even though there's not one word in the show by Swerling. When the show was revived in the 1990s, Swerling's son wrote to the *New York Times* and asked why no one mentioned his father, whose contribution to *Guys and Dolls* is largely underestimated. Ernie and I wrote to the *Times* and straightened it out.

Now we had a book and a score, and we had to cast. When you write a show, you have to have some prototypes. You have to have in mind the flesh and blood of the characters. We wrote Nathan Detroit with Sam Levene in mind. Nathan had to be Sam. If Sam hadn't been available, we would have postponed the show until he was ready.

ALVIN COLT: Sam Levene was an accomplished actor, but he had never done a musical. He wasn't a musical person at all. It didn't matter. He had such expression, was so endearing. He was perfect.

CY FEUER: We call Sam down to the Forty-sixth Street Theater to establish his keys, find out what his voice range is. We had sent him a recording of "Sue Me," which he was to learn. "Sue me, sue me, what can you do me? I love you." And we put him up on the stage, and we say, "We want to find out what your key is, Sam."

"OK."

We pick a note.

"Do . . ."

"Fa . . ."

"Jesus," we say, "he's tone deaf!" Finally Frank changed the beginning of the song so Sam could speak his way into it. He says, "Call a lawyer and—," then goes into "sue me, sue me . . ." Next line he says, "Give a holler and—" then goes into "hate me, hate me . . ." He just croaked it out. But it didn't make a difference. It was Sam Levene, and it worked.

ALVIN COLT: Vivian Blaine as Adelaide was a typical Broadway doll, vulnerable, adorable.

CY FEUER: She had starred in a couple of movies but had never quite made it. But as Adelaide, Vivian was great. She played her sweet, really sweet.

You're out. Three people make a committee. And, besides, we don't need you.

She's this blue-collar girl, working in this crappy nightclub, but she's sweet. Against Nathan Detroit, this momza. That's what made it work.

B. S. Pully was cast by accident. He came in with a friend of his, a well-known comic who was auditioning for the show. You could hear him talking to his friend offstage: "That's it, kid. You're doing good," in that gruff voice.

And Kaufman said, "Who *is* that?"

They bring Pully out, and Kaufman says, "That's our Big Julie."

Stubby Kaye was a tenor who worked in the borscht circuit: "And now here's Stubby Kaye to sing 'Ah, Sweet Mystery of Life.'" Stubby'd come out, sing the song, take a bow, and walk off. He sang "Sit Down, You're Rocking the Boat," but never spoke a word onstage.

That's what happened in *Guys and Dolls;* we had a stage full of Runyon characters, many of whom were non-actors.

ALVIN COLT: Cy and Ernie worked very closely with me in getting the characters' touches in costumes. No detail was overlooked. For instance, Nicely Nicely is a big fat man. We figured someone that size probably has foot problems. So I had him wear perforated shoes for ventilation. Arvids, the old Salvation Army character, always wore white socks, and Big Julie had an irritating acid green tie with a huge white *J* on it. Adelaide was the typical doll, engaged for fourteen years and not married. We thought, Where would she buy her clothes? They had to be a little too busty, a little flirtatious.

The dolls were to be scantily dressed. They came up to Cy and Ernie's office and were shown the "Bushel and a Peck" costume sketch before they signed their contracts. "This is what you're going to wear," they were told. "If you have a problem, don't sign the contract." They all signed.

There had never been a hairdresser for a Broadway show before. But I felt we needed one to make our girls look like dolls. I was told about a young man working at the Roxy Theater who knew the Times Square look, and we brought him down to Philadelphia, where the show was playing.

Ernie Adler had magic fingers. He had our girls looking so great in a half an hour, you wouldn't believe it. Although he went on to do many shows afterwards, *Guys and Dolls* was Ernie's first Broadway show. It established how important hair design is to the theater. Today no show is without a hair person; it has developed into an art form.

We played a long time in Philadelphia. The week before New York, they added "Take Back Your Mink." I had four days to do the costuming.

OPPOSITE PAGE
Vivian Blaine rebuffs Sam Levene's plea, "Sue Me," in the original Broadway production of *Guys and Dolls* (1950).

We decided to have the dolls wear gold lamés with dark fake mink stoles and high-heeled shoes. The girls protested. "We can't dance in high heels," they kept saying. Finally the choreographer, Michael Kidd, put on a pair and performed the whole number. "If I can do it, you can do it," he said.

CY FEUER: We couldn't do "Take Back Your Mink" until those special costumes were ready. Everything had to be breakaway. They had to tear off the furs, jewelry, headpieces. We had the number rehearsed, ready to go, but we were waiting for the costumes. They arrived on Friday. We played Friday, Saturday matinee, Saturday night, closed in Philly. Then we came in and played three previews in New York. And that first Friday night the girls took all their stuff off and threw everything into the pit. It was such a mess.

We said, "Kids, don't worry about it. We'll clean it up. It works." And it did.

Another number we added at that time is "The Oldest Established Permanent Floating Crap Game in New York." Originally it was a line of dialogue. Frank said, "Abe, I want that line. Write something else for the scene." And Frank wrote it as a hymn, an all-male chorus, and we put it on in Philadelphia.

But "Fugue for Tinhorns" was written early on. Frank came in one day and said, "Listen to this song I've come up with," and he began: "'I got the horse right here, the name is Paul Revere . . .'"

We said, "Terrific!" But we didn't know what to do with it. The show is about crap shooting, not horse racing. Everyone is preoccupied with a crap game. We can't stop to sing about a horse race.

We were out of town with this thing still on the side when Ernie finally came up and said, "Listen, let's open the show with it. Nobody will know what we're doing. It's generic; it'll sound like Damon Runyon."

So that's what we did. First thing you hear is the Broadway ballet, and then the newsstand comes down, with the guys looking over with the tip sheets: "I got the horse right here, the name is Paul Revere," and then Miss Sarah Brown comes on and does "Follow the Fold" and is a flop evangelist, and off we go.

Opening night New York, after the ballet, there was the sound of the bugle announcing the horses at the gate. And it got a great burst of laughter. The biggest laugh of the evening. I turned around and said, "We're home. They're waiting for us."

Cy and Ernie worked very closely with me in getting the characters' touches in costumes. No detail was overlooked.

Ernie had been right. He had said, "Let's do it up front and get it over with." And to this day, nobody has ever questioned it.

Everything worked. We knew we'd be a hit. I don't know why. It was in the air. In those days the opening-night audience was the opening-night audience. All the critics. You banked everything on that night.

ALVIN COLT: Opening night in New York, I stood out front and watched my sketches come to life, moving around on the stage. That's your gratification. Seeing what you dreamed of, what you created, on an actor up there on the stage. The audience, the critics, they never know what you've gone through to reach this goal—your research, the work at the drawing board, in the costume shop, what it cost or didn't cost. It's what's onstage that counts. What your audience is seeing. That impact. That's what counts. That's the magic.

Three of the guys from the original *Guys and Dolls:* John Silver, Sam Levene, and Stubby Kaye (1950).

CY FEUER: After *Guys and Dolls,* Ernie and I were out in California, talking about what to do next. I was so steeped in Frank Loesser and Abe Burrows. But Ernie said, "You can't have Frank and Abe for everything. You got to spread out a little. What about Cole Porter?"

I said, "Well, Cole Porter's a little fancy for us."

He said, "Are you knocking Cole Porter?"

I said, "I can't be knocking Cole Porter, for Chrissakes. He's terrific."

So we got ahold of the phone book and called Cole Porter. We said, "We're Feuer and Martin and we just produced *Guys and Dolls.*"

He said, "Terrific! I meant to write you guys a letter."

We said, "We want to see you about a show."

He said, "Come on over." We went over and told him we had an idea to do something based on the Lautrec period in Montmartre. He said, "I love it. I'm on."

We did a lot of research and found there was a Society Against Sidewalk Licentiousness in 1892. A guy wanted to clean up Montmartre in time for the Exposition when the Eiffel Tower opened. He wanted to get all the prostitutes off the streets of Montmartre. His attempts were comical because people were coming to see the prostitutes as much as the Eiffel Tower.

As it turned out, we got Abe Burrows to do the story. Cole Porter did the words and music. We went to Paris to see Lilo. She had a big barrel-chested voice; she was tough. We brought her over. We cast Gwen Verdon for her first speaking part. Michael Kidd did the choreography; he was part of our team.

That was *Can-Can,* and it was the runaway hit of the season.

FRED GOLDEN: A few years after *Can-Can,* Feuer and Martin did *Silk Stockings,* with Cole Porter once again. It got terrible notices on the road, and everyone said, "Oh, they'll have to close it. It's gonna break their streak." Not those fellas. They toured it all over the country and kept making changes and recasting it, and finally about a year later, it opened at the Imperial, and it was a great big hit.

CY FEUER: In between *Can-Can* and *Silk Stockings,* we brought *The Boy Friend* over from London along with Julie Andrews, who was under eighteen at that time. Ernie had to sign on as her guardian. We kept the original production intact, except I turned the four-, five-piece orchestra into an old 1920s band, with two pianos, banjo, tuba, soprano saxophone, twelve or thirteen men. We called them the Bearcats, dressed them in black-and-yellow blazers, and put them in the pit to play an overture. And they stood up and sat down like an old-fashioned band with clarinets, saxes.

We played the opening number with the lights on the orchestra, and they finished it to a tremendous burst of applause. We raised the curtain. The maid is on the telephone: "Hello, hello?" But we couldn't go on. We had to stop the show for the orchestra, have them stand up and take a bow while she was waiting on the stage. That was one of the two showstoppers in our career. The other was with Gwen Verdon in *Can-Can*. They talk about showstoppers, but these two really stopped the show.

Ernie and I didn't go back to working with Frank until *How to Succeed in Business without Really Trying!,* which opened in 1961. Some years before we had tried to get him to write the score for a show we were working on based on *Cannery Row*. "We'll call Frank. It's a natural for Frank," we had said.

But Frank didn't want to do it. "I don't want to do any more joke shows. I want to be Puccini," he said.

We said, "Frank, for Chrissake, don't do that. You're the greatest joke writer in the world." But Frank had some kind of problem with his brother, some sibling thing. His brother was a well-educated musician and all that. Couldn't touch Frank for beans. But at any rate, Frank wouldn't do it. He was off doing *The Most Happy Fella* and things like that.

After *The Most Happy Fella,* however, Frank Loesser came back to us for *How to Succeed in Business without Really Trying!* a very different kind of show. It's a musical that has just one ballad: "I Believe in You." Only, the guy is singing it to himself while he's looking in the mirror. He starts to shave, and the electric razor picks up the melody. You know how we did it? We put kazoos in the orchestra.

Abe Burrows, who was one of the writers of the script, directed the original production. You had to pay attention to his jokes. There's an office with a lot of chairs and a lot of typewriters. It's morning, and the girls all come in: "Good morning, good morning." They take off their things, sit down at the typewriters, put in a piece of paper, and are just settling down to work when a guy sticks his head in and shouts, "Coffee break!"

They get up and line up right across the stage. They're standing there. And then the guy says, "There's no coffee!"

"No coffee?" They all turn into junkies: "If I can't have my coffee break,

Cy Feuer had admired Gwen Verdon for a long time when he cast her in *Can-Can.* It was her first speaking part on Broadway.

my coffee break, my coffee break . . ." There's no dancing, no moving. The lyrics alone carry the number.

MERLE DEBUSKEY: Cy Feuer had snapped, "goddamn, we need a button on this coffee break number," which means it had to end clean and sharp and on a high, and Bob Fosse came up with the idea that one guy in the chorus would come out with a cup in his hand, needing a fix, and walk up to the lip of the stage and jump into the pit.

Soon after Jack Kennedy was elected president, he came to see *How to Succeed.* There were security men in the flies, the wings, the balconies, and in the pit. I was standing in the back, watching the show, when suddenly it occurred to me: Holy shit! What happens when they see a guy jump off the stage?

I found the head of security and told him what was going to happen. "Oh, my god," he said. Next thing you know, security guys are running all over the place and talking to each other to make sure that nobody has a quick trigger.

Across from the Forty-sixth Street Theater was the Hotel Edison, which had a big marquee. I had tipped a couple of photographers from the *Times* that they could get up there and take some pictures of Kennedy coming into the theater. But it didn't occur to me to tell security. About twenty minutes before the president arrived, security ran the photographers off. There was a whole to-do.

DONNA MCKECHNIE: *How to Succeed in Business without Really Trying!* was the first Broadway show I saw, and the first Broadway show I was in. I was the second understudy to the two leads: Rosemary, the secretary, and Hedy La Rue, the bombshell, and I was in the chorus. I thought, This is what it's like. You go from show to show to show . . .

I had auditioned for an Oldsmobile show. The choreographer was Bob Hamilton, of the Bob Hamilton Trio, and the producers were Cy Feuer and Ernie Martin. Without my realizing it, Feuer and Martin were actually auditioning me for *How to Succeed.* It was Cy who took me out of the industrial show and put me on Broadway in what turned out to be my only chorus job.

During rehearsals I could make out this figure in the darkness of the audience. It was Hugh Lambert, the original choreographer. They didn't think he was achieving what they wanted, so they replaced him with Bob Fosse. But they couldn't fire Hugh because he was under contract, and he got full credit along with Bob Fosse, even though he only did one great dance number that remained in the show. It was sad. Hugh had to be there, but he had no work to do. At that time I did not understand all those dynamics. What I did understand was that I had to work on acting and dancing and singing or I'd never get out of the chorus.

Cy Feuer was one of my first mentors. He was a trumpet player, a tough little fighter, his hair always styled in the famous brush cut. "You've got to sing every day, every day," he'd tell me. He knew that it takes years for back muscles to develop and that's why women don't come into their own as singers until their late thirties and forties.

Frank Loessor was my first vocal coach. He could be the most romantic of men—he wrote those lush melodies—but he was also like one of those guys standing on the corner in *Guys and Dolls.* Once he came down the aisle to the stage: "Hey, honey, make the gesture first."

"What?" I asked. I didn't quite understand.

He repeated. "Make the gesture first."

He was right, of course. The gesture comes first; it works that way. You mimic your organic response, do whatever your physical impulse is, then follow it with your voice. Like in *A Chorus Line,* you cross your arms and grab your chest before you sing "God, I'm a dancer . . ." I began thinking about my physical life, what I do with my body.

In *How to Succeed* I had masters around me: Bob Fosse and Gwen Verdon, who came along with Bob as dance captain, Loesser and Burrows, Feuer and Martin. I learned from all of them.

In 1995 I went to see the *How to Succeed* revival. It was in the same theater where we had opened in 1961. Maybe I was sitting in the same seats my parents sat in when they came opening night. It was nearly thirty years later, but all I could see was our old choreography, our costumes, Charles Nelson Reilly, Rudy Vallee, Bobby Morse . . .

CY FEUER: Robert Morse had played the lead very broad. He was wild, all over the place. You couldn't control him. So we played everybody else absolutely serious. Wonderful juxtaposition of Morse against this serious business background. When I heard Matthew Broderick was going to do the role in the revival, I thought it was a mistake. He seemed too contained. But the director hit upon the reverse of what we did. Matthew played the lead absolutely straight, and the company was wild. It worked just as well as ours.

What I did understand was that I had to work on acting and dancing and singing or I'd never get out of the chorus.

In other ways, though, I felt they didn't appreciate what Abe Burrows had put into the original. Their production was fixed up with technology. It had more spectacle. But some of the jokes went right by, and, sociologically, I think the director didn't understand the casting. They had this big Jewish guy playing Biggley. Ours was a WASP with a homburg hat. And their Heddy La Rue could have killed you. Ours was tougher than Adelaide, but she was really sweet. Whenever we did bimbos, they had to be sweet. You had to love them. When Virginia Martin and Rudy Vallee sang "Heart of Gold," they sang it straight. The audience was in hysterics over these seemingly serious ridiculous people. That's where the humor was.

Sometimes the old ways work the best. When they were rehearsing the 1992 revival of *Guys and Dolls,* Tony Walton and Jerry Zaks called me. "Listen," I said, "I staged the show myself recently, and I opened it up and it hurt the show." It's an old-fashioned show, in-one—you can change the scenery in the back. You didn't have winches in those days. And Tony said, "Jesus, I've been pondering that one in depth." And he did it the old-fashioned way, and it worked.

During the 1970s somebody got an idea to do a black version of *Guys and Dolls.* Abe Burrows was at the beginning of Alzheimer's at that time. I didn't know it. He called me: "Help me out with this one." So I went to the producers, and they signed me on.

The arranger put in something at the end of "Sit Down, You're Rocking the Boat," what we call a ride-out. You hold the number, the band drives. I said, "What is that ride-out at the end? It's a great sound."

"That's gospel," the arranger said.

I said, "Listen, we do an encore, let's do a gospel encore." That was a big thing in that revival; it got the audience up and standing on their seats.

But even though the performers were wonderful, the show didn't work. It was a black *Guys and Dolls,* but not to a black man. The black audience didn't take to it. It didn't feel black to them. Fosse made the same mistake of trying to do *Big Deal* in black. Sociologically it was wrong.

But we were the right team for *Guys and Dolls.* It's like when I saw the group for *My Fair Lady;* I knew they were right. The whole little effete gang, all a little on the homosexual side. Perfect. It was exactly the group for that. It wouldn't have smelled right coming from us. We were *Guys and Dolls,* New York; the essence of New York.

7 | LOOK, LOOK, LOOK WHO'S DANCIN' NOW

JAMES HAMMERSTEIN: Because my family was so heavily involved in musical theater, I didn't know it was a golden age that came and went. I thought it was normal. The golden age did not go out with a bang. Basically, the ranks thinned. Cole Porter, Frank Loesser, Lerner and Loewe, Rodgers and Hammerstein died. They died. And replacements were not coming at any steady rate.

But then there were the Jerry Robbinses, the Michael Kidds, the Bob Fosses, and the Michael Bennetts. We went from a book era to a dance era. The choreographer was the last thing on the totem pole in the book musical, pushing it to more of the visual. Little by little, as the choreographers finally got into the position of being choreographer-directors, all that frustration was unleashed. With Jerome Robbins in *West Side Story* and Michael Kidd in *Li'l Abner,* there was a real breakthrough in dancing. Robbins integrated book and dance, but he used a great deal more dance to tell the story.

SUSAN STROMAN: Jerome Robbins crossed over and made musical comedy and the ballet world jell, first with *On the Town* and then with *West Side Story*. Robbins used behavioral dance; he made those Jets and Sharks fight and react to each other through dance, yet you still believed they were gangs. *West Side Story* is the ultimate musical. It's a political story with racial problems told through dance, a beautiful American love story with great music and important characters, all of whom dance.

GWEN VERDON: It used to be that a show needed eight dancers and eight singers. Today a performer in a musical has to be multifaceted, able to dance, sing, and act as well. While I may have gone on to personify that multifaceted performer, the field was opened up by Agnes de Mille, Jack Cole, Michael Kidd, Jerome Robbins, and Bob Fosse.

OPPOSITE PAGE

Jerome Robbins made musical comedy and the ballet world jell. Here he rehearses Ethel Merman through a number for *Gypsy* (1959).

Just about everything you see on Broadway today is there because of Jack Cole and Agnes de Mille. Jack Cole introduced what today you would call jazz. It was actually African dance, but we did it in high heels. Agnes said that dancers are not animated wallpaper. They've got to be carried through in the show. So each of her dancers, whether he or she had lines in the show or not, was given a character to play.

CELESTE HOLM: Agnes de Mille was blunt, but blunt is never anything to be afraid of. She told me, "Everything you are doing is fine, but do it bigger. Oklahoma is a great big state. Great big sunlight." Even the polka dots on my costume were big. That was the idea.

HOWARD KISSEL: Gower Champion was apparently a control freak. Someone once called him a Presbyterian Hitler. Bob Fosse was also not a piece of cake. But they had this high degree of professionalism.

Each of Agnes de Mille's dancers was given a character to play. Here she rehearses Tommy Hall and Gemze De Lappe for *Juno*.

MARGE CHAMPION: Gower Champion had grown up as a one-man show in a cabaret, and he didn't want us to be just another dance team. He wanted us to tell stories through dance and song. We never had any scenery. Most of the time we didn't even have any costumes. I never changed from the basic evening dress that I wore. Nevertheless we had thirteen years all over the country, honing our talents in the biggest places—the Sheraton circuit, the Hilton circuit, the Palmer House, the Waldorf.

Our image just happened to fit in with the postwar period. We were like Doris Day and Rock Hudson, the all-American girl and boy, the young couple next door. We didn't have to pretend; that was what we were. Marge and Gower Champion wouldn't have become what we became if it hadn't been at that particular time. Not a few years earlier— the thirties—nor a few years afterward, because as soon as Elvis and all of that came in, there was no place for us.

CHARLES STROUSE: Gower directed and choreographed *Bye Bye Birdie* and contributed mightily to the staging, but Marge was always on the scene, buzzing in his ear. She was responsible for many of the best ideas.

I never got close to Gower. I found him to be a very cold man, very controlling and very controlled. Each day he ate the same lunch: a bacon, lettuce, and tomato sandwich and a glass of milk. He was immaculate, exceedingly neat. His rehearsal outfits, with everything just so in cashmere pastels, made us feel like we were homeless.

Flipping the set is a conventional idea today, but when Gower devised it in 1960, it was quite an innovative staging concept. He had the teenagers say good-bye to Birdie in New York, take off their coats, and turn them inside out—and the set flipped to Sweet Apple while they continued singing the same song. We wrote to the concept. That was typical of Gower.

MARGE CHAMPION: I never thought that Gower was a great choreographer, but he was a great concept person. Whatever story value needed to be illuminated, be it text or song, he was able to do it. In his four or five really great hit shows, the scenery danced, the lighting danced.

CAROL CHANNING: Mr. Merrick told me he was going to have a musical version of *The Matchmaker* written for me. He asked whom I would like to direct me, and I said Gower Champion. I adored Gower. I had done *The Vamp* before *Hello, Dolly!*, and it was a terrible flop because it didn't have a Gower Champion. It had nobody at the helm. You must always have a benevolent despot in charge who stands there and says, "You are all going to look at this show through my eyes."

But Gower was tied up with Rodgers and Hammerstein, and so I turned *Dolly!* down completely because I wanted to work with him. Then all of a sudden the Rodgers and Hammerstein thing fell through, and Gower took on *Dolly!* But he said that I couldn't do the role because all I could do was grin like Lorelei.

I wasn't crushed. You don't get crushed. You don't have time to get crushed and still succeed. I called up Gower and said, "Look, Gower, you owe me this. I gave you everything I had in *Lend an Ear.* I want an audition. I want you to come and listen. I'll jump out the window if I don't do this part."

I auditioned for him at the St. James. I stood there and read my part and had the stage manager do all the other parts. We went through the whole of *The Matchmaker*. *Oliver* was playing across the street. Gower would go across and look at *Oliver,* and then come back and look at us. This went on for an hour and a half. Finally he said, "I buy that," and he embraced me. From then on, we never disagreed.

Gower choreographed the scenery and the flowers and the hat shop scene. He would pin the colors of the scenery and props onto the costumes we were wearing. He wanted to weave what we were wearing into the rest. Thornton Wilder told me, "I've rewritten *The Matchmaker* for thirty-six years, and I never got it the way I wanted it until Mike Stewart and Jerry Herman and Gower Champion fixed it and got it where it should be."

MARGE CHAMPION: Until he got the idea for the ramp, Gower wasn't even interested in doing *Hello, Dolly!* It was one of those ideas that he'd wake up with in the middle of the night and talk into the machine. The ramp was used to track through the show—where Dolly could talk to her husband, where the people came out when Dolly came back from retirement.

CAROL CHANNING: "You come down the ramp," Gower would say to me, "and I want you on this spot here, in fourth position. I don't want third. I don't want second. I don't want fifth. Fourth!" And by golly, I can't do it any other way. The way Gower directed *Dolly!* is riveted in my brain.

At one time during rehearsals for the 1995 revival, Lee Roy Reams, who was the director, said, "Carol, I think you should stand in the middle of the ramp instead of on the right to talk to your dead husband."

And I said, "All right." I wanted to be the spirit of cooperation. I started to go. But I couldn't. "Lee Roy," I said, "it isn't that I mean to be disobedient to you. But Gower won't let me. I couldn't go against him."

LEE ROY REAMS: I wanted to try out for the lead in *42nd Street*, but the casting director told my agent they wanted someone young, fresh, and new and that I should audition instead for the secondary role of Andy Lee, an older character who doesn't have a number but does dance in the show. I didn't want to do it, but my agent said, "Go. Do what you do. They'll see it."

I went right into the ballad and then segued into the tap dance without giving them the chance to say "Thank you, Lee Roy." I put on a performance. When I finished, there was dead silence. Then this very elegant gray-haired man started coming down the aisle.

Recording the original cast album of *42nd Street:* Lee Roy Reams, Wanda Richert, Jerry Orbach, and Joseph Bova (1980).

"You're really not right for the role of Andy Lee," Gower Champion said. "I know that."

"But you are very right for Billy Lawlor."

42nd Street was my introduction to David Merrick as well as to Gower. I said, "Hello, Mr. Merrick." And he said, "I'm not your father. Call me David." He paid us very low salaries. His feeling was, if you don't like it, you can be replaced. But I was working with Gower Champion, so who cared? I would have paid Gower to let me work with him. It was like Gower and I had met in a previous life. I knew instinctively what he wanted.

Gower had had a bad history of working with David, and as a result he protected himself with all kinds of contractual things. David could not come to the rehearsals until Gower said he could. But by the time we came to New York, Gower was often ill and not always at rehearsals. We all knew that Gower was not well. Every once in a while he'd go and have a blood transfusion. He looked rather peaked and thin, and sometimes he would lose his energy, but his mind was sharp as a tack, and he was extremely creative. He incorporated into *42nd Street* things from all his other shows. It was a living tribute to the man's genius.

MARGE CHAMPION: I first saw *42nd Street* just before Gower went into the hospital. I was just bowled over by it. He had an overall vision for making a classic show work in the 1980s. I think it is absolutely one of the best things Gower did in his entire life.

LEE ROY REAMS: Before *42nd Street*, Gower had done *Rockabye Hamlet* and all that; he went through that drug thing. Then one day, he told me, he was walking the beaches of California stoned, and suddenly he realized what he truly was: an old-fashioned song-and-dance man. And rather than try to compete with what was happening culturally at the time, he decided to go back to what he knew best: the old-fashioned musical.

Ironically, opening night of that old-fashioned musical, August 25, 1980, David Merrick interrupted a thunderous curtain call to announce that Gower Champion had died earlier that day.

Some time later, I ran into Bob Fosse. We were talking about his film *All That Jazz.* I was surprised because it was so personal, so autobiographical. I knew how insecure he really was. "Gower once again did me one better," he said. "I filmed my death. Gower Champion had the nerve to do it on opening night."

CY COLEMAN: Fosse was a skinny little guy, always dressed in black, introspective, intensely funny, always smoking. He liked to talk about how he started out as a hoofer. He loved literary people. Paddy Chayefsky and E. L. Doctorow were good friends.

MERLE DEBUSKEY: He was an original, the apogee, the zenith of a professional at work. Nobody worked any harder, loved what he did more, was more critical of his own work. But since he was not a producer, he was in great turmoil, because he didn't like not having absolute control.

ROBERT WHITEHEAD: There was something in Bobby that wanted to do it all. He wanted to play the part, dance the part, conduct the orchestra, produce the play. It was a kind of obsession with him.

GWEN VERDON: In terms of use of the stage and movement, Bob Fosse left a powerful image. He was similar to a painter, but not any single painter. He could be surreal, like Dalí, but he could also be very lyrical and beautiful, as in the pony dance in *New Girl in Town* or parts of the Roxie dance in *Chicago*. By "lyrical" I don't mean just pretty—it was poetic. He was also a fabulous tap dancer; he had that enormous range.

SUSAN STROMAN: Every step Fosse choreographed had a motivation behind it so he could reinforce the dancer's acting. Agnes was more balletic, Fosse more jazz oriented and with more of a sexual quality.

LEE ROY REAMS: The sexuality really became pronounced in Fosse's later works. I was interested in seeing the little wiggles suddenly became grinds and forward thrusts. That was not as obvious in his early work, which was a little more comedic.

MARTIN RICHARDS: Bobby never made wisecracks. He was never unkind to chorus people. Yet he was probably the toughest taskmaster, more so probably to his leading ladies. They all respected him. They never moved one iota from what he said. But he was very, very shy, and that made it seem that he was standoffish.

JULES FISHER: He tried awful hard to not let you know that underneath he was a warm man. He pushed me a lot. He would say, "That's not good enough. I want more." His attitude was, I can be demanding with you because I'm demanding with myself. He was never satisfied with himself.

WAYNE CILENTO: Bob's roots come out of the Jack Cole and Hermes Pan era. He danced for them in movies. When Gwen and Bob got together, the influence of Jack Cole had to have rubbed off on them.

Fosse was a skinny little guy, always dressed in black, introspective, intensely funny, always smoking.

Choreographer Bob Fosse: nobody worked harder, loved what he did more, was as critical of his own work.

GWEN VERDON: I had been working as Jack Cole's assistant on the film version of *Gentlemen Prefer Blondes.* Michael Kidd, who was on the next lot, asked me if I was going to New York to audition for *Can-Can,* which he went on to choreograph. "Go ahead. It's a free weekend in New York," Jack said. So I went, and I got the job.

My friend Carol Haney was starring in *Pajama Game* at that time, and through her I got to know Bob socially. Everyone was talking about his choreography for the "Steam Heat" number. Carol was more than a dancer in the show; she was an actress who played a character. That was revolutionary.

It was not the first time Bob and I met. I had done at least one movie at MGM when he was around working with Debbie Reynolds. All dancers know one another. But as soon as we began working together in *Damn Yankees,* I realized he was unique. The first night we rehearsed, Bob did the entire choreography for "Whatever Lola Wants, Lola Gets." I think that was record-breaking time. When he showed it to me, I was so nervous, but I thought, Dance is dance. I'll try to do it exactly like him—although it seemed quite amazing to do the scene and the dance as the same character.

The movement of the first chorus was very simple, although by "simple" I don't mean easy to do. Bob told me exactly what to do, down to the second joint of my little finger. He was absolutely specific about every single detail. When I finished the part of the dance where I have to go back into singing, he even choreographed how I would push my hair back off my face. There was not a movement left to me alone. I think that distinguished Fosse. With the exception of Jack Cole, I don't know another choreographer who worked in such great detail.

WAYNE CILENTO: Bob taught me that it's OK to be perfectly still onstage and just move one little portion of your body in an isolated movement.

GWEN VERDON: He liked the absence of sound; he'd have you stand there with no music and maybe wink one eye.

He was very knowledgeable about classical music. We would rehearse to Aaron Copeland, even though we never performed any of his music. He liked the Copeland sound; he liked the space.

WAYNE CILENTO: When I auditioned for *Dancin'* he brought me into this room and had me dance this stylized piece with him and Ann Reinking to the music of "Tea for Two." He was using that song for all his auditions then.

AL HIRSCHFELD: Fosse had a way of defying the bones in his body. Somehow he managed to twist and turn in a way that communicated to an audience exactly what he meant. It's so difficult to describe dancing in prose; it's easier in line. I think I caught his spirit in my drawings.

LEE ROY REAMS: The movie versions of the Broadway shows *Damn Yankees, Kiss Me Kate, Pajama Game* were my first exposure to Fosse. I was excited by what he did with "Who's got the pain when they do the mambo . . ." and also what he did staging-wise with Gwen in "A little brains, a little talent . . ." He would take bodies and put them in positions of posturing that were not normal. Gwen used to say, "If you walk in with a limp one day, you might find it in the choreography five minutes later."

Fosse's body was almost like a question mark. He'd gotten into that stooped position. So many things came from that. Gwen had one foot that was turned in. To hide it, she would bend her knee. After the training and dancing straightened her foot, the bent knee and turned-in foot had become a habit. You would see a lot of the turned-in foot, the bent knee in Bob's choreography. His style was immediately identifiable.

DONNA McKECHNIE: Fosse developed his style out of his limitations. He choreographed around them, out of what he saw in his own body. He tried all his dances on himself. He did a lot with hats, which looked really great on him.

GWEN VERDON: He liked black floors and black legs—that is, the side panels on the stage. It was almost the way a puppet show is presented, where you don't see anything except the character. It gives such depth. Black goes on and on. It's infinity.

JULES FISHER: I remember a bare stage, all black velour, and out front Ben Vereen with a follow spot. Bob Fosse turned to the designer and me. "Now, that's a set," he said.

One of the reasons a lot of his sets were black is that Fosse was learning about motion pictures, seeing the power of film and trying to capture that power onstage. The camera can be selective. The camera can come in and give a close-up. He asked, "How can we do that in the theater? How can we show just a face? How can we see just this person's finger?"

It was exciting for me to give him dissolves through lighting. In film one image is overtaken by another image, and the first image disappears. In theater the effect is achieved spatially. There's an object here that's lit, and slowly five other objects become lit and the first one is no longer lit. Some of it was tricky.

Bob loved what light could do, particularly for a kind of Felliniesque theater. He loved the startling effects light could achieve, the kind of power and punch it could deliver.

In *Pippin,* there's that famous photograph of Ben Vereen's face and all the dancers' hands in a very thin curtain of light that comes out of the floor. It was Bob's idea, which I implemented. If an actor stood upstage of this light, the audience saw nothing, because there was no light there. If he stood downstage of the light, the audience saw nothing. But if he put his hand in that curtain, it was like a wall of lit fog; all of a sudden the hand was visible.

FRED GOLDEN: It was Fosse's idea to advertise *Pippin* on television in 1973. Nobody had done it before, because it was too expensive. The idea was, You've just seen sixty seconds of *Pippin.* If you want to see the other 119 minutes, go to the Imperial Theater.

MICKEY ALPERT: Suddenly this show which was a good show, but not a great show, discovered a much larger audience because the selling was expanded.

ROY SOMLYO: The curious thing was that the beautiful little moment Fosse staged for the commercial wasn't even in the show. It became so popular that ultimately he did put it in, and whenever that moment came up, the audience broke out in wild applause.

SUSAN L. SCHULMAN: Bob Fosse would sit in the orchestra and say to Jules Fisher, "Lighting: Cue eighty-seven, bring it up two notches, and add two counts to the cue." That's the kind of technical expertise he had. Or he'd say, "Bring up the sound on the oboes two points." Who can hear that? Such was the level of his sophistication and theater knowledge.

GWEN VERDON: He would have people up the rails, the side of the proscenium. In *Chicago* he had the orchestra up on a platform. We danced down the platform.

When we were rehearsing *Sweet Charity,* Bob would say, "I need something lopsided." That's how he would talk. And Cy Coleman, who has a classical background and who I think is a musical genius, would know immediately what he meant. Cy did things that were structured with that sort of lopsided sound to them.

CY COLEMAN: Bob wanted to do *Sweet Charity* for Gwen. Of course you couldn't do it for a better star. You wouldn't want anyone else.

LEE ROY REAMS: I auditioned for *Sweet Charity* because Gwen Verdon and Bob Fosse were idols of mine. During rehearsals I used to sneak in and watch Bob and Gwen work through the numbers. One day he was just exasperated. "I don't know whether any of this is any good or not. Everything you do looks good," he said. And it was true. You would give her something, and it just looked right.

Out of town with *Sweet Charity,* Bob was upset that the Irene Sharaff costumes weren't what he had envisioned. Those for the "Big Spender" number were made of incredible silks and expensive fabrics. He thought they were too bright, and not tacky enough. So he had them sprayed with dulling paint.

GWEN VERDON: They came up with elaborate costumes for me as well, but what they had not taken into consideration was that I hardly left the stage and therefore didn't have time to change. My one costume change, into the red for "Something Better than This," had to be made onstage.

Bob loved what light could do, particularly for a kind of Felliniesque theater.

Gwen Verdon in the number that really stopped the show in *Can-Can* (1953).

LEE ROY REAMS: During rehearsal Gwen had always worn this little black slip. Bob Fosse struck all of Gwen's elaborate costumes and told Irene to make her a black slip like that to wear through nearly the whole show. Irene Sharaff was very upset, but being a professional, she did what she had to do.

We reopened the Palace Theater. The front of the house looked fabulous. The backstage was terrible. There was a lot of dust, and Gwen had allergy problems. We dressed down in the basement with sheets put up. They dragged in old carpeting and taped mirrors on the wall. That was my introduction to Broadway. It was nothing like the movies I had seen. But it was thrilling. It was 1966. It was the Palace. And it was me with Bob Fosse and Gwen Verdon.

AL HIRSCHFELD: Gwen is a reincarnation of Bob Fosse, a female Bob Fosse in the look and everything.

JAMES HAMMERSTEIN: Everybody fell in love with her. I was no exception. When I met her, I was twenty-three years old and stage manager of *Damn Yankees.* She was funny, warm, unspoiled, talented as hell. She could make sex on the stage so funny. She could move her tail and get a laugh.

LEE ROY REAMS: For my taste the best theater dancer is Gwen Verdon. She has training but also style. She has a humor with her fluid body and an incredible theater face that also dances. Gwen dances from the neck up as well as the neck down.

CY FEUER: We had had our eye on Gwen from the time she was the lead dancer with Jack Cole. In *Can-Can,* we found a perfect role for her. Michael Kidd staged a comic Apache dance in the second act, where Gwen, in slow motion, takes a knife out of a cheese a waiter is carrying, kills her lover, puts the knife back in the cheese as the waiter goes by again, and slow-motions off the stage.

Opening night in New York, Gwen does the dance, exits, and the number finishes. She gets an enormous hand. I always tell my stage manager, "Don't wait. At the top of the hand, go on. Call for your next scenery and lighting. Kill the hand." That way you get pace in your show. Otherwise you get bogged down.

The stage manager does just that. The set changes, curtain goes up, actors come on. Only they're standing there—in the new set. The audience doesn't stop applauding. They want Gwen. I rush up the aisle. Gwen had already taken off her costume. I grab a robe, hand it her, she puts it on, and we push her out onto the stage holding a robe around herself. They went wild. You can imagine.

The next morning on the cover of *Life* magazine, there's a picture of Gwen with her leg straight up in the air and the heel out. She was off! That's old-fashioned show business.

DONNA MCKECHNIE: I met Gwen during rehearsals for *How to Succeed.* She was Bob's assistant and my first dance captain. By this time Gwen was a big star, but between shows, she loved to work as a fixer-upper. She would tell me how she and Bob would work the numbers up at night, thinking them through on their bed, jumping up and down all over the bedroom. Next day, the choreography would be all set.

RICHARD KILEY: I worked with Fosse and Gwen in *Redhead,* which was Bobby's first directorial role. His style was already being talked about on Broadway. I was leading man, and we crossed swords a couple of times. Coming from choreography, he expected an actor to behave like a dancer and just do as he was told. Occasionally I would ask, "Why?" There were a few sparks but our mutual respect overcame that.

JOEL GREY: Since I thought that Ron Field's choreography for *Cabaret* was perfect and brilliant, I was somewhat apprehensive to learn Bob Fosse would be completely restaging the numbers for the movie. My fears were unfounded, however, and quickly allayed. Both Field and Fosse had night-club backgrounds that found their way into the choreography of *Cabaret.* Yet Fosse as director and choreographer had his own vision and his own brilliance to bring to the film.

TONY WALTON: Bob had just come off *Cabaret* and was finishing the editing of *Lenny* when he began *Chicago.* He was at the peak of his powers. He asked me if I would design the poster for *Chicago.* "It makes me crazy that the posters never have the look of the shows," he said.

"I'll have a crack at it."

"But I've got a real predicament for you. Gwen has poster approval. She's always been the solitary figure in the poster, whether it's been for *Sweet Charity* or *Damn Yankees* or whatever. But I would like you to try *not* to feature her, because she's now of a certain age and doing a very demanding show. If she should get sick, we'd have to cancel it and return the ticket money. So try doing one without featuring her and see if you can get her to accept it."

I did five different versions, all variations on the same theme—and none of them included Gwen.

OPPOSITE PAGE

One of Tony Walton's five

variations of the *Chicago* poster.

"I see what you're up to," Gwen said. She was a real sport about it. She picked one, and that was the one we used. The idea was also to incorporate it into the show, and we used it as the scrim show curtain.

MARTIN RICHARDS: Bobby Fryer asked me, "Would you like to work with me on producing a show with Gwen Verdon, Chita Rivera, and Bobby Fosse?"

"Are you out of your mind?" I said. "Of course. What do I have to do?"

"Raise the money."

When *Chicago* opened in 1975, it was the most expensive show up to that point in time: eight hundred thousand dollars. I raised all of it.

The story of Roxie Hart had been a book and a movie. Going back to the 1930s, everybody had tried to get the rights to it. Fifteen years before we began working on *Chicago,* Gwen and Bobby had tried unsuccessfully to get the property from the mother of the writer, Maurine Dallas Watkins. Watkins had been a sob sister, and she felt it was because of her stories that so many murderers got off without going to jail or the chair. She ended up in a mental institution, and her mother ended up with the rights. By the mid-1970s, however, Watkins and her mother were dead, and the property belonged to some cousins who wanted money and their percentage. We got the rights.

The second day of rehearsals, Bobby Fosse had a heart attack. We stopped everything. Jerry Robbins, who never wants to do any show, was kind enough to offer to step in and help. But we all said, "No, we started this with Bobby. We owe allegiance to him." Bobby told Gwen and Chita that he would be fine, that we should keep the original cast together. We had insured him. I don't know why. They had never insured a director before. But it gave us the time to wait.

Right after Bobby's heart attack, our conductor had one. Out of town, I got an attack of colitis and had to be hospitalized. We thought, Maybe

" 'Chicago' is a marvel."
—Time Magazine

"Easily one of the best musicals of the season."
—Clive Barnes
New York Times

" 'Chicago' is a landmark musical."
—After Dark Magazine

"The songs are show stoppers."
—Rex Reed
The Daily News

"Kander's score is superb, as for Ebb's lyrics, they are masterful."
—New York Post

"The Broadway musical at its best."
—Newsweek

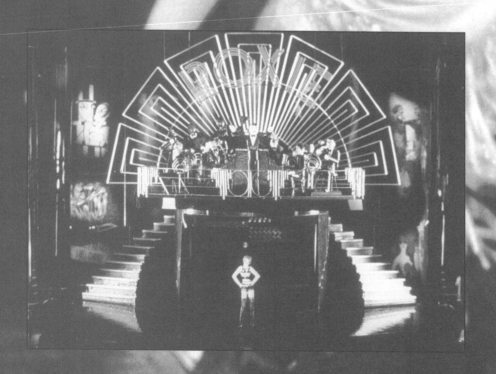

there's a curse on *Chicago*. We kept saying, "Do you think Maurine Dallas Watkins is trying to tell us something?" At our first preview, at the end of the first act, the elevator smashed thirty feet to the ground just before Chita and a whole bunch of people in the chorus were ready to step in. I ran back like a meshuggener. I'm down there with a screwdriver, and I can't put a screw in the wall. Bobby says to me, "What are you doing?"

"We're trying to get this up so we can go on with the second act," I say. And he says, "The second act is canceled. There is no second act."

During rehearsals, nobody knew who I was. I never went to the auditions for the chorus dancers, wasn't allowed into the rehearsals. In fact the first day I went to the theater, Bobby Fryer said, "Take a seat as quickly as possible, and don't say a word." It astounds me now. But this was my first big show, my first Broadway musical. I sat down two rows in front of Bobby Fosse—I didn't know that was a no-no. Not according to Bobby Fosse; he couldn't care less.

It was very hard for me to get to know Gwen Verdon. I was overwhelmed by her. But then, the first Christmas Eve, I got a call from her. She was deliciously dear on the phone. She invited me to her Christmas party. I said, "Thank you very much. But I usually spend Christmas with my family." My family didn't know what the hell Christmas was about.

"No, no, no," Gwen insisted. "You must come, even for fifteen, twenty minutes. Bobby is here. He just got out of the hospital, and he wants very much to see you." So I go to the party. By this time I have become extremely friendly with Fred Ebb and John Kander. And my best friend is Chita Rivera. The three of them are leaving the party just as I come in. I say, "Oh no, you don't. I am not going up there alone. You're the only ones I know to talk to."

We all ride up in the elevator. Gwen opens the door. "Oh, you're coming back," she says to Chita, Fred, and John.

I enter the apartment, and there is the whole cast. They applaud and hug me. Everything is hunky-dory. It was really like an old movie.

Still, despite the fact that I raised every single nickel for the show, my name was brought down below the title. It's Robert Fryer and James Cresson above, and Martin Richards down below. Did I feel bad? I was suicidal. I thought we would win the Tony and I wouldn't be going up for it. It took a lot of years and a lot of therapy for me to get over it.

Opening night. Bobby Fryer and Jimmy Cresson are standing to the

PRECEDING PAGES

INSET (TOP)
The reviews for the original production of *Chicago* were in, and they were raves!

INSET (BOTTOM)
The model of Tony Walton's set design for the "Roxie Sunburst" scene in *Chicago*.

A dynamic duo: Chita Rivera (left) and Gwen Verdon in the original production of *Chicago* (1975).

left side of the theater. I hear the overture, and I envision my mother being there. She had died. I sob like a baby. The curtain goes up, and, as I have continued to do the rest of my career, I don't watch the rest of the show. I pace the lobby, go to Sardi's, have a drink, go back, wait to hear the big laughs, the applause. In every show there is what they call the cigarette number, the number you know won't work, the number where you go outside and meet everybody else who escaped for a smoke. But not in *Chicago;* no cigarette number there.

The reviews come in: "Roxie Hart has no heart." We have a meeting with the whole cast. Bobby Fosse says, "Any heart that is left in the show, we're taking out."

Little did we know that Bobby was way, way ahead of his time. What he saw in *Chicago* came to be: the O. J. Simpson case, the Menendez brothers . . . It's happening right now, exactly. The song "Nowadays" ends with the lines "In fifty years or so, it's gonna change I know, but oh, it's heaven nowadays." What's happened is that *Chicago* has found its time. Life is imitating art.

During the courtroom scene Fosse had all of the dancers in sexual positions. He had them dressed unisexually or asexually, men as women, women as men; half man, half woman. It was a brilliant concept. They were a Greek chorus. But Bobby Fryer said, "We're going to lose the matinee audience," and it was cut.

Bobby Fosse quoted a lot of the dialogue that went on around *Chicago* in his autobiographical movie *All That Jazz.* Remember the scene where the producers and writers watch that sexually explicit dance, and one of the producers says, "We're going to lose all the matinee audience"? There's all that kind of inside stuff in the film. Fosse swore to me, "Everyone is in it but you. I love you."

They always picked me to do the lovely things. Bobby Fosse said to me, "I understand there's a little show being played down at the Public called *A Chorus Line.* I'd like to know how it's doing. Are we in trouble?"

I went down and saw it, came back. "It's brilliant. I think we're in trouble. But I don't know. It's so different."

We went head-to-head with *A Chorus Line.* We were nominated for eleven Tonys. They were nominated for ten. We won none. We were robbed. But we ran four years. We won best musical in Los Angeles, in London. The show has longevity; I still get checks from all over the world.

Any heart that is left in the show, we're taking out.

In the 1996 revival, Ann Reinking, who was Bobby Fosse's girlfriend at the time of the original production and who replaced Gwen in 1977, came back to play Roxie and choreograph the show in the same theater where we played it. I still call it the Forty-sixth Street Theater. It's come full circle.

Two weeks before he died, Bob Fosse and I began preproduction of the movie version of *Chicago*. He had met with Madonna twice. "I'll win her an Oscar," he said.

JULES FISHER: The last thing I did with Fosse was *Big Deal,* based on the movie *Big Deal on Madonna Street*. It was very dark and black, the look that Fosse loved. It used existing music, pop and contemporary. It was his last major work, and it showed a different dimension of him.

WAYNE CILENTO: I think that the producers and theater owners wanted Bob to do *Dancin' II,* but Bob had something else on his mind. He wanted to tell a story through 1930s music. The vision was beautiful, but I don't know if it was commercial enough. The Sunday before we closed, he won the Tony for best choreography.

GWEN VERDON: *Big Deal* is one of the most extraordinary pieces Bob ever did. It was taking the old-time songs and putting them into the Broadway show in the way they could have fit into a Broadway show. No one really knew what he was talking about. Producers would sort of nod their heads and say, "Oh yes, I see." But no one did. He had people seated on wires. They flew over the orchestra and landed onstage. It was a show before its time.

But that was true of all his work. Bob would do a show and it would not get great reviews. He would be very disappointed, devastated. But he wouldn't show it; he would joke about it. And then the next Broadway show would come out, and it would have things in it that had been in Bob's show. It was like Jack Cole said, "If I were to quit doing East Indian groups, I'd put nine other groups out of work because they would have no one to copy from."

LEE ROY REAMS: When they were doing the revival of *Damn Yankees,* Bob Fosse received the Fred Astaire Award. It was a bittersweet moment for him. That *Big Deal* had not been a success was very disappointing. He was very proud of its choreography. In accepting the award, he mentioned how difficult it is for dancers to survive in the business, as it is such a short life. He looked at those of us who were there in the audience and he said, "I'm mostly proud of what has happened to my dancers: Lee Roy Reams,

Donna McKechnie, Ann Reinking . . . ," and we all stood up. I just sobbed. To be singled out by Bob Fosse as one of his dancers.

That was the last time I saw him. He had a bad heart and was told to stop smoking. But he smoked cigarettes end to end. He smoked them as he danced. I was told about the drugs. But a lot of creative people during that period did them, and it was culturally more acceptable. Nobody knew the consequences then.

TONY WALTON: To this day, I'm always conscious of Bob Fosse. I'll decide to set a scene a certain way, nag a lighting designer, or suggest to an actor what to do. And I'll feel him beside me, looking over my shoulder and asking, "Are you sure?"

DONNA MCKECHNIE: In a way Bob Fosse–Gwen Verdon and Michael Bennett–Donna McKechnie are the two archetype couples of Broadway. Bob and Gwen had a daughter. Michael and I had a show.

Michael had been in one of the first tours of *West Side Story,* and so he was strongly influenced by Jerome Robbins. He danced with much more abandon than Bob did. Where Fosse's energy went down and inward, Michael's energy went down and then opened up and out. He was expansive; he had that sense of abandon. Fosse created detailed steps; Michael worked in a more abstract way. He would let you move on to the next stage by yourself, and then he would be the editor.

WAYNE CILENTO: Michael was more of a choreographer of the whole picture; he wasn't very specific about the individual steps. I was one of his core of people who would go into rooms and experiment. He would come in and pull all those pieces together into a number. Bob, on the other hand, did everything himself, every single step. He was very specific in what he wanted.

A lot of people said that I danced like Michael when he was young, which may be why he related to me. During rehearsals for *A Chorus Line,* he'd have the company sit on the stage, and just the two of us would dance together.

DOUGLAS WATT: I thought Michael was a better choreographer than Fosse. He was more steeped in ballet, and there was more variety to his work. Fosse had certain devices that he used over and over again very effectively, like "Me and My Shadow," but Michael had a much bigger picture of dance. He used it to tell a story.

SUSAN STROMAN: Every show Michael did was groundbreaking. He

Every show Michael did was groundbreaking. He took a lot of chances, especially in melding dance with the set.

took a lot of chances, especially in melding dance with the set. They both moved. In *Dreamgirls* he collaborated with set designer Robin Wagner, having people dance on those towers.

LOUISE LASSER: Michael's dance numbers propped up *Henry, Sweet Henry,* a musical based on *The World of Henry Orient.* Every one was a showstopper. He directed the dancers like actors. He motivated them. That's where people got to see his beauty, his sensitivity, how so much of his life went into his work.

MARVIN KRAUSS: Michael was one of my favorite people. Crazy sometimes—but all creative people walk that fine line between being a mother and father and being Hitler.

LEE ROY REAMS: He was a little guy with a Jewish-Italian look and moles on his face, extremely sexual. He wanted to have everybody; it was this Napoleon thing. If you were new on the block, he wanted to take you to bed, mostly men. That was part of Michael. I met him when we were both doing a number in the Kraft Musical Hall, and I was struck by his incredible intensity and energy. To work with him was infectious.

MERLE DEBUSKEY: He endured another person's power over him with great difficulty. He liked the hold of power himself. He was one of the most Machiavellian characters I've ever encountered. Extremely talented, very ambitious.

DONNA MCKECHNIE: I had known Michael for years. We were friends but we never talked about things like relationships and sex. It was too personal. I was basically this out-front dancing doll raised in the Bible Belt.

Michael created this dance for me in *Company:* "Tick Tock." It was to be my first big solo dance number on Broadway. Then when we were in Boston, they decided it wasn't working. There was talk of cutting it. I felt very threatened. I didn't want to be in the show if I couldn't dance. I persuaded Michael to give it another try, and he trusted my instincts. David Shire was brought in, and the three of us worked one day from noon to midnight revamping the music and the choreography. The number stayed in the show.

At one point, Michael said, "Maybe we should try her nude with just a sheer thing."

I said, "Oh, my god, I don't think that is going to work."

He said, "Well, maybe something on the bottom, but the breasts could be seen through this nice filmy gray blue."

"Michael," I insisted, "I don't think that's going to work."

"Why not?"

"Well, you know, there's something about the mystery of dance and music. If you show too much, it becomes too graphic. Besides, you don't want people to be self-conscious when they watch." Luckily I talked him out of it.

We used to get together in coffee shops, and he was always talking about doing a show about dancers. Then one day he asked me to come to a get-together with a whole bunch of dancers.

WAYNE CILENTO: When I was doing *Seesaw* with Michael Bennett, a group of maybe twenty-five dancers would get together after our shows and actually dance a class. Then we'd sit around and talk. That started the process of the tape sessions.

DONNA MCKECHNIE: We all sat on the floor. There was a jug of red wine and one of those big old tape recorders, and Michael said, "I don't know what this is going to be—a book, a movie, a script, a play, a musical—but what I want you to do is tell me your name, where you were born, and why you wanted to become a dancer."

A true Broadway couple: Donna McKechnie, the star, and Michael Bennett, the creator and director of *A Chorus Line*.

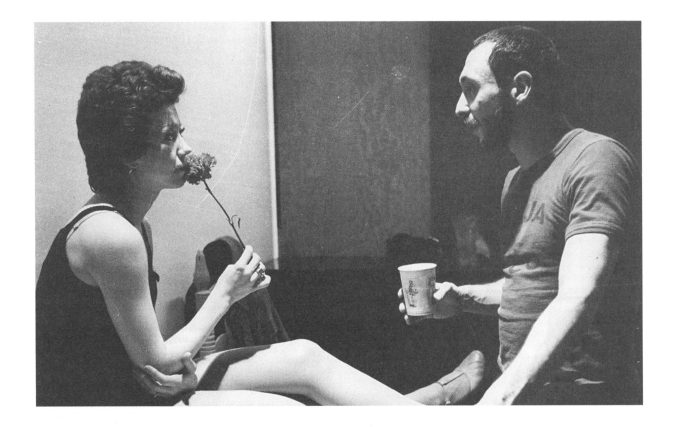

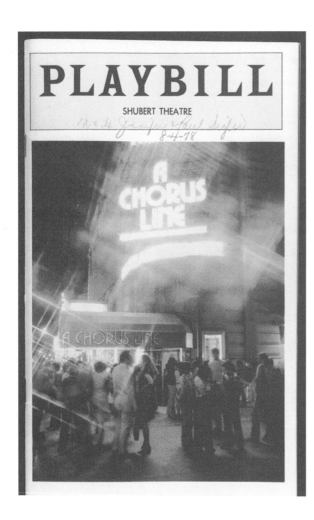

PLAYBILL

SHUBERT THEATRE

He turned the tape recorder on, and it was boom, boom, boom, right down the line. There were all these common threads: when you're eight years old and you see yourself dancing, how you get to the point where you have nothing else on your mind, how you become tenacious about it, how you feel you're not going to live if you don't do it.

Before that night I had never told anyone my story. I ran away from home in the 1950s before graduating from high school. I had a lot of unresolved conflicts, a lot of guilt. I thought what I had done was unique to me. I thought if people knew how I felt, what my dreams were about, they would laugh. But that night I realized it wasn't just me. "You felt that way, too?" we said to each other. "You were growing up, and they didn't understand you, either?"

Twenty-four hours later everyone had headaches and hangovers. But we kept getting together, doing it over and over for a couple of weeks, until Michael wound up with some forty hours of tape, which he brought to Joe Papp.

At first Joe wasn't interested, but then he went along. He gave us the luxury of time. We did what became *A Chorus Line* as a workshop for six months.

WAYNE CILENTO: The tapes were turned into monologues, and the monologues became audition pieces. After workshop we went into production. Although I ended up doing "I Can Do That" in the show, it was actually the story of Sammy Williams, who played Paul.

HOWARD KISSEL: According to Michael Bennett, Joe Papp never liked *A Chorus Line* because it was about Broadway . . . albeit the *proletariat* of Broadway.

Michael was rehearsing it at the Public Theater downtown on the understanding it would be produced in the Newman, a proscenium theater in the Public with perfect proportions. There was a strong feeling among people associated with it that it would then move to Broadway. At that time Joe was running not only the Public downtown but also the Vivian Beaumont in Lincoln Center. He had given the Lincoln Center subscribers one disaster after another (including a ludicrous *Richard III* that Neil Simon later lampooned in *The Goodbye Girl*), and suddenly he told Michael he wanted to put *A Chorus Line* in the Beaumont.

"You can't do it there," Michael told Papp. "The stage has too big an apron. The audience will seem so far away. This show has to be framed in a proscenium." But Joe said unless Michael could raise two hundred thousand dollars, it would be done at the Beaumont or not at all.

So Michael called the Shuberts, who had an inkling this would be something big.

He and Marvin Hamlisch and some of the cast went up to audition the show for them. While Marvin and the cast were singing, the Shuberts had their heads buried in the paper—they were involved in some business. "We'll give you the money," they said. "Don't worry."

They ended up offering one hundred thousand dollars. So Michael went to Jimmy Nederlander, who had sent him and Hamlisch each a case of champagne when he learned they were collaborating on a new show. He agreed to contribute the other hundred thousand. When Michael told Joe, Joe called the Shuberts. Once they found out the Nederlanders were involved, they agreed to give the entire two hundred thousand dollars.

Still, Joe made Michael's life so miserable that he got to the point where he was ready to give up the whole show. He was in a limousine headed for the airport to fly to Paris, but then he thought about all those people who had given their time, talent, and memories. He couldn't let them down. He came back and fought with Joe and got *A Chorus Line* to Broadway.

In his office at 890 Broadway, Michael had a sign that read something to the effect of, "This will be as if we signed it in blood. We will not divulge all that happened in the creation of *A Chorus Line*." And it is signed by Michael and Joe. Obviously Michael didn't care, but Joe didn't want that known.

BERNARD GERSTEN: One of my jobs at the Public Theater was taking care of Michael, because Joe Papp was never close to *A Chorus Line*. When it seemed to have the potential to be a successful Broadway show, his interest stopped. He didn't want to appear to be involved with what was going to be a commercial hit. However, before *A Chorus Line,* the Public Theater was in debt for about a million and a half dollars. The show left the Public with an endowment of over twenty million.

DONNA MCKECHNIE: Although later on there was a lot of talk that Michael didn't write the show, that there was a lot of collaboration, it could not have been done without Michael's vision. Numbers like "Give Me the Ball" and "Hello Twelve, Hello Thirteen, Hello Love" were products of Michael coaxing Marvin Hamlisch and Ed Kleban to write songs out of the dancers' words. Michael allowed himself to take all the wrong roads. He always took risks, and more often than not, he came up with gold. Just think of it: a show with no stars that begins on a bare stage with only a rehearsal piano. And then the full orchestra comes on. It knocked people off their seats.

CHARLES DURNING: *A Chorus Line* is an actor's play about actors. When that girl starts singing "What I Did for Love," it has nothing to do with sex. It's the love of the theater—the horror, the heartbreak, the disappointments. We've all had our share.

When I saw *A Chorus Line,* and I saw it several times, I broke down and cried. My wife does not understand why; she hasn't gone through what I have.

RONNIE LEE: The curtain went down, the lights came on. Everyone had left the theater, and I was still sitting there weeping. My wife was holding me in her arms.

I was remembering the cattle calls. Hundreds came. They'd teach you one step, everybody would do it, and they'd eliminate. Then they'd teach you another step, perhaps two steps, and eliminate again. They would eliminate for size, for looks, for color, you name it. What we did for love—*A Chorus Line* really caught it.

JANE SUMMERHAYS: I was doing a television special when I auditioned for the part of Sheila. The auditions were like the show. Michael would constantly refer to them in directing: "Remember the auditions."

At my first rehearsal, when I started to sing "At the Ballet," I broke down. The song touched something in my life. Michael came over and put his arms around me. He could be fierce, but he was very gentle with me then.

I believe in the healing power of the theater, that it is a place where we all come together, where we take refuge, where inexplicable things become explained. It's a second-chance family. And all that is in *A Chorus Line.*

DONNA MCKECHNIE: Although it was specific to the theater community, the metaphor was universal. You're singing about this rarefied existence of a dancer: "God, I'm a dancer." But the metaphor resonated in different ways: "God, I'm a teacher, an accountant, a husband . . ." People connected with it and came back again and again.

When I saw
A Chorus Line,
and I saw it several
times, I broke down
and cried.

The show was a product of the mid-1970s, the confessionals, the "me" generation. Everybody has a painful adolescence. Nobody escapes the pain of growing up. We're all in the same boat, all dancing on the same line.

MERLE DEBUSKEY: The fact that you didn't have to be a dancer to know what it felt like to be on the line made *A Chorus Line* unique.

When it broke the record for the longest-running Broadway show, Michael Bennett put together a celebration, a performance that involved all the people who had ever performed in it. The press of the world wanted in on this. I had a mobile unit from a construction site set up in Shubert Alley just for press. I don't know how many television cameras there were.

Three companies existed at that time: the one in New York, the national, and the international, which had just returned from England. I think there were three hundred or so people, and they had to be gathered together for an extra performance on a Sunday, costumed, and rehearsed into a fantastic event. Special supports were constructed to hold the stage up under the crushing weight of all those performers.

Each company would do something. They would come at you in waves. The finale saw them all over the theater: at the top of the balcony, down all the aisles. They formed the kick line at the end, they fed in, fed in, so that the line and the circle and the wedge kept getting bigger and bigger. It was monumental.

After *A Chorus Line,* Michael did *Ballroom* in 1978. The Shubert organization was convinced that it was going to be a bigger hit than *A Chorus Line* because it had a plot, so they opened a box office in Shubert Alley just for that show. I thought it was magnificent—but a failure nevertheless. The book was never very good. The average age of the dancers was fifty-something. It didn't work.

But in 1981 Michael did *Dreamgirls.* Working with him on it was the pure fun of show business. And it was a big success for him.

DONNA MCKECHNIE: Ten years after I originally appeared in *A Chorus Line,* I returned to the same production, the same theater, the same run, the same role. No actor had ever been able to do that before, because no show had ever run so long. I came in for eight weeks and stayed for eight months.

People think the role of Cassie is my story. Finally I got so tired of arguing about it, I said, "Yes, it is my story." But the truth is Cassie is really about someone else's life. It was the last part to be written and the most fictionalized. Michael and I didn't get together, get engaged, until after the show opened.

Between my first and second runs, I had worked in the Public Theater and around New York. I had gone to California with the rest of the company. I came back. Then it seemed my whole life fell apart. My father died. Michael and I got divorced. But now I was back, a better singer, a better dancer, a better actress, a full person who could leave the part in the dressing room. Michael was sick by then. He tried to give me a couple of clues, but I didn't want to know about it.

LEE ROY REAMS: Drugs became a big part of Michael's creative process. He felt he could not be creative unless he felt he was under the influence. On five-minute breaks, he was doing a joint in the john. Dealers would come in with suitcases, and Michael would encourage his dancers to use cocaine to lose weight. It was the insecurity. He could have done all he did without the drugs.

DONNA MCKECHNIE: The only time I saw Michael cry was on his forty-fourth birthday. "I made it," he said.

JANE SUMMERHAYS: I was sitting in a coffee shop in Manhattan, and the radio was on. They broke for news and the first item was that Michael Bennett had died. My god, I thought, he was only forty-four years old.

I remembered how I loved working for him, how incredible his instincts were, how very quixotic he was, how fearful I was of letting him down. "Let's take out the improvements"—that's what he used to say.

DONNA MCKECHNIE: When Michael died I was in a revival of *Sweet Charity* at the National Theater in Washington, playing the role Gwen Verdon originated and taught to me.

Some time after, I bumped into Gwen on the street. We both started crying. "Gwen, are you OK?" I asked. "We're worried about you."

"I'm fine. I'm OK," she said. And then she added, "Just remember, we keep them alive inside."

It's important for me to pass on Michael's legacy, Bob's legacy: the way you act in a class, behave in a show, the basics that a lot of kids don't have. And it's also important for me to keep the legacy of the great women I've known and worked with. If not for Gwen, I would not have a career. I needed someone to inspire me besides Betty Grable—whom I always thought I should be, only I was born too late.

Chita Rivera once said to me, "Just remember, there are only a few of us ladies who are triple threats, who can sing and dance and act. You can count us on one hand. And out of the few of us, Gwen stands alone."

Gwen is a beacon. But Chita is an inspiration to me as well.

I keep part of these women in me. I keep Michael there, too. When I have the need, I ask, "Michael, what would you do now?"

WAYNE CILENTO: It's amazing how much of an impact Michael Bennett and Bob Fosse have had on my life and what I do. It's all interwoven into what I am; I always feel their presence. When I created the "Coffee Break" dance for the 1995 revival of *How to Succeed,* I used the jerky quality of Fosse's original staging. And all along I kept hearing him saying, "Go ahead, Wayne, do it. Go there."

I used to watch those MGM musicals as a kid, and my fantasy was to go out to Hollywood and become another Fred Astaire or Gene Kelly. But I went to Broadway instead, where I worked with Michael and Bob. In *Dream,* I got the chance to put it all together, to re-create that whole Hollywood-MGM world and combine it with the theater world. I incorporated yet another dimension: MTV. Today music video has taken theatrical license in making minimusicals. While some are a series of cuts and edits just for effect, others tell amazing stories through the songs. I used elements from MTV to make something from the past contemporary. *Dream* became my own dream.

In the past the choreographers were basically pushed aside, viewed as support staff. When I first began I was basically collaborating with the director and his vision, inserting my vision somewhere. But now the choreographer is right in there. As a director-choreographer, I can actually physicalize what is in my mind.

At a certain time, dance on Broadway was very popular. Then it reached a place where there wasn't enough. But now we're on a major upswing.

GEORGE C. WOLFE: One of my theories about musical theater is that in the past there was always a dark world offstage waiting to come onstage and grab the singing and the dancing. In the more modern musicals of Jerome Robbins, Bob Fosse, and Michael Bennett, a little bit of that dark world had started to creep onstage. What I wanted to do with *Jelly's Last Jam* was to bring it all onstage.

PAM KOSLOW HINES: Margo Lion had the idea of a jazz musical about Jelly Roll Morton and wondered if Gregory Hines would be interested in directing a workshop. But Greg wanted to play the character rather than direct him, and so we started on this long journey to theatricalize Jelly's life.

Ultimately Gordon Davidson put a version of the play in his season at

One of my theories about musical theater is that in the past there was always a dark world offstage waiting to come onstage and grab the singing and the dancing.

the Mark Taper Forum in Los Angeles. It didn't have tap dancing; it didn't have Greg, who was committed to a movie at that time; and it didn't have Savion Glover. Nevertheless the reviews were excellent; we sold out. But nobody wanted to move it to New York, because it's a black show that's about a black man's racism toward his own people. Not necessarily the kind of show that people want to see.

LUTHER HENDERSON: As I was working on the musical arrangements, I could see how difficult it was to do a story about a fellow who was a world-class shit. Nobody got a good word in for Jelly Roll Morton. Also, the show was envisioned as a vehicle for Gregory Hines, but we had trouble figuring out how a tap dancer could play a piano player.

PAM KOSLOW HINES: When we came back to New York, Greg began working with George C. Wolfe. They literally redid the show, putting in all those tap numbers, traveling numbers.

LUTHER HENDERSON: George finally figured it. "Honor the source," he said. What he meant was, the play would be about how a man could convey such joy, such humanity in his music, and at the same time be what he was.

BILLIE ALLEN: There was a change in direction. The play had become more sardonic, more surreal. It had become *Jelly's Last Jam.*

GEORGE C. WOLFE: It was definitely a complicated journey. At first there was tension between Gregory and me because of some of the darker aspects of the character that I wanted to deal with. But all the complications ended up making the work richer.

PAM KOSLOW HINES: When *Jelly's Last Jam* opened on April 26, 1992, it was nine years after the time we had started. Sitting in the tenth row of the Virginia Theater, I watched it unfold. I did it, I thought. This thing was born out of myself, like a child.

It was through *Jelly* that George C. Wolfe met Savion Glover, who played the part of the young Jelly Roll Morton. That was a very important connection.

I think that was the time when George began to see tap dancing as one way to express his visions. That influenced *Bring in da Noise, Bring in da Funk.*

GEORGE C. WOLFE: *Funk* is just an extension of my theory about the dark side of musicals. It is the dark and the joy coexisting perpetually all evening, until you realize that they are all part of the same human dynamics. Aside from the talent of the artists, that is what people are responding to, and that's why the work is so immediate and emotional for audiences. It's not fake. It's joyous and dark and dangerous and emotional—all the things that life is.

JOHN LAHR: To me the most interesting musicals in the last few years have been things like *Jelly's Last Jam* and *Funk*. What is great about these black musicals is that they don't have to sing about disillusionment. They embody the betrayal of the culture. They are irony in action. They are both joyous and disenchanted at once, which is what the blues are. They are ecstatic, and at the same time, they make a comment. They work, and when a musical works, it takes you places emotionally. It's great theater.

MARGE CHAMPION: Savion Glover is the new magic on Broadway. Nobody dances like him; his energy is extraordinary. There is a kind of— I don't know how to really say this—an "up yours" attitude: "You like it, you like it; you don't, tough"—that makes him so much a part of this time. Just as Marge and Gower Champion were right for then, Savion Glover is right for now.

Savion Glover (left) and Gregory Hines in *Jelly's Last Jam* a play at once joyous and disenchanted (1992).

8 | YOU NEVER CAN TELL

ALVIN COLT: I've designed costumes for shows I will never forget. Beautiful productions, terrific casts, and total flops. Like *First Impressions,* based on Jane Austen's *Pride and Prejudice,* with Farley Granger, Polly Bergen, Hermione Gingold. One critic said, "Not since *My Fair Lady* have we seen such beautiful clothes." And *Maiden Voyage*—with a cast that included Colleen Dewhurst, Tom Posten, Walter Matthau, Melvyn Douglas, and Mildred Dunnock, and with such distinguished collaborators as Paul Osborn, Jo Mielziner, and Joe Anthony—it closed in Philadelphia. And *Hellzapoppin,* with Jerry Lewis and Lynn Redgrave. That died in Boston. And my favorite: *Around the World in Eighty Days*, the Orson Welles–Cole Porter musical. What a combination. Big, big flop.

BERNARD GERSTEN: There are all those famous stories of judgment run amok. How could some plays so inferior have been put on? How could somebody have turned down *My Fair Lady*? How could *Oklahoma!* have almost closed in Boston?

MANNY AZENBERG: If you really knew what works, you'd have winners every time.

SCOTT ELLIS: You can get the best people in the business. It doesn't guarantee you anything. You work just as hard on the shows that fail as the shows that succeed. It's a crapshoot. You never can tell.

● ● ● ● ●

HARVEY SABINSON: My brother Lee declared himself a producer while I was still in college, and almost at the outset of World War II he produced his first play: *Counterattack,* starring Sam Wannamaker and Morris Carnovsky, with some great young actors my brother discovered: Karl Malden, Wendell Corey, and John Ireland, in small parts. The play was an artistic success but a commercial failure.

OPPOSITE PAGE

Geoffrey Holder, pictured here with Diahann Carroll in *House of Flowers,* taught the dancers in this show how to play the steel drums. It was the first time these instruments were used in a Broadway show (1954).

Famed press agent and publicist Harvey Sabinson. Coming out of the army, he began his Broadway career as an apprentice press agent for fifty dollars a week.

While I was away in the army Lee produced *Trio,* a play about lesbian lovers. The man in the middle was played by Richard Widmark. His understudy was a guy named Kirk Douglas. My brother knew how to pick them. But Mayor La Guardia threatened the license of the Belasco Theater and closed it.

Next Lee did a play by a young playwright named Arthur Laurents: *Home of the Brave.* Although Laurents has never mentioned it, my brother sat down with him in a Philadelphia hotel room to rewrite that play. Originally it was about anti-Semitism; later on, when it became a movie, the subject was changed to racism. With *Home of the Brave,* Lee had yet another artistic success and financial flop.

Meanwhile I got out of the army, and Lee got me my first job in the industry as apprentice to his press agent, "Honest" Sam Friedman, at fifty dollars a week, just as he was about to produce his first musical.

Although it has one of the greatest scores of all time, nobody expected *Finian's Rainbow* to do anything. The story was a combination of fantasy and politics, with satirical overtones. In those days it was considered left wing since it was about a bigoted senator and a union organizer and it had an interracial cast. When we opened in Philadelphia, we didn't even have a theater in New York. But it was a sensation. We got into the Forty-sixth Street Theater and were an instantaneous hit.

After three flops, Lee at last had his big success. The morning after *Finian's Rainbow* opened, there was a wet snow. Lee and I turned the corner and saw the line at the box office was trailing down the street. "Why don't we let these people line up inside the lobby?" I asked him.

"Fuck 'em," my brother said. "They didn't come to my first three plays. Now they'll pay anything to see this one. Let them stand out in the snow."

Finian's Rainbow and *Brigadoon* opened within weeks of each other—the Irish musical and the Scottish musical. That was the first year of the Tony awards. None were given for best musical. It would have been a tough choice. David Wayne, who played the leprechaun, got it for best featured actor, and Michael Kidd got it for choreography. So we got some recognition. Nevertheless *Finian's Rainbow* only ran 723 performances—not nearly as long as it should have.

• • • • •

GEOFFREY HOLDER: My first Broadway show, *House of Flowers,* opened in 1954. Book and lyrics by Truman Capote, music by Harold Arlen, company of great stars, like Juanita Hall, Pearl Bailey, Diahann Carroll, dancers like Arthur Mitchell, Louis Johnson, Donna McHale, Claude Thompson. Peter Brook was the director.

At the start, George Balanchine was doing the choreography; he tried to teach us the mambo. Balanchine was Balanchine. Brook was Brook. They were wrong for the show. Both were replaced with Herbert Ross as choreographer-director. Ross brought in Carmen de Lavallade (who became my wife; I proposed to her four days after we met) and Alvin Ailey. Carmen, Alvin, and I became the three principal dancers of the show.

I had grown up in Trinidad and danced in my brother's company; we performed dances of the Caribbean at American naval bases. When my brother left for England after the war, I took over his company. In 1952 we were invited to the first Caribbean Festival in Puerto Rico, where we saw dances of Haiti, Martinique, Guadeloupe, Suriname. All these cultures entered into my dancing in *House of Flowers*. I taught the dancers how to play the steel drums. It was the first time Broadway ever heard of steel bands. And Harold Arlen wrote a melody for them.

Harold was a lovely, elegant man. The music he wrote for *House of Flowers* is all in a minor key. I still think it's the best Broadway score ever.

We opened at the Alvin Theater. The audience was chic. Frank Sinatra was there with Gloria Vanderbilt. A lot of excitement. But we only ran about six months. The critics said the story was too weak and undramatic, but I think they sabotaged the show because they were out to kill Truman Capote.

● ● ● ● ●

Although it has one of the greatest scores of all time, nobody expected Finian's Rainbow to do anything.

KITTY CARLISLE HART: The summer we were renting a beach house on a little spit of land off the Jersey shore, Alan Jay Lerner and Frederick Loewe came down with the score of their new play to see if Moss would be interested in directing it. A couple of other directors had already turned them down.

Across the weeds in this godforsaken spot was a kindergarten the local population used in the wintertime. And in the basement of this school was this big, old upright with some missing ivories. That's where Moss and I heard the music to *My Fair Lady* for the first time. They did "I Could Have

Danced All Night" and "Why Can't the English Teach Their Children How to Speak?" And I tell you, it swept everything else away.

"I've got to do this," Moss said.

"You do indeed," said I.

Rex Harrison was in a play in London at the time, but they got him. He is the only person I know who ever did *Sprechstimme* (talk-singing) successfully. He made it look so easy all actors think they can do it, but of course they can't. Rex was brilliant but also arrogant. He never tired of telling Moss he was not the first choice for director.

Julie Andrews was not first choice, either. The part of Eliza was initially offered to Mary Martin. After the third rehearsal, Moss said to me, "Is Julie Andrews as bad as I think she is?"

"I think so," I said.

The stars of *My Fair Lady:* Julie Andrews, Rex Harrison, and Stanley Holloway chat with Princess Margaret after a performance (1956).

"What am I going to do? If I were Belasco, I would hire a hotel suite, lock the doors, order up room service, and rehearse her for the weekend. I would paste the part on her."

Later Moss swore I said, "Why don't you?"

What he did was give the company twenty-four hours' leave. Moss and Julie had the theater to themselves from nine-thirty in the morning until seven-thirty that night. For the first ten, fifteen minutes, Moss explained what he wanted. Julie was very green. She was twenty years old and had only done one show here: *The Boy Friend*. She was obviously intimidated by the responsibility of this role. Moss told her, "I will show you how to play this part. But you must trust me, put yourself into my hands."

It's funny. I could hear Moss's inflections, the sound of his voice, in every line that Julie spoke for the first two weeks. And then she made Eliza her own.

I was at home in New York with a frightful cold when *My Fair Lady* opened in New Haven. I waited and waited for Moss to call. Finally, at a quarter to one the phone rang. "Well?" I asked.

"It's some kind of a hit. I don't know how big," Moss said.

Opening night in New York, I stood against the back wall while Moss and Alan paced in front of me. Fritzy Loewe was sort of ambling around. I knew him from the beginning. He had been the pit pianist in *Champagne Sec,* the first show I did on Broadway, back in 1933. Every night he'd climb the two flights of stairs up to my dressing room at the Morosco, stand behind me while I was putting on my makeup, and in a guttural German accent say, "I am going to wraite da beest musical on Broadvay." And I would say to myself, You and who else? In those days there were forty musicals on Broadway and a lot of pit pianists. Now, in the middle of the first act of *My Fair Lady,* Fritz turned to me. "Vell, I wrrote da beest musical on Broadvay."

And I said, "You certainly did."

My Fair Lady is my favorite musical, the best ever written. I've seen it a hundred times, and every time they start "The Rain in Spain," no matter who is playing in it, the audience is lifted two feet off their seats. They levitate, and they stay up there for the rest of the performance.

Camelot was quite a different story. Fritzy never wanted to do it. He felt the only part that was any good was the first act when King Arthur learns from Merlin how to fly. And that was enchanting. They invented the rest, but it didn't quite hang together.

When we opened in Toronto, the curtain didn't come down until a quarter to one. They began to cut the show, and they began to have bad luck. Alan was hospitalized for an attack of ulcers. Just as he was getting out, Moss had his first heart attack. Alan did the best he could, but he was not a director. The show continued pretty much the way it was until Moss was able to go back and fix it.

The score of *Camelot* was one of the best. And then the play took on the connotation of the Kennedy years, so it has that poignancy. Nevertheless, *Camelot* was never quite what they had hoped for.

● ● ● ● ●

CHARLES STROUSE: I felt this terrible lack of being anyone. I was a graduate of the Eastman School of Music in Rochester, New York. Serious music had been my life. But I hadn't made it as a serious composer. I worked as a rehearsal pianist and vocal arranger. But I hadn't made it as a theater composer. To say the least, I hadn't been part of the Broadway scene. But together with Lee Adams, I had written for resort shows and off-Broadway revues. And an incipient producer, Ed Padula, liked our work and wanted to produce a show about teenagers. That, in essence, was the genesis of *Bye Bye Birdie*. We spent five years on it, going through five book writers until we finally settled on Mike Stewart.

One day Ed Padula told us he had this guy, Slade Brown, coming up from Texas. We were playing auditions for anybody then, and we arranged a private audition for him and a gentleman friend.

"I like that," he said when we finished. "Those are really nice songs."

I thought to myself, What a fool.

"How much money do you need?" he asked.

"Seventy-five thousand dollars."

He wrote out a check on an account with Brown's National Bank of Orange, Texas. Then he flew us down to Texas and got a lot of his friends to put money in. And *Birdie* got off the ground. It was like a Judy Garland–Mickey Rooney movie.

The show was originally written for Carol Haney. We were at her place going over the score when the doorbell rang. It was Gower Champion. Carol said, "Hello, Gower," and she lost her voice right on the spot.

We sat around for a half hour, saying things like, "Oh, don't worry."

But it was clear that she couldn't do the show. Carol was a wonderful talent, full of beans, but she had a lot of bad luck. She originated the "Steam Heat" number in *Pajama Game,* but Shirley MacLaine, who took over for her, got most of the attention. Carol was too soft for life, buffeted about. She was a diabetic and died when she was still quite young.

Now we went to Eydie Gorme, thinking she would do it with Steve Lawrence. But she got pregnant. We couldn't think of anyone else. Then someone came up with Chita Rivera. It was after *West Side Story,* and she was hot.

"You can't," one of us said. "The part is a Polish girl. All the jokes are Polish jokes."

"Can't we change Polish to Spanish?"

So every "Warsaw" became "Mexico," and every "Polish" became "Spanish," and the story became more contemporary.

Although neither Dick Van Dyke nor Chita Rivera were original choices for leads in *Bye Bye Birdie,* they certainly were right for their roles. Here Gower Champion (right) rehearses them through a number (1960).

Birdie would never have been what it became were it not for Chita. Her training is in dancing; discipline is part of her life. No agents came around saying, "She needs another song" or "She doesn't like this." She was just part of the creative process, part of the company, not the star. Chita is a gypsy at heart.

I had become friends with Dick Van Dyke when I was the pianist and vocal arranger for *The Girls Against the Boys* and Dick was the second banana to Bert Lahr. All the while I was writing the music for *Birdie,* I used to tell Dick, "You'd be terrific for this show I'm working on." So when it came time to cast, Dick's agent kept pestering us. But we were looking for a name—Jack Lemmon, Larry Blyden—until one day Dick came in, and he was wonderful.

All the parts were coming together. Still, it wasn't until we were a smash in Philadelphia that the reality of it began to seep in. Did I dare believe that I had written a successful show?

I had been a student of Aaron Copeland's. He returned from Europe and noticed there was a show on Broadway composed by somebody who spelled his name like mine.

He called me. "Is that any relation to you, Buddy?"

TED CHAPIN: You can probably tell how old people are by knowing their introduction to Broadway. Mine was *Bye Bye Birdie*. I saw it the year after it opened: May 11, 1961, to be exact. I was eleven years old, and the floodgates opened. It was just so exciting and youthful.

Birdie is a rock-and-roll show, and yet there's a harp in the orchestra. It has one of the best orchestrations ever created for a Broadway show. Robert Ginzler legitimized the kind of high-energy Broadway sound without it sounding like Las Vegas. Listen to "Put on a Happy Face," and you'll hear how much fun the flutes are.

CHARLES STROUSE: During the run, Dick Van Dyke came over to me: "Buddy, I got an offer to do a television series."

"Dick," I said, "you just won the Tony. You've got your choice of roles. How long is the contract?"

"Twelve or thirteen weeks."

"Right now you're on top," I said. "Stay with Broadway. A television series would be a big mistake."

> Birdie *would never have been what it became were it not for Chita. Her training is in dancing; discipline is part of her life.*

• • • • •

FRED EBB: I was sure *Flora, the Red Menace* would be a hit. George Abbott was directing. Hal Prince was producing. Those shows don't fail.

Liza Minnelli came up to my apartment to hear the score. She was seventeen years old, her hair was long and stringy; she was wearing funny-looking clothes. She sat down on the couch, took off her shoes, and tucked her legs under her. I was reminded of my mother's horrified reaction when a girl I once was seeing had done that.

JOHN KANDER: Liza sang through some of the numbers. We saw at once she was very talented. Fred and I wanted her, but Mr. Abbott did not. She had the curse of being Judy Garland's daughter. But as it turned out, the performer Mr. Abbott wanted was not available. "Get the Minnelli girl," he said. And then he fell completely in love. On her birthday he came waltzing in with a cake, which is something he would never ordinarily do.

FRED EBB: We wrote a lot of music for Liza, and it was great to have a voice you could always count on. But once we got on the road with *Flora,* we could tell it wasn't going well.

During one rehearsal Hal turned to me and said, "How would like you like to write a musical version of *I Am a Camera*? I'll direct it." I had seen the play, and the idea of a musical didn't make any sense to me at all. But it was a chance for John and me to write another show and be in the business, even if *Flora, the Red Menace* was going to be a failure.

* * * * *

JOEL GREY: *Cabaret* was one of the first of the dark and sinister musicals. We were aware of that as we were working on it, and that's why none of us expected it to be particularly successful. At best, we thought, it would be of artistic interest.

There was a fleeting character in Christopher Isherwood's *Berlin Stories* (the source for the play *I Am a Camera,* which *Cabaret* is based on) who was a master of ceremonies in a cabaret, but Hal Prince enhanced the role by drawing on his memory of an actual emcee he had seen in Germany. To create the character, I called on those actors who had such a great influence on my life: Laurence Olivier as that dark-underbelly night-club performer Richard III, James Cagney, Peter Lorre, and all those crummy comics I had seen as an eighteen-year-old working in nightclubs. I despised the nightclub scene, and I thought the comics were awful. But now they provided a background for me to create my character. I also called on my father, Mickey Katz. While he was very funny and bright in his point of view, his material had a middle-European sensibility that proved invaluable. And to all that, I added the soul, or the soul-*lessness,* of this guy. As a Jew, I felt an obligation to make the role of the emcee disgusting, evil, very dangerous. I wanted that.

Originally the emcee was only to be seen in Act Two, in a twenty-minute production number made up of five cabaret acts—a kind of kaleidoscope of 1930s Berlin nightclub entertainment. But by the time rehearsals began, they decided to break up the numbers and spread them throughout the show in such a way that the cabaret numbers became reflections about what was happening in the story. The emcee went from being merely an entertainer to a commentator on the times.

There's the scene where the older couple played by Lotte Lenya and Jack Gilford are in his fruit shop, and someone throws a rock through the window because he is Jewish. They stand there wondering what to do, whether they will have to leave Berlin. And the next thing is the number where the emcee dances with a gorilla. The song ends with the line, "If you could see her through my eyes, she wouldn't look Jewish at all."

FRED EBB: That line got the exact reaction I wanted. First there was a collective gasp from the audience, followed by a moment of silence, and then applause.

However, when we were getting set to open in New York, we received a letter from a rabbi who claimed he represented millions of Jews. He found the line decidedly anti-Semitic and threatened he would tell all the Jewish groups to boycott us if it were not changed. Soon after, I was walking through the lobby of the theater when a lady wearing a checkered skirt and carrying a pad and pencil accosted me. "Do you have anything to do with this show?" she asked.

"Yes, I wrote the lyrics."

"Well, I represent B'nai B'rith," she said, "and we're here to protest the use of that line. If you don't take it out, we'll withdraw all our theater parties."

The truth is, we ran scared. I was frightened. Hal Prince was frightened, and he is not a man who frightens easily. *Cabaret* was one of his early chances at being a successful director. He was also the producer, and a producer depends on theater parties, especially at the beginning of the run. We were all so desperate to succeed. We did things that we would never agree to today.

Coming up with another punchline was about the most difficult task I've ever faced in the theater. I rewrote it as "She isn't a *meeskite* (ugly person) at all." However, whenever he felt he could get away with it, especially when he knew there was somebody important to us out in the audience, Joel Grey would sing, "She wouldn't look Jewish at all." The stage manager would yell at him, and he'd say, "It just slipped out."

Bob Fosse put the line back in for the movie. The screen goes absolutely quiet, and Joel says it. It was shot that way because if, on an outside chance, there was any protest, Joel could dub in another line. But in the movie it was accepted.

None of us knew what we had with *Cabaret* until we opened in the Shubert Theater in Boston. After the first number, "Willkommen," the show could not continue. The audience applauded and applauded. And all of us just stood there in awe. We realized we were on to something very special.

Joel Grey with two of the cabaret girls (Sharon Lawrence and Ruth Gottschall) "each and every one of them a virgin."

• • • • •

Richard Kiley knew the part of Don Quixote in *Man of La Mancha* would be the role of a lifetime.

Joe Darion, the lyricist for *Man of La Mancha*.

RICHARD KILEY: Mitch Leigh was hardly the kind of guy you'd expect to come up with the idea of a musical based on *Don Quixote*. He was a wealthy businessman, but also a highly trained musicologist. There was this side of him that goaded him to do this thing.

MITCH LEIGH: *Man of La Mancha* was a gift to myself. It took more than three years to write the music. I did unusual things with meter. "The Impossible Dream" is in $\frac{9}{8}$ time. There is $\frac{10}{8}$, $\frac{5}{4}$ time. Initially it was very difficult to find musicians who could play the music I had composed. Our first lyricist was the great poet W. H. Auden. It was inhibiting to work with someone like that. Ultimately, he wasn't right. He wrote poetry, not lyrics, and that was a problem.

JOE DARION: They called me down to a meeting and asked if I could work on Auden's lyrics. "Are you out of your mind?" I said. "Me touch Auden's poetry? I wouldn't have the guts."

"What do you think has to be done?" they asked.

"You have to start all over. The whole thing has to be done again, fresh."

They threw me out. I came home to my wife. "I just ruined myself, Helen. I just lost out on the most magnificent thing I've ever seen in my life." I sat down and chewed my nails. I don't know for how long—maybe weeks.

Then they called me back.

MITCH LEIGH: Joe Darion turned out to be the absolutely right lyricist.

JOE DARION: The lyrics had to be sixteenth century, yet suitable to the modern ear. My job was to get inside that crazy, marvelous man's head and heart and guts. If I heard my own voice, I knew I was in trouble.

It took a very long time for Dale Wasserman and me to come to an agreement about the book. The show ground to a halt for days because Wasserman and I realized that we were writing Aldonza/Dulcinea differently. She is the focal point of the play; she is the only one who changes. We had to grapple with her. Did she learn from this crazy old man to be something else, or did she have something inside her waiting to be lit?

I ended up with 1,008 pieces of paper for nineteen songs. The last song I wrote was "The Quest," which everyone calls "The Impossible Dream." Helen pulled the paper out from under my pencil. "Don't you know when you're finished?" she said.

RICHARD KILEY: I was playing straight man to Buddy Hackett in *I Had a Ball*. I wasn't happy, but I had a family to take care of, and it paid well. I was sitting in my dressing room feeling sorry for myself when Albert Marre, who had directed me in *Kismet,* dropped by and gave me a script to read. I gave my notice that night.

I always thought I was a character man who was caught in a leading man's body. Now I was offered the opportunity to work my way out. I knew Don Quixote would be the role of a lifetime.

As a boy I had been given a record of the great Russian bass baritone Shlapin singing little bits and pieces of various operas. One was the death scene from *Don Quixote*. All these years, it had lingered in my mind. I felt the part was out there waiting for me. Joan Diener and I had worked together in *Kismet*. She had a trained operatic voice and was able to do incredible things, go from the most awful kind of chest sounds of someone from the gutter to the wonderful thread of sound in the reprise of "Dulcinea."

MITCH LEIGH: Joan Diener had a three-and-a-half octave range. We tailored the music to her voice.

RICHARD KILEY: At the Goodspeed Opera House in Connecticut, we were a smash. Doug Watt was enthusiastic, but he said on Broadway it would die.

MITCH LEIGH: Apparently the world was not anxious for a musical version of *Don Quixote*. We couldn't get a recording company to record the score. We couldn't get a Broadway theater. Finally, we managed to get the ANTA Theater on the NYU campus, down in Greenwich Village.

RICHARD KILEY: Our opening-night party was at One Fifth Avenue. I arrived a little late, just as the television reviews were coming in. Edwin Newman had been pressed into service as a theater reviewer, and as I worked my way through the crowd to the bar, I heard him say, "But the lowest point of the evening came when Richard Kiley stood up and sang an awful song called 'The Impossible Dream.'"

With that the whole bar emptied, like someone had flushed a toilet. Well, I thought, back to the old drawing board. At that time I was living in Tuxedo Park, which is about fifty miles from Manhattan. It was a long drive home that night.

Playbill for *Man of La Mancha,* the play Richard Kiley said was doomed to succeed.

JOE DARION: While the play was on, Wasserman and I made a ring around the theater and hit every bar there was. I won't give a name, but one of the critics who killed us was inside one of those bars. He wrote his review from the program.

RICHARD KILEY: The morning critics' reviews were not bad as much as they were indifferent. But all the afternoon papers were filled with smashing raves.

MITCH LEIGH: It was like Kennedy and Nixon. JFK went to sleep thinking he had lost it. We went to sleep thinking we had a flop.

JOE DARION: At first there was a misunderstanding about what the show was about. Women were dragging in their husbands, who were protesting, "I don't want to see Shakespeare."

HELEN DARION: I got in a cab. The driver was such a huge man, the steering wheel looked like a plaything in his hands. "Where to?" he asked.

"The ANTA Theater."

"That's where *Man of La Mancha* is playing," he said. "Have you got any connection with it?"

"Some. My husband wrote the lyrics."

"You mean he wrote 'The Impossible Dream'?" he said. "The little woman tried to get me to see the show. I didn't want to go. She went again and again. I still didn't want to go. Finally she dragged me. I heard that song, and I tell you what was on that stage is in my heart."

RICHARD KILEY: "The Impossible Dream" is my very favorite song. People are always asking me to sing it at hospital openings and everyplace else, although I don't enjoy singing in a tuxedo. I feel I have to be wearing armor to do it right. But it has had an impact. I can't tell you how many people have told me it's changed their lives.

JOE DARION: I still receive letters from all over. A man whose son was killed in Vietnam. The father of a little girl who was dying of leukemia and would sing it. The Czechs used it as an underground song against the Russian occupation.

RICHARD KILEY: From the stage I was able to see people being moved by various scenes. They walked out feeling transformed, which is what theater is really about. The play is written in an easily accessible style, yet there is a profound Aristotelian catharsis. At the end Don Quixote/Cervantes has made his peace with himself. The man and the creation have become one—maybe not beating, but certainly defying, the unbeatable foe.

From the stage I was able to see people being moved by various scenes. They walked out feeling transformed, which is what theater is really about.

MITCH LEIGH: We moved up to Broadway and had a total run of seven years. There are continuous touring and international productions. The album has never been out of print.

RICHARD KILEY: *Man of La Mancha* was an odd success story. I always say it was "doomed to success."

• • • • •

PETER STONE: Alfred Drake talked the agent we shared into producing a musical based on the Sartre play about England's greatest actor, Edmund Kean. They asked if I'd like to write the book. I had never written the book for a musical, but I agreed.

Kean was a triumph in Boston, but then Alfred got sick. We opened in New York, in a theater too large for the show. Alfred was not at full steam. We got respectable reviews but closed after a few months.

Four years later I got together with Feuer and Martin for a musical based on Elmer Rice's 1945 hit *Dream Girl. Skyscraper* starred Julie Harris and Charles Nelson Reilly. The main problem was that Julie, one of the great actresses of our time, never really landed as a musical performer. Although the show was nominated for a Tony, it ran for less than a year.

Then, in late 1967, I was asked to write yet another musical book. A teacher turned songwriter, Sherman Edwards, had written a musical about the Declaration of Independence. Stuart Ostrow wanted to produce it, but he felt the book needed work. I tried desperately to avoid it. It seemed to me audiences would never go for a play where an all-male cast debated the Declaration of Independence. People would fall asleep before they heard the "six" in the title, *1776.*

However, after nearly a year of persuasion, I went down to Stuart's office in the Paramount Building. Sherman Edwards, a very brusque man, walked in. He sat down at the piano and, in a rotten voice, sang "Sit Down, John, Sit Down." And I was entranced. I learned more about the Continental Congress from that song than in all my years in school. Sherman had composed a score that had an attitude, a kindly irreverence to these vaunted characters.

But the book was not right. Sherman's friend Meredith Wilson had written the music, book, and lyrics for *The Music Man,* and Sherman was determined to do the same for *1776.* At first he refused to allow it to be touched, but finally he relented. We cut the number of songs from twenty to ten. Still the proportion of book to music is double what it is on any other show, and a full forty minutes of dialogue passes with no singing.

Difficulties abounded all through rehearsals. The part of Martha Jefferson wasn't working. It wasn't the actress's fault; she was quite good. But the book and the score weren't coming together in this naughty song sung by a very dignified person: "He plays the violin / He tucks it right under his chin / And he bows / Yes, he bows . . ."

We had to replace her. Five actresses came down to audition. The last one was Betty Buckley, just off the bus from Fort Worth, Texas. Instead of singing "bows" like "fiddles," Betty sang it like "bows from the waist." She had an attitude and a freaky voice, sang head range in the chest voice, was enchanting. This was our Martha.

Howard daSilva played Ben Franklin. He was a great performer but a trial and tribulation. In the weeks leading up to the opening, he kept quitting on us. Finally we said, "OK, good-bye," and got a replacement. Only, Howard never left. The replacement stood in the wings every night. In the final preview before the opening night, Howard suffered a very serious heart attack, but he was determined to open in the show, even if it killed him. It nearly did. The first few performances, he was physically leaning on Billy Daniels, who played John Adams. Then he checked into the hospital for a month or two.

Everyone discounted us. We didn't have an advance of five beans. We had no real stars, a director who had never worked on Broadway before, a writer whose two previous shows had not done very well, and a composer-lyricist who was even more of an unknown quantity. And there were all kinds of questions about the subject matter.

We opened in New Haven in a blizzard, with almost no one in the audience. But then we moved on to Washington, D.C., where the *Washington Post* gave us a great review. And when we opened at the Forty-sixth Street Theater, we got incredible raves. Many people expected something stodgy, but *1776* was full of fun and surprise. The calendar onstage with each date being ripped off as time moved closer to the Fourth of July put a kind of a clock on things. And the tally board showed the progression of colonies agreeing to sign the Declaration: five colonies holding out, four, three, two . . .

1776 came out during the Vietnam War, when a lot of people were selling patriotism. Our logo capitalized on this: a little eaglet with an

American flag in its beak, hatching out of an egg decorated with a British flag. We won Tony awards for best book, score, show, and supporting actor, ran about three years on Broadway, two on tour, and had a successful London tour. Not bad for a show that everyone discounted at the start.

• • • • •

CHARLES STROUSE: I had met Martin Charnin when he was an incipient lyricist and singing in the chorus in *The Girls Against the Boys*. He called me up one day: "Buddy, I got a great idea for a show. But I can't talk about it over the phone. You gotta come over to my office."

"C'mon, tell me," I said.

"Little Orphan Annie."

What a resounding thud that made.

MARTIN CHARNIN: I had been Christmas shopping in Doubleday's and came across a coffee-table book that was a collection of the *Little Orphan Annie* comic strips by Harold Gray, edited by Al Capp. I bought it for a friend, but since there was a big line at the counter, I didn't bother to get it gift-wrapped. That night I read it through. The next morning I called my attorney and asked him to contact the *Chicago Tribune* to see if the rights were available. It took a year and a half before I got them.

I asked Tom Meehan from the *New Yorker* if he'd be interested in doing the book. I asked Charles Strouse if he'd collaborate with me on the music. Neither responded favorably, but I convinced them. "We'll do it real. We'll put flesh and blood into the outline of the comic strip."

Six years later, I was seventy-five thousand dollars in debt. Every producer had turned us down. Then Michael Price agreed to do *Annie* at the Goodspeed Opera House in East Haddam, Connecticut, for a ten-week tryout. Mike Nichols saw it and decided it would be the first play he would produce.

ANDREA MCARDLE: I was a twelve-year-old pint-sized tomboy when I auditioned for *Annie*. I wore a little dress and kneesocks, with my hair pinned up in curls, and sang the Rodgers and Hart song "Johnny One Note" because I could really belt out that "one note" and hold it. The veins were popping out of my neck. I got to be one of the orphans.

CHARLES STROUSE: We had a sweet, pretty girl playing Annie, but then we began to think the show was getting saccharine and that we needed a tougher kid.

ANDREA McARDLE: Martin asked me if I thought I could play Annie. "No problem," I said. The girl who was in the title role was terrific, but she wouldn't have survived two seconds on the street.

"You'll have to learn the part," Martin said.

"I know the entire show," I told him. So did every other kid in the play.

MARTIN CHARNIN: Kids have an interesting habit of learning everyone else's material, and Andrea had the role down cold. I worked with her over a weekend, and on Sunday night we told her she had the part. She was letter perfect.

ANDREA McARDLE: We were the last show that did not use any microphones. You had to have chops that could reach the back of the house.

CHARLES STROUSE: Originally "Tomorrow" was a song that took place during a very clever scene change. Annie sings "Tomorrow, tomorrow, I love ya, tomorrow, you're only a day away" and walks off with the dog, ducking behind a flat while another scene comes in. When the song got such a tremendous hand, I thought they were applauding the set change.

MARTIN CHARNIN: But "Tomorrow" broke out of the show, instantly wrapping itself around the vocal cords of every singer in the country. The song is the root of what the kid is all about, what the play is all about. It's still as valid a theme today as it was in 1976, which is why Andrea sang it at the 1996 Democratic National Convention and in Little Rock after Clinton won. They didn't ask her to sing anything from *Les Mis*.

Annie had a five-week tryout at the Kennedy Center in Washington, D.C., and then moved on to previews in New York. By then we'd sensed that we had something on our hands. The audience wanted the show to work. They loved the kid and what she stood for. They loved the satire. They loved Miss Hannigan, her rage and anger.

Annie is really about heroes and villains, with the good guys winning after a lot of travail. It's also about extremes: the richest man in the world and the poorest child in the world. Audiences buy into that.

The first review that came in after we opened in New York was Stewart Klein's "On the Aisle" on Channel Five. He didn't like it. He thought it was corny. Oh, my god, I thought, have we been deceiving ourselves? But from then on it was unanimous, to the point where your mother couldn't have written those kinds of reviews. Afterward Stewart Klein kept calling every week to try and get house seats for his relatives.

CHARLES STROUSE: Soon after we opened somebody sent me an editorial from a newspaper in New Mexico. In essence it said, "Last night, a jaded Broadway audience leaped to its feet when a little girl, fully dressed, said, 'Daddy, I love you.'"

MARTIN CHARNIN: *Annie* was right for its time. We were coming out of Nixon, Watergate, Vietnam, recession, that cynical spirit in the country. When we opened, Carter had just been elected. There was a glimmer of hope. That's why the political part of the play works so well.

CHARLES STROUSE: Martin was convinced *Annie* would be a big hit and he was right. It's probably the biggest hit I've ever had. When we were in Washington, D.C., I was being called by senators for tickets. It's still the fourth- or fifth-longest running show.

MARTIN CHARNIN: *Annie* was one of the last shows that relied exclusively on the strength of its text, its emotions, and its simplicity. It is helicopterless. It is chandelierless. It is pure Broadway.

Andrea McArdle was a twelve-year-old tomboy when she was picked from the chorus of orphans to replace the lead in *Annie* after the powers that be realized they needed a tougher kid (1976).

Two stars of the original Broadway production of *Barnum*: Jim Dale, who came out of the British musical hall tradition and could sing, dance, play the clown, ride a unicycle, and walk a tightrope; and Glenn Close, who went on to become a Hollywood star (1980).

CY COLEMAN: "I want you to think about doing a musical about P. T. Barnum," Michael Stewart said to me.

"Michael, I turned it down five years ago. Barnum's life isn't particularly interesting."

"Rethink it. We can make it work."

So I thought about it and decided to do a show using the three rings of a circus. Every time Barnum's life gets dull, I thought, we can bring in another chase. I can write fast music, and I love to do chases. I also know what circus music is. We got a book together and a score, and we began casting. It was no good. We needed the real stuff, circus performers who could also act and dance and sing. But the casting people had no idea where we could find them.

Then one or two heard about it and auditioned. And with that, suddenly the word spread. There is an underground of circus performers, we discovered as these kids started coming in from everywhere. They were amazing. One was a virtuoso on the violin who, at the same time, could walk a wire, do the trapeze, perform every physical trick you could imagine.

Jim Dale comes out of the British musical hall tradition, and he not only sings and dances, he can play the clown, ride a unicycle, walk a tightrope, perform magic acts. As far as I was concerned, there was never anybody else to play Barnum.

Glenn Close auditioned for me six times. Everybody wanted her because she's a fabulous actress. But I kept telling her she didn't sing right. She was determined. "What do you need? What do you want?" She went to work with a vocal coach and built up the range. *Barnum* started it for her.

MARTIN RICHARDS: Cy Coleman asked my wife, Mary Lea Johnson, and me to produce *Barnum*. Michael Stewart had asked David Merrick to produce it. Merrick sent me a contract with the clause, "When we win the Tony, I accept it." We walked out. We just didn't want to work with him. Then he walked out, and Judy Gordon, who had never done a show in her life, did it together with Cy.

CY COLEMAN: It is very difficult to be both producer and creator. Your fellow creators don't trust you because you're a producer. The producers don't trust you because you're a creator. You're caught in a crossfire.

Our problems abounded. The set was too big and too expensive. We had Jenny Lind and Barnum ride hobbyhorses on a merry-go-round until I found out it would be a criminal offense if so much as a screw fell off and hit somebody. The next day, director Joe Layton came up with the idea of a wire walk. That was better and cheaper. The whole idea became, Let's get away from the scenery. Let's get back to being inventive.

An underground of circus performers came out from everywhere to audition for Barnum.

We decided not to go out of town. The previews were our first exposure. First night of previews, every guy that wants to kill you comes in. They were there in droves. To top it off, there was a strike, and half the costumes didn't arrive.

The word was so bad that during the first week, we lost ninety thousand dollars. The next week we lost thirty thousand, and the *Times* canceled an interview with Jim Dale. Evidently some editor had snuck in and didn't like what he saw. The next week we lost only fifteen thousand. Progress. I walked into a meeting and said, "We're a hit."

Then Frank Rich put us on the map. It was his first review of a musical and one of the great reviews of all time. He just loved the show. After that we got unanimous raves. We were a big hit.

● ● ● ● ●

MARTIN RICHARDS: Mary Lea Johnson, Bobby Fryer, and his partner, Jimmy Cresson, formed a company called the Producers Circle. Hugh Wheeler and Stephen Sondheim came to audition the music and tell us the story of *Sweeney Todd*. Mary Lea and I flipped out over it.

LEN CARIOU: I got the script for *Sweeney Todd* when I was back home in Winnipeg. During my lunch hour, I began reading it, and I came to the lyric "There's a hole in the world like a great black pit / And it's filled with people who are filled with shit."

What the hell is this? I wondered. Who ever heard such lyrics?

Over the weekend, when there were no distractions, I read the script again. I thought, This is as bizarre a subject matter as one can imagine: a mad barber who kills his clients and has them made into meat pies. But if Stephen writes a very romantic score to such a subject, it will work like gangbusters.

The script was in my head way before rehearsals began. I realized that it was an extraordinary opportunity for me. The character is so interesting, so tormented, the role so demanding as an actor and as a singer. It's my favorite, hands-down.

MARTIN RICHARDS: Hal always does a run-through for friends in the business, chorus kids, gypsies, to get a reaction. Usually they're a positive audience. But at the run-through for *Sweeney Todd,* it all went down the toilet.

OPPOSITE PAGE

"The demon barber of Fleet Street" (Len Cariou) and Mrs. Lovett (Angela Lansbury) rehearsing for the original Broadway production of *Sweeney Todd* (1979).

Stephen Sondheim came over to me. "Where's the show? Where's the show? What are we going to do?"

Sondheim doesn't speak to everybody. I was honored.

We got together in his townhouse. There was a big controversy. People said to each other, "I didn't want to do the show in the first place," and this and that.

Stephen and Hal had words. Finally Hal said, "If everyone stays out of my hair for forty-eight hours and leaves me alone, I will restage this whole thing." He decided to place the show in the middle of the Industrial Revolution, when machines were dwarfing the whole world. That's when everything came together.

Quite often Hal starts by getting a whole picture and saying, "This is the way I want the set to look." For *Sweeney Todd* he wanted us to buy a steel factory. We had to buy the whole thing in order to get the pieces that we needed. It cost a fortune.

We used as much Grand Guignol—the horror theater of France—as the audience could take. We had these special trick razors that made blood come out of the razors. One time in previews the blood ran down the shirts. There was a very heavy reaction. So we cut it down to a little drip, just the suggestion.

LEN CARIOU: *Sweeney* scared the shit out of a lot of people. But for me the most wonderful thing was to look out from the wings and see the little kids who sat in the first few rows. Their mouths would be wide open from start to finish.

MARTIN RICHARDS: The people who came to previews said, "How brilliant, how brilliant!" But the theater-party ladies did not want to buy tickets, and when they did they walked out in droves. One lady hit me with a shopping bag right in the lobby of the theater, yelling, "What kind of thing is this, to show people eating people for a musical?"

Uh-oh, I thought, maybe we're in trouble. But once the reviews came out you couldn't get a ticket. *Sweeney Todd* was like chic. All those people who had been turned off to the show were now lining up for tickets.

Still, none of us knew what we had. Like *Oklahoma!*, *Sweeney Todd* has gone down as a landmark musical.

• • • • •

MARVIN KRAUSS: Allan Carr walked into my office one day and said, "I want to do *La Cage aux Folles* as a Broadway musical." It took five years from that time to get it off the ground. All shows have a story.

MARTIN RICHARDS: This is a true story. Screw it—once and for all it's going to come out. Jerry Herman came to visit me in the Hamptons. "I just saw a movie, *La Cage aux Folles*," he said. "It is so incredible. You've got to go see it.

"Marty, not since *Mame* have I wanted to do a musical. Everything else has been fed to me, forced on me. But I feel for this. I've already written two songs for it. Will you buy it for me?"

So the next time we were back in New York, Mary Lea and I went to an art theater on Second Avenue where the movie was playing. It was in the afternoon, and we found ourselves standing on line with all these old ladies with blue hair and shopping bags.

We go in and watch the movie. There's the scene where Albin, the drag queen, is sitting on the bench. He's been hurt and he's leaving his lover, Renato.

Renato asks him where he is going.

"I'm going to the cemetery to get a plot."

"But we already have a plot," says Renato.

"I want to be buried alone," Albin says.

"Whom will I laugh with?" asks Renato.

The old ladies in front of me go, "Ohhhhhh!" Two men talking together, talking about being together for an eternity. Remarkable.

I learned Allan Carr had bought the property three months ago. I called him up. "Allan," I said, "if you let me do this, I'll let you do the film of *Chicago* with me. And I've got a surprise for you. Jerry Herman is sitting right next to me, and he is dying to do the score."

Allan Carr said, "It's brilliant! It's brilliant! What a great idea! Bring Jerry and bring Jimmy Kirkwood (who wrote the book for *A Chorus Line*) with you."

Mary Lea, Jerry Herman, Jimmy Kirkwood, and I go to the Plaza Hotel to meet Allan and his female secretary. He serves strawberries and crème fraîche. We have this very long conversation. Finally he says to Jerry, I have this great idea. You write one or two songs. Cy Coleman can write one or two songs. So and so—"

Before he could finish the list Jerry was up and out, with Mary Lea and me following him.

"Marty, where are you going?" Allan asked.

"If Jerry Herman is not doing the show, I'm not doing the show."

Allan's option was up. He went to Marvin Krauss, who brought in Barry Brown and Fritz Holt. On the strength of Jerry Herman doing the score, they convinced Jean Poiret, who wrote the play the film was based on, to give back the rights. They brought Harvey Fierstein in to do the book, but they were going to do the show without me. Jerry called me and said, "I won't do it without you." I came in, but I was no longer owning half of the property.

Emotions heighten when you musicalize a scene.

MARVIN KRAUSS: No shows are easy. If you've been in the trenches out of town with anyone and come back friends, you will remain friends until the day you die. But once we began working on *La Cage,* it was a lovefest.

The first time I heard "I Am What I Am," I was overcome. The irony is that this song has become a rallying cry not only for gays, but for anyone with a cause. It has become an anthem.

JERRY HERMAN: It was a very easy song to write, but only because Harvey Fierstein had written a very moving scene to end Act I, and I said, "Oh, boy, that has to be a song." Emotions heighten when you musicalize a scene. Still, I was blown away. I'd never seen a song affect an audience quite like that. People stood up and cheered; they cried as they walked up the aisle at intermission.

"I Am What I Am" has become a truly important song, and I'm not known for important songs. Leslie Uggams sang it in *Jerry's Girls,* and a black woman doing that song made as much sense as a gay man.

MARVIN KRAUSS: We opened in Boston. I thought it was such a conservative town, they'd be the most antihomosexual. Instead we were given the key to the city. We had people handing out sheet music to "The Best of Times," and everyone was singing in the streets. Opening night in New York was like a snowball going down a mountain, getting bigger and bigger. But how successful it would be was anybody's guess. There were many moments that we were concerned about, like when Gene Barry and George Hearn touch hands. This was a first, a breakthrough.

Early on, there was a very elderly crowd at a matinee. If only we can reach these people, I thought. When it was over and the entire audience stood up, I knew we had a big hit. *La Cage* remains the only show that my mother-in-law ever asked to see twice.

After it was established, everybody and his brother auditioned for replacements. There wasn't a star who came into town who didn't want to do it. I watched Sid Caesar audition in drag.

La Cage had everything: heart, spectacle, humor, great music, a wonderful cast, and a "Good Housekeeping Seal of Approval" for a difficult subject. It brought homosexuality out from under the bed and onto the coffee table.

SHIRLEY HERZ: The day Rock Hudson died, TV cameras were down at the theater asking the matinee audience if they thought they might contract AIDS by being in the audience. That cut into business. There were people who were afraid to sit in the theater with a gay chorus up there—even though they weren't all gay, by the way. The show broke new ground, but it closed much too soon.

In all my years as a press agent, I never had a show like *La Cage.* We were joined at the hip; there was so much love. It was one of the few productions where the chorus was a major part of it. They still come around to see me.

• • • • •

DAVID SHIRE: Richard Maltby and I did two off-Broadway shows together, *Baby* and *Closer than Ever.* People from the theater community were saying, "Wow, these guys are comers." Therefore I think an expectation was set for our next collaboration, *Big.* People thought it was going to be groundbreaking.

RICHARD MALTBY, JR.: Yet there was an inexplicable hostility to *Big,* even before previews. In the old days, a big new show would be welcomed with excitement. If you got a bad review—it happened with *Fiddler; Hello, Dolly!; Forum*—you did some work, changed the show a little, and it became a hit. But with *Big,* there was all this sniping. The *Variety* out-of-town review hammered away at the idea that *Big* existed to publicize FAO Schwarz.

DAVID SHIRE: We couldn't destroy this false perception that FAO Schwarz had creative control of the show. In the movie, the store scene is set in FAO Schwarz. What were we supposed to do? Put it in Toys 'R' Us?

RICHARD MALTBY: During rehearsals the *New York Times* assigned this guy to do a Sunday piece. He was dour looking, always with a long face.

We didn't quite get it at the time, but when he called to fact check, all his questions were about the FAO Schwarz connection.

DAVID SHIRE: It turned out he was a political reporter, and the thrust of his piece was about the tie-in with FAO Schwarz. It was a hatchet job.

RICHARD MALTBY: We got raves from the *New York Times, USA Today,* and Joel Siegel. But the other reviews were very hostile, much more so than the material, which is kind of benign, seemed to warrant. You get a rave review in the *New York Times,* and it should counter almost anything else. Nevertheless we were perceived as a show that got bad reviews.

DAVID SHIRE: From the day we opened, our approval rating was as high as 85 or 90 percent. Yet only 8 percent of our audience was coming from Manhattan. It seems that sophisticated theater people wrote us off. Out of town, the fact that it was a kids' show was a plus. But in New York that was somehow turned into a minus. We were nominated for a Tony in five categories, but not best musical, and as soon as the news of the Tony nominations came out, business dropped thirty thousand dollars a day.

RICHARD MALTBY: Although we ran about six months, we lost more dollars than any show to date. And that got the *Times*'s attention. They gave us more space for closing than we ever got for running.

DAVID SHIRE: They did a piece in the "News of the Week in Review" about how *Big* lived up to its name as an enormous financial flop.

Originally we planned to open in the fall of 1995. If we had, we probably would have been all right. But instead of coming up at the same time as *Victor/Victoria,* we came up around the same time as *Bring in 'Da Noise, Bring in 'Da Funk* and *Rent.*

RICHARD MALTBY: There seems to be a sense that American know-how has not produced anything groundbreaking of late. Then these two little off-Broadway theaters come up with *Rent* and *Funk,* shows that have real energy and excitement. They get praised, and *Big,* a conventional book show, gets dismissed.

Yes, the world was hostile. Yes, the FAO Schwarz tie-in was attackable. Yes, the Tony awards committee behaved inexplicably. Yes to all of those things. Had *Big* been astonishing, they all would have been blown away, but we weren't good enough to counter all that.

Big was not a revival. It was a new show with a new score. It was entertaining and nice. But Broadway is no longer in the business of doing nice. We're in the business of amazing, of causing audiences to gasp.

• • • • •

JOHN GRIESEMER: Some time in late 1995 I received a call from my agent: "Tony Randall's National Actors Theater is putting on a revival of *Inherit the Wind,* with Charles Durning as Bryan and George C. Scott as Darrow. They want you to audition for the role of the jury foreman."

I knew about the National Actors Theater. It had been around for five, six years and done maybe seventeen productions. One or two had gotten good reviews, many had been creamed. But with Charles Durning and George C. Scott, *Inherit the Wind* might be the company's breakthrough. Also, I thought it was interesting that Tony Randall was producing a play he had once performed in; he played the cynical reporter Hornbeck in the original production some forty years before.

NORMAN BEIM: In the original production Paul Muni played the famed lawyer Clarence Darrow and Ed Begley played the populist politician and local hero William Jennings Bryan. I played Bill Snellings, one of the townspeople. All of us townspeople were given names, characterizations, and backgrounds, even if we had no lines, because it was felt that helped create an atmosphere and made us relate to one another better.

MERLE DEBUSKEY: The great moment in *Inherit the Wind* was the short-paced, emotionally violent scene when Clarence Darrow got William Jennings Bryan on the stand, cross-examined him, and broke him down. During the run Muni developed cancer of the eye. He left to have surgery on a Saturday, and Monday night Ed Begley took over the role of Darrow. How anybody could have switched roles and performed that intense scene in only forty-eight hours was really quite phenomenal.

NORMAN BEIM: Shortly after, Melvyn Douglas was brought in to play Darrow. The director spoke to Melvyn Douglas like a chorus boy, ordered him around. I was astonished. This was a man who had played opposite Greta Garbo. But Melvyn Douglas took it and played the part very well for several months.

No one knew when Muni would return, not even the cast. Then one night the manager went out in front of the curtain and announced, "Melvyn Douglas will not be appearing tonight."

The audience went, "Uhhhhh."

The announcer continued, "Instead, a special guest star will play the role of Clarence Darrow."

Charles Durning (left) confronts George C. Scott in the 1996 revival of *Inherit the Wind*. "George is the only one I have been awed by," said Charles Durning, "the only one who makes me think, I wish I could buy some of that."

The curtain rose. We townspeople were standing in the wings, watching for Darrow's entrance. A shadow appeared first, followed by Paul Muni. He walked to center stage and climbed to the top of the hill. Everyone recognized him. The place went wild.

CHARLES DURNING: Muni orated, gesticulated, and was very grand. But there wasn't an ounce of truth in his Clarence Darrow. It worked for the time. It wouldn't work today.

JOHN GRIESEMER: I arrived for my *Inherit the Wind* audition at Eighth Avenue and Forty-seventh Street in Manhattan on a gray, wintry afternoon. A bunch of actors, eight or ten, in a waiting room. Sitting at a table, the director and various other functionaries. "Sign in here," sit and wait.

Nice audition. Fine. They seemed to be politely receptive. Another day on the audition trail.

Three, four weeks passed. I didn't hear anything. I started wondering about the whole enterprise. Finally my agent called: "You got it."

I had been on Broadway once before, played the milkman in *Our Town,* pictured Lyme, New Hampshire, where I live in my mind. Now I told myself, Small part, a three-month commitment. Do it. You're not going to get on Broadway many times in your life.

Late January, I went down for the first rehearsal, way, way out on Forty-second Street, almost to the Dayline dock. Icy wind blowing off the river. You could see Jersey across looking dirty and snowy. Ahead of me a couple of figures were walking, all bundled up, carrying shoulder bags. *They must be other actors. Nobody else is out here.*

You go into the rehearsal hall. Right there the glamour stops. It's rats and everything else. This is a warehouse, an old garage. A big gas heater in the upper corner makes a huge racket. A couple of toilets are out back. One room out front is sort of the green room for the fifty actors in the cast. A lot of them know one other. A lot of mingling, bussing on the cheeks.

We learn that both George C. Scott and Charlie Durning won't be with us for the first four days. So we start working the crowd scenes, tedious work with fifty people, how to get on and off, how we move around. The rehearsal hall is cold. We sit in our jackets when we're not on. On a break, they crank up the gas heater and blast everything, and then it cools down again.

One day at the end of rehearsal, I overhear the director and stage manager talking. They're trying to decide when to bring in the live organ-grinder monkey. The stage manager says, "We have to work this out. We have to get the schedule exact, because the monkey costs us more than the actors do."

Not everyone in the cast was Equity. A lot were interns earning points. Because it was a nonprofit show, we were making top regional theater salary rather than Broadway minimum, something like eight hundred bucks a week for the length of the run. If the run got extended, we would get bumped up. Since there was a subscription audience, it was going to run no matter what. I knew I had a job for at least three months.

After a few days, Charlie Durning showed up. His character had to blend with the crowd. Having him there kind of galvanized everybody. He was very personable, affable, always of good cheer. Through all the ups and downs, he was an exemplary trouper. He set a tone that made it enjoyable for us to go to work.

George C. Scott came in the second week, wearing a nylon Detroit Tigers warm-up jacket over a T-shirt. He was cordial but a little distant. Clearly he wasn't well. His complexion was very gray, and he moved slowly. You could tell that he'd driven himself, put a lot of hard miles on.

But you could also tell how much of a theater animal he was. In rehearsal he would grab the lines and work. He was trying to get off book and often had trouble remembering the lines, but if his memory was not that acute, his sense of where he was and where he had to be for the best effect for the line was always dead-on. Terrific instinct.

At one point the director, John Tillinger, said, "It's not a matter of directing you, George. It's just a little more or a little less of what you've already got." George was a natural fit for that role, and he wanted to do it. He never floundered or searched; he just bore down on it.

CHARLES DURNING: George is one of the few male geniuses I have ever worked with, the only one whom I have been awed by, the only one who makes me go, "I can't do that. I don't know how to do that. I wish I could buy some of that."

Offstage, he is quiet and introverted. But at the same time he has more rage than anybody I know. And it works for him onstage. People come up to get him to sign autographs, and he dismisses them. He told me, "I don't like people."

JOHN GRIESEMER: You don't learn a lot working with George C. Scott. What he's got, you can't copy or learn in a class. Even when he was weak and tottering, even when he had his back to the house, he was still the figure you'd look at.

In late February, about ten days before our first preview, George came down with the flu. He was out. We would come in and rehearse more crowd scenes with Charlie.

We would get reports. *How is George? He got up. He's getting better. He passed out. He had to go back to bed.* What was going to happen with the show?

Tony Randall was producer, manager of this company, everything. He was also the understudy for George and the role of the reporter, the part he had played in the original production. Now Tony was up, walking the role for George, doing it, learning the part. We were still piecing the show together, but the opening date was doubtful, and there was talk about pushing the first performance back. There were all kinds of rumors on the street.

Then we moved into the Royale Theater on Forty-fifth Street and started doing the technical rehearsals. They were aiming the lights and fixing this and that, working on the crowd scenes with Charlie and Tony. George was still sick, not getting better. What were we going to do?

The day of the first performance, we arrive at around noon to do some run-throughs. Still no George, but we learn that he is now on an IV. Before he had refused it. Incredibly, this makes management happy. You've got a guy who is going to play the lead in a three-act Broadway play who is on an IV, and they're happy. Oh, my god, what's going to happen?

Tony was doing manfully, holding this whole thing together. A producer with his star sick, a huge investment in the balance. It was quite heroic. Some people think he's quixotic, but on the other hand he does this kind of stuff. It takes guts.

Night of the first preview. Supper break. Be back here in a half hour. We come back at seven-thirty, and George is there. He had gotten up off his bed, took out the IV, and came to the theater in his T-shirt and Detroit Tigers jacket. We go out and do the show with him to a pretty full house. There were a lot of friends.

It was pretty grim, really shaky, kind of like watching a corpse being reanimated. It was very difficult for him to move. He had to hold on to the steps. There were long pauses while he searched for lines. But he got through it. I think it was very important that he did. The average person wouldn't think of going to work in that condition, especially that kind of work. But George just ripped out the IV and came and did the whole play.

The next day was a Wednesday matinee for schoolkids, early, like eleven in the morning. George's contract stated that he didn't have to do such shows. We were ready for the audience to hiss when they heard that Tony Randall instead of George C. Scott would be playing the role of Clarence Darrow. But this was an audience of high school kids, and they all cheered. Then somebody said, "You know, none of these kids have ever heard of George, but they've all watched reruns of *The Odd Couple*." They were just tickled pink to see Felix Unger playing this lawyer.

Now George seemed to be getting healthier. It was amazing how he went from walking around a rehearsal studio in a warehouse on Forty-second Street with taped lines on the floor to performing on a Broadway stage with no transition, no chance to try on the costume, no time to get used to the space. We were beginning to get up a head of steam. But by the scheduled opening night he was sick again, and the critics were told not to come.

That night I headed to the stage door, passing by the marquee in the front of the building. I noticed early arrivals there, picking up tickets for the titular opening night. A limo was parked out front of the stage door. The door opened and one of our company managers came out with a walkie-talkie. He looked up the street and down the street, and then motioned to the alley of the stage door. Coming out, obviously dazed and weak, leaning on the arm of another one of the stage managers, was George C. Scott, in his Detroit Tigers warm-up jacket and T-shirt. He passed right by me, not really seeing me.

He was full of tricks, and the simplicity of his acting was something to behold.

Less than half a block from the marquee, where the crowd was starting to line up, George C. Scott was being snuck into a car. He had somehow willed himself to come to the theater. He had tried to go on for opening night. He was too weak.

They were able to cancel the critics, but they could not cancel the opening-night party at Gallagher's Steak House. The walls of the restaurant were decorated with show-business memorabilia, but the mood was melancholy. There were no critics. There was no George. Then Charlie comes in, and we all applaud, as is the custom for the star on opening night. He takes his party over to a reserved table. Ironically, there on the wall beside the table is a huge movie poster of George C. Scott as General George S. Patton, saluting the American flag. The guy who couldn't make it that night was right there on the wall in his greatest movie role.

A couple of weeks later George was back. The critics showed up. The reviews were great, like, "You don't get to see this kind of theater very often." Before, we had been this struggling, floundering show: George in, George out, from the sickbed to the stage. We didn't know where we were. But once those reviews hit, it was like going through the looking-glass. We were getting standing-room-only houses, standing ovations. *Inherit the Wind* was the same show it had been three or four nights before, but now we had become something great.

CHARLES DURNING: "I'll see you in reality," George would say to me as we got ready to go onstage. He was full of tricks, and the simplicity of his acting was something to behold. Being with him onstage, it was sometimes difficult for me to stay in the play. I wanted to observe what he was doing as an actor. He threw the words out like he wrote them himself. That's not acting, I'd think. I'd wonder whether he was ad-libbing or speaking the lines that were written. After, I'd go and check, and sure enough, they were the lines.

JOHN GRIESEMER: When George was healthy enough, he could be great. But there were the days when he was really under the weather, and he would blow his lines. One night he went up to the judge's bench and very forcefully said, "Do you mean, your honor, that you will not accept any expert testimony on Charles Darwin's *Design for Living?*" Everybody onstage gasped. The guy playing the judge couldn't believe the malaprop. He slammed the gavel down and said, "The court so rules." George immediately knew he had made a mistake, but he kept his poise and just barreled on.

After the scene ended, the director was livid. "*Design for Living,*" he shouted. "*Design for Fucking Living*! They should have let me direct Noël Coward's *Origin of the Fucking Species*!!!!"

We were all thinking, What's going to happen next?

The first time Tony Randall had to go on for George, he walked out onstage before the show began, wearing a maroon V-neck sweater and slacks. "Ladies and gentlemen," he said, "*Inherit the Wind* first opened April 21, 1955," and then he went into this long speech about how Paul Muni, who played the Clarence Darrow role, had gotten sick and was replaced by his understudy and ultimately with Melvyn Douglas. Back then, Tony said, the director told him, "You go out and make the announcement." And tonight, Tony told the audience, he was out there reprising his announcement that the star wasn't going to be appearing. Just like in the original production, another man would be coming in. Only that man would be he—Tony Randall. Then he added that because he'd had to make that announcement so many times back in 1957, the director gave him a maroon sweater as a gift. "And that is the sweater I am wearing tonight," he said.

What Tony did is perform a sort of bait-and-switch job. He was out there telling the audience that they weren't going to get what they paid for, and they were cheering. They felt they were part of Broadway history.

The cast stood in the wings, listening. "Wow! Wow!" The next night George was out, and Tony did the same bit, wearing the same maroon sweater, delivering the same vivacious speech, totally extemporaneous. And he did it again and again, charming the audience every time. It was a real bit of showmanship, and it became part of the play.

George functioned as best as he could. There were nights when I knew he really wasn't well, when he would look really drawn and peaked. But when he would get to the climax, bearing down on Charlie, making all those points and grinding, he summoned stuff that would just come up from somewhere. It would just roll to the back of the theater and roll right back. Oceanic. This was the same man I had seen a couple of hours before, shuffling in from his car service in a warm-up jacket and T-shirt. Where he got the stuff to do that, I don't know. But where he was really alive was onstage.

One night in the middle of the court scene where Darrow is trying to entrap Bryan, he holds up a rock with a fossil in it and asks, "How old do you think this rock is?"

Charlie gives him an answer. And George says, "Excuse me, ladies and gentlemen. I think I'm going to have to leave."

Someone in the audience laughed, but everyone else knew something was terribly wrong. George leaned against the judge's bench and said, "I'm going to faint." We all froze for a second. Then the actor playing the judge and the actor playing the bailiff jumped up, got on either side of George, and helped him off stage left. The audience began to rustle and mumble.

The stage manager in the wings got on the public address system and said, "Ladies and gentlemen, we are experiencing some slight difficulty. We will take a short intermission and then will resume the show."

At that, a voice from the rear shouted out, "No, no, we won't!"

It was Tony Randall, up in the mezzanine. He ran downstairs and in a flash was up onstage. "We're not taking an intermission," he said. "What was the last line?"

Charlie, sitting in the witness box, said, "Darrow asked me how old that rock was."

Tony grabbed the rock, took off his jacket, loosened his tie, and said, "How old do you think this rock is?"

It took all of forty-five seconds. One actor exited stage left, another entered stage right, and we were right back doing the play. Somebody told me that never had happened before in the history of Broadway.

By late April, things were on again. We were doing so well, we were extended into June. And then a scandal erupted between George and his twenty-six-year-old personal assistant, who filed a $3.1 million sexual harassment lawsuit against him. Paparazzi were all over the place, getting pictures of George. Everything crashed around him. He began having trouble with an aneurysm in his leg and said he would go out to California for a quick operation and be back in four or five days. But everybody knew he would not come back, not with the pack of wolves that were around.

After a long weekend, I came back to the theater and saw the signs. The Tony nominations were in. We were nominated for best play, and George was nominated for best actor. Nevertheless, though the show went on for another week, the box office went into free fall. They wanted to see George. Tony did not have the clout. The following week it closed.

• • • • •

MAURY YESTON: *Titanic* was three years in the making. Peter Stone, who wrote the book, and I thought the subject was very much the stuff of theater: the greatest and most indestructible ship on the face of the earth hits an iceberg its first time out and there aren't enough lifeboats; the movers and the shakers of the world, like John Jacob Astor and Benjamin Guggenheim, stand aside to put women in the boats. The *Titanic* held the dreams of every group on it: the immigrants, the new middle class, the privileged upper class, the believers in progress and technology. The ship hits that iceberg, and every one of those dreams goes down forever.

I had written the best possible music and lyrics I could, but I was a cog in a very big wheel. I didn't know how it would turn out. As our opening at the Lunt-Fontanne drew near, I thought to myself, Here we go again, for better or for worse.

• • • • •

MANNY AZENBERG: Some time ago I chose to do a play called *Einstein and the Polar Bear*. It failed. A major critic came up to me afterward and asked, "What did you do that for?"

I said, "You really think I did it because I hated it? I did it because I loved it." I still do. Plays like that aren't the real failures. The plays that you have no commitment to, that you produce for other people's reasons— even if they are smashes and make a fortune—those are the failures.

I've done three or four of them. Still, I'm thrilled that in the accounting of my soul it will say I produced plays with Tennessee Williams, Neil Simon, Tom Stoppard, Stephen Sondheim, Brian Friel . . . That's enough, and I was there.

The plays that you have no commitment to, that you produce for other people's reasons— even if they are smashes and make a fortune—those are the failures.

9 | THE X FACTOR

MORTON GOTTLIEB: When I was a student at Yale I would go to all the opening nights at the Shubert Theater in New Haven. One night in the fall of 1938 I saw Cole Porter's *Leave It to Me*. There were four names above the title: Tamara, Sophie Tucker, Victor Moore, and William Gaxton.

I was sitting in the first row of the second balcony, enjoying the talent and the great score, when this unknown young lady dressed in furs and sitting on a trunk started to sing "My Heart Belongs to Daddy." I was overcome. After the show I waited at the stage door for her to come out. "Oh," I said, "you were just wonderful. You're going to be a brilliant star someday." She suffered through my praises.

That Saturday night was the last performance before they went on to Boston. I went to see it again, I waited at the stage door again, and I told the young lady how wonderful she was again. We walked together to the hotel next door, where the company was staying. We sat in the lobby and talked for a while, and I gave her advice on how to conduct her career.

When, on November 9, *Leave It to Me* arrived on Broadway, there were not four but five names above the title. Already Mary Martin was a star among stars.

Decades later I was seated next to her at a posh dinner party in New York City. "Do you remember that we met in New Haven all those years ago?" I asked.

"Yes," she said. "You gave me advice on how to conduct my career. And I've been following your advice ever since."

MARGE CHAMPION: Mary Martin had that wonderfully crackly soprano voice, but what made her truly unique was beyond that. It was something in the face that asked, You want to know my secret?

She had a quality that I can't define, except to say that those who have it come onstage with a secret. I call it the X factor. It has very little to do

OPPOSITE PAGE

Something in Mary Martin's face asked, You want to know my secret? She autographed this photo of her in the Honeybun costume from *South Pacific* to Richard Rodgers: "Dick–See! You're my honeybun *today* and every *day*–Love Mary" (1949).

with looks, or even basic talent for that matter. You can train yourself until you're blue in the face, but you can't get it that way. Your name may be over the title, but that won't do it, either.

There is certainly nothing wrong in not having it, in being what I call a working actor/actress for your entire life. If you look back, you'll find many personalities that had it all—except for the X factor that makes for a Julie Andrews, that made for a Robert Preston. And they enjoyed great careers. On the other hand, there are those who cannot sing, cannot dance, cannot act, and yet they have that something that draws you to them.

You can have the X factor for the Broadway stage and not for movies; witness Ethel Merman and Mary Martin. They were not movie personalities, although they did get over on television extremely well.

Jim Dale has the greatest facility with his body, but there are a lot of physical people. He has that something else. Chita Rivera has it; Gwen Verdon has it. Carol Channing doesn't sing too well; she certainly would never claim to be a dancer. But she has it, too.

LEE ROY REAMS: I turned to Marge Champion, sitting beside me opening night of the 1995 revival of *Hello, Dolly!,* and said, "We will never see this again in the theater. We will have terrific stars, standing ovations. But not this, not this legend coming back at this age, better than she was before, with that concentration, that energy, that charisma." I was blown away.

LESLIE UGGAMS: I was popping up and down out of my seat applauding. Carol's comedic timing is the best. The woman is a hot ticket.

LEE ROY REAMS: Directing that revival, I had decided to do the play in a much more sexual context than it had been presented in the past. Dolly was living at the turn of the century, when women were repressed. She had had a wonderful time with this man who had died. Now she had to do something to earn a living, so she adopted and adapted his lifestyle. The only thing she had working for her was her sexuality, and with that she managed to snap up Vandergelder.

So I had to make Carol Channing more sexual. It had to be deliberate. We restaged "So Long, Dearie" with this in mind. It was angrier. It had more of a vampy quality. When Dolly reenters in the last scene, she just glares at Vandergelder, and we magnified it.

CAROL CHANNING: How did I feel playing to that New York audience? Like I feel playing to anyone. An audience is an audience. People outside the theater say it must be glamorous to be on Broadway. Yes, it is. But why is it different from anywhere else? All any actor wants is to be going into his next show. They don't care where it is.

LEE ROY REAMS: I'm sorry. The conditions in New York made it different. Although she'd never admit it, that opening night, Carol gave the performance of her career.

CAROL CHANNING: It wasn't until a year or two ago that I learned Ethel Merman was offered the original role of Dolly and turned it down. All I knew was Mr. Merrick told me he was going to have a musical version of *The Matchmaker* written for me. Thornton Wilder told me he wrote *The Matchmaker* about a woman he knew who had sandy hair like mine. "She was a tall, handsome figure of a woman, like you," he said to me. "You even look like her."

JERRY HERMAN: I had been told that I was writing a score for Ethel Merman. But when she heard about it, she apologized, "Please don't even make me come hear the score. I'll be very frustrated if I like it, because I really don't want to do another show. I've spent my life in dressing rooms."

The minute we met Carol Channing, however, we all realized *Hello, Dolly!* would have a much more unique flavor with her. She brought an unusual and now legendary talent to the role. There are other marvelous women who have played Dolly. Pearl Bailey was adorable. There was also Ginger Rogers, Betty Grable, Phyllis Diller. When Merman finally did it, she was magnificent; I think she was sorry that she did not take it on originally. But for me, frankly, there is no other Dolly but Carol.

CAROL CHANNING: How often in your life does a part come along where you have these wonderful songs and these wonderful things to say? I could do *Dolly!* every day of my life until I die.

CHARLES LOWE: After *Dolly!* had been on Broadway for seven years, Mr. Merrick asked Ethel Merman to come and play it. The night of the last show, Carol was playing across the street in the Abe Burrows show. She went over to see Miss Merman. The *New York Times* was there and asked, "Oh, Carol, won't you come backstage so we can get a picture of you and Ethel in her dressing room?"

CAROL CHANNING: All the press was there, and they wanted to take a picture of the first Dolly and the last Dolly before I went on tour. I rapped on the door. And Ethel said, "I'm not coming out." She wouldn't have her picture taken with me. It threw all the sympathy to me.

I said, "Ethel, don't be so dumb."

I could do Dolly! *every day of my life until I die.*

"There are other marvelous women who have done Dolly," said composer and lyricist Jerry Herman.

Clockwise from top left: Betty Grable, Ginger Rogers, and Pearl Bailey.
"But for me, there is no other Dolly but Carol [Channing]." (left)

During a break in rehearsals for *Call Me Madam,* Ethel Merman poses with some of the people who made it happen: (left to right) set designer, Raoul Pene du Bois; producer, Leland Hayward; director, George Abbott; authors Howard Lindsay and Russel Crouse; composer, Irving Berlin; and leading man, Paul Lukas (1950).

But she said, "Naw, I don't want to take a picture." So they took a picture of just me, in front of the theater, and that was what was on the front page of the *Times.*

CHARLES LOWE: That gave Ethel pause.

CAROL CHANNING: It did indeed. Anyway, we became best of friends. I adored Ethel. She was the funniest thing I ever heard, funnier than she knew.

JERRY HERMAN: I was devastated that Carol did not get the movie role in *Hello, Dolly!* My belief is that when someone makes such an indelible mark on a role, it belongs to that person. I felt the same way when Ethel Merman did not get the movie role in *Gypsy.*

JOHN KANDER: I had been working on *Gypsy* with Jerry Robbins until late in the afternoon, and when we got back to the theater, it was near the end of the first act. We stood in the wings and watched Ethel Merman singing "Everything's Coming Up Roses," and we could see the tears running down her face. When the curtain came down, she turned and saw Jerry. "See, I'm acting, I'm acting," she said.

People often speak of Merman as being on automatic pilot. Supposedly she'd say, "The show is frozen." I don't know if it ever got to be routine for her, but I saw her put her guts out there during the out-of-town time for *Gypsy*.

FRANK GOODMAN: *Gypsy* was her show. She got 15 percent off the top. She knew what she wanted and usually got it. She did not want Sondheim to write the music. "He's a protégé of Hammerstein, so let him write the lyrics," she said, and insisted they get somebody who understood her style. They got Jule Styne. She was comfortable with him.

She was a pro beyond belief. If a guy in the orchestra was off pitch, she would know. If a chorus boy started to step out of line, she would have the stage manager whip him through more rehearsals. She did not just play for opening night.

DOUGLAS WATT: Ethel Merman's voice used to go right to the back wall of the theater, for god's sake.

ELAINE STRITCH: She made a lot of enemies because she wanted to get it right. She was a selfish old broad. Still, it's a sin that they haven't named a theater for her.

Ethel Merman's voice used to go right to the back wall of the theater, for god's sake.

• • • • •

HARVEY SABINSON: As the story goes, when Barbra Streisand auditioned for *I Can Get It for You Wholesale*, David Merrick was late. Everyone was sitting around waiting for him to come in before they would let her sing. She was bantering with them, being very funny, with that Brooklyn-Jewish inflection that was so perfect for the role of Miss Marmelstein.

Then Merrick walks in, and Barbra starts to sing, and she knocks them on their asses. After, Merrick calls his people to the back of the theater. "If you hire her, it will be against my wishes," he says.

Later they were casting for *Funny Girl*. Anne Bancroft was the first choice, then Carol Burnett. All the time, Barbra's manager, Marty Ehrlichman—with the help of my partner, Lee Salter, and myself—was trying to sell Barbra. We were getting her more and more television shows where she was coming off as the amiable kook with that great singing voice and not the great lady she is today. Finally they gave in and cast her.

FRANK GOODMAN: David Merrick had called me with the news that he was going to do *Funny Girl* with Ray Stark, a big Hollywood producer who owned the property. Fanny Brice had been Stark's mother-in-law.

HARVEY SABINSON: But something happened. Merrick never did co-produce that show. One day he called me up: "Ray Stark is buying me out. He's going to produce the show himself."

"What happened?"

"Well, I guess that Ray felt his mother-in-law always hated him. And now that he's on the verge of doing this show, she will be looking down at him from heaven, and she will say, 'Ray, I was wrong about you. You are a great producer.' He doesn't want her to look down and say, 'Hey, David, you did a great job on this show.'"

FRANK GOODMAN: Once *Funny Girl* opened, Barbra was a star. After the show, there'd be crowds waiting for her to come out the stage door. Elliot Gould would be waiting for her, too; he'd pick her up in a white Bentley, like a chauffeur. Barbra and Elliot had first met in *Wholesale.* They lived together in a walk-up on Sixty-seventh and Third. She couldn't stand the smell from the fish market. He used to buy her a rose every day.

HARVEY SABINSON: I was working for Merrick then. So once he was out of *Funny Girl*, so was I. But I had plenty to do with two other shows that opened that season: *Hello, Dolly!* and *High Spirits.*

The stars of these three shows, Barbra Streisand, Carol Channing, and Beatrice Lillie, were nominated for the Tony that year of 1964. That was before the awards were televised. I was sitting at Merrick's table with Carol, and when they announced her as the winner, her husband, Charles Lowe, asked me to take her arm and escort her up to the stage. As we walked past Barbra's table, her manager said to me, "Hey, this is your fault."

I loved Barbra in those days. I talked her out of getting a nose job. "You're one-of-a-kind," I told her. "You don't want to be just another pretty face."

LUTHER HENDERSON: Barbra was difficult, although I don't know if I've ever worked with a performer worth their salt who was not difficult in one way or another. She had great talent and wanted to break through right away. She was very emphatic and strong, not afraid to take risks. She even took on Jerome Robbins.

FRANK GOODMAN: Even back then Streisand knew what she wanted and usually got it. She didn't have the weight and the power, but she worked very hard at becoming "the greatest star." Eventually Ray Stark had to give her more money, better billing.

OPPOSITE PAGE

"The greatest star," Barbra Streisand, with the man who wrote the music for *Funny Girl,* Jule Styne (1964).

MARVIN KRAUSS: When I saw Barbra on the opening night of *Funny Girl,* I said to myself, A star is born. No question about it. It was a great moment, seeing a very talented person who could do anything.

HARVEY SABINSON: Performing live was always a little terrifying for her. After *Funny Girl,* she never did another Broadway show.

• • • • •

CHARLES STROUSE: Sammy Davis, Jr., was the Sugar Ray Robinson of the musical theater. He did everything incredibly well. He was a real star.

I got to know him when we were working together on *Golden Boy.* I could see he wanted very much to be an actor, and when he put his mind to it, he was quite good. Primarily, however, he was a singer. So I, as the composer, was important to him. He liked my songs and sang them well. But sometimes he tended to fall into nightclub patterns, and I would tell him, as I'd tell any actor, "I really would like it better if you would sing the note as I wrote it," or, "I don't think you should hold that note so long."

Then he would become very impatient with me: "Please don't tell me the fuck how to sing." I always had the feeling that he didn't like me as much as I liked him, and I wanted him to like me. There was something about the situation where the only way we connected was if I was a little bit obsequious to him. That's not my nature, so there was always that discomfort.

Sammy always traveled with an entourage. His lifestyle and his needs were such that you kind of automatically fell into his world, which was one of late nights and never-ending parties. When we were working out in Las Vegas, we would often meet at four in the morning to go over things.

He smoked, he drank. To my mind, he was virtually an alcoholic. At noon, somebody would be slipping a Coke into his hand that I'm fairly certain was laced with bourbon. He'd go on doing this all day. Yet he was in great physical shape. His body was trim; he had superhuman stamina. Although I think the misuse of all that energy ultimately shortened his life.

He missed shows. When he showed up he was invariably late and often in a bad mood. But he never apologized. He'd become nice if I blamed myself. He wanted you to apologize for making him feel guilty. Then his laugh became too uproarious, and he became almost smothering in his interest, which I felt went beyond his real affection for me. It was like I was being brought into an orbit of the way he wanted things to be.

Sammy played in *Golden Boy* for two years on Broadway and toured it a couple of years. At the end of every show, he'd come out and say, "I don't know how to thank you," and he'd make this little speech of appreciation to the audience. People thought this was something spontaneous, that it hadn't happened before. Some guy would yell out, "We love you, Sammy." And that would set him off into this whole nightclub routine. He ate it up.

Sammy Davis, Jr., the Sugar Ray Robinson of the musical comedy world, on stage in *Golden Boy* (1964).

• • • • •

ALVIN COLT: Of all the actresses I have dressed, Tallulah Bankhead was something else. I did the costumes for her in a play called *Crazy October,* which closed prior to New York. Besides Ms. Bankhead, Estelle Winwood and Joan Blondell were in the cast. Quite a trio to costume!

I went to see Miss Bankhead at her East Side townhouse one afternoon. The place was darkish, with curtains drawn and a sea of ecru slipcovers. She asked me my name and upon hearing it said, "Don't be ridiculous, dahling, no one can be called Alvin."

Tallulah Bankhead. She was something else.

Miss Bankhead was to play a rather slovenly woman who ran a bar-grill and gasoline station somewhere in the Midwest. She told me she wanted to look very different for this play. She didn't want the audience to recognize her. There was to be no big slash of a red mouth, no Tallulah swinging hair; everything was to be as un-Tallulah as could be.

I suggested a red wraparound apron over a long-sleeved sweater. "Do put me in red, dahling," she said. "They won't look at anyone else on the stage."

But the apron was custom-made by Ray Diffon, and the sweater was specially dyed cashmere lined in silk chiffon. And when the curtain went up in New Haven, there was the old Tallulah, red mouth, flowing hair, and all.

The day of the fitting, she came in wearing a huge mink coat. A large woman named Rose, who was her confidante and secretary, came along. Miss Bankhead stepped onto a little platform for the fitting and dropped the mink coat. All she had on was a small pair of pink step-ins. "It was all I could do to get Miss Tallulah to wear those step-ins!" said Rose.

She had brought along her two Pekingese dogs, which she had clipped herself. They were the nastiest little weasels you'd ever seen, scampering, yapping, getting into everything. Their faces were full of threads and spangles. "Miss Tallulah treats those dogs something terrible," Rose explained. "You know what she gives them for breakfast every morning? A cup of black coffee and a package of Lifesavers."

Miss Bankhead had a television set in her dressing room, and every afternoon rehearsals were stopped while she watched her favorite soap opera. In New Haven the fire marshal at the Shubert Theater told the stage manager he would have to tell Miss Bankhead she was not allowed to smoke in her dressing room. To which he replied, "You tell her!" Truly, of all the actresses I have worked with, Tallulah Bankhead *was* something else.

• • • • •

MARTY JACOBS: Of all the memories I have of the theater, Helen Hayes in *Victoria Regina* stays with me. There must have been about fifty curtain calls that night. She was sitting on the throne, just exhausted. Finally she said, "I don't know about you people, but I'm going home."

What made her extraordinary—and I saw her in three or four different plays—was the fact that it seemed she was not acting, she was just being. It seemed so effortless. When I got to know her a little bit later on,

I asked what her secret was. "I just learn my lines, listen to the director, and do it," she said.

● ● ● ● ●

Ethel Waters with Julie Harris on her lap and Brandon De Wilde at her shoulder in *The Member of the Wedding.* "She was rooted in the earth of that character," producer Robert Whitehead said, "and I wanted her" (1950).

ROBERT WHITEHEAD: Ethel Waters had had some bad years during the war, even though she'd done many marvelous things on the stage. She was singing in this depressing nightclub in Detroit when I went to see her to offer her the part of Berenice Sadie Brown in *The Member of the Wedding.* She was rooted in the earth of that character, and I wanted her. I waited until she did her last set, and then we went to her rooming house and up to this shabby little room. "Mr. Whitehead," she said to me, "I have been on my knees by this bed here saying, 'Dear Lord, when are you going to get me a good booking?'"

And I said, "I've come here to give you a good booking." I told her about *The Member of the Wedding* and the part of Berenice. But she turned me down because she said that God wasn't in the play. It actually is a deeply religious play, but Ethel wanted God in it specifically. I couldn't persuade her to do it.

When she finished in Detroit, she had a booking in New York, and I got her to come to my apartment on Thirty-eighth Street. It was a spring night, and suddenly there was an earsplitting crack of thunder, followed by a crashing thunderstorm. We were all startled, but Ethel remained perfectly calm. "Everything is just fine," she said, because she had an inside track to God. And sitting there on a chair in my living room, she began to sing, "His eye is on the sparrow / I know He watches me . . ."

Suddenly I thought, We'll put that hymn in the play.

Ethel agreed. If God was in the play, she would do it.

And so, at the end of act I, Berenice gathers Frankie and John Henry onto her broad lap and sings that song. There's no musical accompaniment, just the pure voice of Ethel Waters. A beautiful and moving moment. It gave the act an incredible curtain.

After running for about a year in New York, we were back in Detroit, rehearsing to open at the old Cass Theater. Julie Harris's replacement for the tour was going on that night for the first time. Ethel had not been easy to work with. She felt Harold Clurman, the director, and I were a little square. She called us Humpty and Dumpty. Now I saw she was doing nothing to help this actress. "Ethel, please—don't just mark your place and drop the lines," I said. "Rehearse with her."

But she continued to ignore her. Then, in the middle of the rehearsal, she just stopped. She came over to me. "Since you're worrying, I want to tell you a little story from a Hoagy Carmichael song. All the animals in the woods were having a big party. They were frolicking in the sun and having a great time, except for a jackass who stood under a tree. The other animals tried to get the jackass to come down and participate. They said to the jackass, 'We're having so much fun. Why don't you become part of the party?'

"The jackass said, 'I'm happy just standing here in the shade. But don't worry about me. In the cool of the evening when the fucking begins, I'll be there.'"

Ethel was such a primitive soul, all instinct. You couldn't talk to her about developing a character and a role. She didn't want to hear all of that. And she had a terrible time with the lines. But when she got them, it struck something in her bloodstream that made her extraordinary.

BILLIE ALLEN: In the 1950s I was offered the opportunity to work with Ethel Waters in the revival of *Mamba's Daughters*. She was Brechtian, bigger than life, a force of nature, a geyser. I had heard she had affairs with young girls, and when we got together at the Empire Hotel, where she lived, I would always let her sit down first, and then I would take the chair closest to the door. I thought I was being very slick. Until she said to me, "I know you've heard a lot of things about me, and most of them are true. But I know when to, how to, and not you. So relax."

I picked up the script, and we started to work. She wrote out her part in longhand. That helped her to memorize it. She thought I was a kid, kept Twinkies around for me, which I dutifully ate.

Once she asked why I kept going upstage of her. I explained I didn't want to stand in front of her. "Big as I am, how is anybody going to miss me?" she said. She had just finished her autobiography, *His Eye Is on the Sparrow,* where I learned they used to call her Sweet Mama Stringbean because she had been slim and stylish when she was young.

At this time, which was before *The Member of the Wedding,* Miss Waters was down and out. Friends had gone or left her. She took a risk by coming back.

Once during rehearsals, someone began extolling Mahalia Jackson. I thought it was insensitive to carry on about this new phenomenon when Miss Waters was obviously not doing so well. But her eyes began to twinkle. "Yeah, I guess Mahalia sing right good," she said. "But I don't know about swinging the Lord's songs, you know. There's something very blasphemous about that. One day Jesus is going to see her walking down the street and slap the shit out of her."

And I thought, Amen, Miss Waters. She was nobody's fool.

● ● ● ● ●

ROBERT WHITEHEAD: Across from my office was the old Globe Theater, which had been turned into a movie house at the beginning of the Depression. They boarded up the original beautiful entrance on Forty-sixth Street and made an entrance on the Broadway side. We made a deal, took over the theater, redid the interior, turned the Broadway entrance with the lobby into a shoe store, and reopened the original entrance. We called it the Lunt-Fontanne, and in 1958 we brought in Alfred Lunt and Lynn Fontanne to star in the Friedrich Dürrenmatt play *The Visit.*

HOWARD KISSEL: I saw *The Visit* in Milwaukee after its Broadway run. It was the last thing I saw before I left for college, and it was from that performance that I got my understanding of theater.

I can still picture the scene where Alfred and Lynn meet. It's before you know what the play is all about. They are pointing to this deer that is crossing, and they say, "A deer," together in a fluttery sort of voice. It was orchestrated, one of those things that you know they worked very hard on. They had very old-fashioned notions. It probably was a little artificial, and yet so many years later, I remember it.

I remember the scene when the character that Alfred played realizes he's going to be sacrificed. At first the townspeople say, "Oh no, we're not going to turn you in." But then at a certain point, when he tries to get on a train and they stop him, he understands that they will. Then the townspeople and the train disappear. And he just kind of curls up on the floor and retches. I still can hear it.

Offstage as much as onstage, Alfred Lunt and Lynn Fontanne projected an inimitable presence and charisma.

I remember Lynn Fontanne's first entrance. She was wearing a red dress. I was a high school senior at the time, very naive, very impressionable, and I remember thinking her legs were tremendously sexy. Years later, I read her obituary and discovered that when I saw her, in the spring of 1960, she was seventy-two years old.

Once I met someone who had been one of her stage managers. I told him of this recollection, and he laughed. "Miss Lynnie was always very self-conscious about her legs," he said. What I realized was the Lunts took care of every detail to the *n*th degree. Lynn Fontanne knew exactly where that dress had to be cut and what fabric it had to be made of so that when it rippled, it gave the impression she wanted.

ROBERT WHITEHEAD: The character Lynn played was written as a cripple with a wooden leg, someone who was put together in pieces. That was Dürrenmatt's point: She was assembled by all the destructive forces of a rotted and rotting capitalism. But Lynn wouldn't play that. She was an actress and didn't want to get herself involved in that political thing.

The Visit is a very depressing play. In England everybody thought the play was so desolate we had had trouble getting a theater, and ultimately we ended up doing it in Manchester instead of London before bringing it to New York. There is one particular portion that is terribly cynical but nevertheless has a truth about it. After the hero is murdered and carried away, there's a chorale that informs the audience that now the village has all these wonderful things, like new schools and an opera house; Brahms is played, art thrives. It is devastating. I thought we should do it, but we didn't. Lynn didn't want it, and she influenced Alfred a great deal. They were both great actors.

One night during *The Visit,* Alfred got stomach trouble forty-five minutes before curtain time. An ambulance came and took him to the hospital. Lynn refused to go on. "I can't appear without Alfred. I feel shaky," she said. Meanwhile the theater was beginning to fill up. I told Lynn that I would go out and tell the audience that Alfred was unable to perform. We would wait ten or so minutes and anyone who wanted to could get a refund. "If half the house leaves, we'll cancel," I told Lynn. "But if the bulk of the audience remains, you can play it with the understudy."

There were about 1,350 people in the house, and only about 40 of them left. Lynn went on with the understudy, and he was very good.

It's one of those things. When an understudy goes on, the first night you always rejoice. He is a hero. The second night, he is not as big a hero.

When an understudy goes on, the first night you always rejoice. He is a hero. The second night, he is not as big a hero. The third night, the feeling is, When is that son of a bitch coming back?

The third night, the feeling is, When is that son of a bitch coming back? Alfred got out of the hospital fast. The next night he was on again.

I wanted to do a musical version of Giraudoux's *Madwoman of Chaillot* and thought Lynn would be wonderful as the madwoman and Alfred as the director and ragpicker. I took Bob Fosse with me up to their farm in Genessee Depot. We stayed there for a couple of days, trying to persuade them. Alfred was sort of interested.

We were talking to Alfred about the play one afternoon while Lynn sat at a table playing solitaire. Suddenly she turned over a card and calmly said, "It is really not my sort of play." No eye contact. And I knew that was the end of this conversation.

The Lunts spent their summers up at their farm. Alfred loved gardening. He was always bringing me peas and eggs and saying, "You can't do the theater in the summer." Lynn agreed. She admired my wife, Zoe, and warned her, "You must never act in June or July. You have to have a decent life. The people will come back in the fall." It was such an old-fashioned thing. It reminded me of the time when I first came to New York, how people would put white sheets over their furniture and go out to spend the summer in some place like Cedarhurst, Long Island.

I loved the Lunts and loved working with them. They were such professionals. Every moment was devoted to making something better. It went on at night, in the morning, all the time.

● ● ● ● ●

HARVEY SABINSON: My brother Lee was representing Walter Slezak when he appeared in *Fanny,* the first big hit produced by David Merrick. Ezio Pinza, the Metropolitan Opera basso, was the costar. Saturday afternoons, I used to hang around at the theater where both stars, when they weren't performing, would usually be listening to the radio—Slezak to the Metropolitan Opera broadcast and Pinza to the Red Barber broadcast of the Brooklyn Dodger games. Onstage, Ezio was this great presence, but offstage, he was something else. Once I was sitting with Walter in his dressing room while the opera was on. Pinza, about to make his entrance onstage, stopped in the doorway. "What you listening to, Walter?" he asked.

"*Don Giovanni,* you fucking peasant," Slezak said. "I only saw you in it ten times."

• • • • •

TONY WALTON: Zero Mostel was an incredible force of nature, totally unpredictable. He might jump into the audience or bounce on and flatten an inattentive actor. No two performances of his were ever the same.

THEODORE BIKEL: There was no stage large enough to contain him.

CHARLES DURNING: One day I was walking down the street when suddenly I was grabbed from behind. "I've seen what you've done to my wife!" Zero Mostel shouted at the top of his lungs. "This is a citizen's arrest." He shoved me into a six-seater Checker cab. The driver didn't know what the hell was going on.

"Where do you want to go?" he asked.

"Drive us to a bigger cab," said Zero.

He used to say, "They talk about LSD. I've been on LSD for years: lox, salmon, and Danish."

The incredible force of nature, Zero Mostel. Here, in the role of Tevye, he stares downstage at Bette Midler playing one of his daughters in *Fiddler on the Roof* (1964).

JOHN KANDER: I worked with Zero in a stock production where the director was very nasty to the kids in the chorus. Once when he was being particularly unpleasant, Zero abruptly stopped the rehearsal. He picked the director up by the necktie and said, "I don't want to ever hear you talk to a member of this company like that again." And that was the end of it. He had a sense of justice about him.

At that time, I had yet to have a hit show. But every so often, Zero would throw his great beefy arm around my shoulder and say, "Kander, I want you to do me a favor. When you get up in the morning, I want you to look at yourself in the mirror and say, 'My name is John Kander, and I'm a talented man, and fuck 'em all.'"

Some time later, after I had gone on to do three or four shows of my own, I reminded him of that. He loved it and went around telling everyone that he was totally responsible for what had happened to me.

TONY WALTON: At one time, Zero had been knocked down by a bus and towed for half a block under it. One of his legs was badly mangled and had been pieced back together with fragments from other parts of his body. It looked like an uncooked hamburger. When we were thinking up the costumes for *A Funny Thing Happened on the Way to the Forum,* we knew Zero would have to wear tights. And since Zero would have sweated even if he were standing bone naked in the Arctic, I designed a pair of striped mohair tights for him, which he loved. They were knitted with drainpipe–sized needles, resulting in a cool open weave, with the fuzz of the mohair concealing all the ventilating holes.

At the first tryout out of town, Zero took a massive deep breath in preparation for singing his first song, and balls of mohair went whirling up his arms and into his vast nostrils. He came choking into the wings, where I was standing, put his hands around my neck, and shook me up and down. We had to switch his costume to a kind of terry toweling that could absorb his sweat. And a fresh one had to be ready for him in the wings every time he came offstage.

CHARLES DURNING: I've seen a lot of people do Tevye, but Zero was the best. During the rehearsals for *Fiddler,* he'd often lapse into Yiddish. If someone said, "I don't understand you," he'd say, "Buy a book." At the feast scene he would bump bellies. He would mess up the conductor, slowing down "If I Were a Rich Man." He'd ad-lib lines like, "They were as poor as *synagogue* mice."

There was no stage large enough to contain him.

JERRY ZAKS: In the mid-1970s, when Zero came back to *Fiddler* for the second time, I played the role of Motel, the tailor. There was a scene where Zero was davening (praying) and I was following him around. He would say, "Just follow me."

This would go on for a while, until he felt the audience was ready. Then he would say, "What is it? What is it?" and whirling around, yell at me, "*What is it?*" Our first time onstage, I started to move. Zero whispered, "Don't move." I stopped. The laughter built and built. There was a lesson: You don't move on a laugh.

At one point, I had to get very angry with him as I said the line, "That's true, Rev Tevye, but even a poor tailor is entitled to some happiness." Zero would give me the cue and say, "Now give it to me, give it to me." I thought I was giving it to him as fully as possible. But Zero kept giving me notes under his breath onstage, something you're not supposed to do.

Finally, one evening I got up on my toes and went beyond myself. I was so angry I spit the words into his face. There was a huge pause, and then an immense laugh. I backed away. I thought I had overstepped my bounds. Then through the laughter and under his breath, Zero said, "That's it."

SUSAN L. SCHULMAN: Although people think of Zero Mostel as a clown, he was also a serious, scholarly man, very interested in Jewishness. It was important to him that he do Arnold Webster's updated version of Shakespeare's *The Merchant of Venice*. But as it turned out, *The Merchant* was one of those shows where if anything could go wrong, it did.

The director, John Dexter, was brilliant but also cruel. He would deliberately call the cast by Jews and Christians—the Jews are called at three o'clock, the Christians are called at four o'clock. That created tension. Zero was the only person who could control Dexter. He had greater power.

The first preview in Philadelphia, the show lasted four hours—too long. The next day, right before the matinee, Zero got sick and was taken to the hospital. The following day, he came out and dropped dead.

John Dexter said he had another star in his pocket. But he had nobody. Zero's understudy, Joe Leonne, inherited Zero's part, Zero's costume, Zero's hair, Zero's hats. But this perfectly capable character actor didn't have a prayer. You sat there and you saw Zero Mostel. *The Merchant* was killed by Zero's ghost.

• • • • •

OPPOSITE PAGE

Zero Mostel, wearing the infamous mohair tights, with Jack Gilford in the original Broadway production of *A Funny Thing Happened on the Way to the Forum* (1962).

CHARLES DURNING: Zero Mostel and Jack Gilford were two of our great clowns. Zero was outrageous, childlike and childish. He would try anything. Jack, on the other hand, was gentle and kind. Sadly, there aren't too many character clowns left in America anymore.

As a kid I worked as an usher in a burlesque house where I became enamored of the girls and in awe of the comics. Ultimately I got used to the girls, but I never got used to the comics. Only, they were clowns, not comics. A comic comes out and tells jokes. A clown can make you laugh just by your looking at him.

Zero Mostel and Jack Gilford were two of our great clowns.

I don't know whether it was my early exposure to clowns that attracted me to all the Shakespearean clowns I have played over the years, or the role of Archie in *The Entertainer.* I based my characterization of Archie somewhat on W. C. Fields, that kind of clown. Laurence Olivier said he based his characterization on a man he knew who was a sort of social clown and never really made it. When I saw Olivier do it on Broadway, I was so devastated I thought I wouldn't be able to stay for the third act. I was sobbing uncontrollably.

For years Archie was my favorite part. When he has that incredible breakdown, it can silence the house. He goes right from comedy to the singing of that spiritual, and it tears your heart out.

• • • • •

JOHN KANDER: Bea Lillie had a sad and lonely life; she had lost a son. But onstage she was a comic genius. She had instincts that told her not only what was inventive but also what was comically right. Once I watched her do a bit with a fur coat. She knew it was funny, but for some reason the audience did not laugh. She went back and did it again, and a third time, right in front of the audience. By then, they were practically in the hospital from laughing so much.

• • • • •

JANET GARI: My father would say, "There is no such thing as a bad audience. You just haven't got to them yet." Eddie Cantor loved his audiences as much as they loved him. He and Jimmy Durante started out together as singing waiters in Coney Island. They sang song requests, and people would always try to stump them. "How about singing 'Standing Outside of Lindy's Looking at the Cheesecake Inside'?" someone would ask. They would sing the title, turn about, mumble some nonsense, then face the person and sing the title again. If anybody complained, "That's not the song," Jimmy and my father would say, "You mean there are two of them?"

Eddie Cantor did the bulk of his work on Broadway in the *Ziegfeld Follies,* where he became good friends with W. C. Fields, Will Rogers, Fanny Brice. And then there was a twelve-year absence that ended Christmas night, 1941, when *Banjo Eyes* opened. The war had begun just a few weeks before and it was the first musical to open on Broadway since then.

A big crowd outside the theater waited for Eddie Cantor's family to arrive. There were so many of us, we took up two cabs. And as we got out, the crowd screamed: "There's Ida! There's Ida!" Then they counted, "One! Two! Three! Four! Five!" as each of my four sisters and I stepped out.

When my father made his entrance out of a rolltop desk, the audience cheered for a full five minutes. The love that went back and forth between them and him was palpable.

My sisters and I saw *Banjo Eyes* quite a few times. Daddy would stand in the back with us before his second-act entrance. We'd hear his cue coming up. "Daddy, for god's sake, you're going on."

"It's all right. I've got time."

Eddie Cantor in striped pants, Irving Berlin at the piano, and Flo Ziegfeld with members of the cast of the *Follies,* probably in the 1920s.

He'd wait till the last possible minute, race around to the wings, and come out onstage breathless. He wanted to raise that adrenaline level to what it had been in the first act. It was his little trick for keeping up the energy.

Before he appeared in a show he would always have a snack and then take a nap. When we would go to wake him he would say, "I'm too tired. Have . . . (and he'd name some ridiculous substitute) go on for me tonight."

He never became a living legend to himself, never took himself seriously. He and my mother would be all dressed up, ready to go out for the evening—he'd be getting some award or something—and they would come in to say good night to us. He would poke my mother and say, "So, Ida, what do you think of the little couple from Henry Street?"

OPPOSITE PAGE

Comedian Bert Lahr—he could get a laugh on a conjunction.

● ● ● ● ●

JOHN LAHR: Ironically, more people remember Bert Lahr as the Cowardly Lion in *The Wizard of Oz* than as the Broadway clown, but my father was a Broadway star for much longer than most of the comedians of his era. Long after the others had gone out to Hollywood, he was still starring with Ethel Merman or Bea Lillie on Broadway, and that was a much bigger thing at the time. In the 1930s there was a decline in live entertainment, and only the best performers were able to get work.

When he played opposite Dolores Gray in one of the last of the great Broadway revues, *Two on the Aisle,* my sister Jane and I would sometimes stay in his dressing room at the Mark Hellinger Theater. His valet, a former prizefighter named Earl, would serve us soda pop and Lindy's lunches that had been wheeled around backstage. The dressing room was dilapidated, but the clean tablecloths and silverplated chafing dishes made the atmosphere exciting.

It was wonderful to watch my dad from the wings, watch him control the audience, be able to hear the audience. He could get a laugh on a conjunction. "Dad, how did you get a laugh?" I'd ask him after a performance. "There was no joke there."

"I listened to the audience and they told me where the laugh was." I didn't understand it at the time. But now I realize that was the genius of my father and performers like him. They were so in tune with their audience. They had the desire and ability to corrupt an audience with pleasure. That is what I love about them. It is their gallantry for me.

10 | THAT'S THE CRAFT

ERIC STERN: In creating and performing in a play, there is a sense of common purpose, of living something outside of yourself, of hauling to one common goal. All these different artistic disciplines are corralled into one purpose, and in the process, incredibly strong bonds are created.

JOHN KANDER: There is a kind of classlessness in the theater. The rehearsal pianist, the head carpenter, the stage manager, the star of the show—all are family.

CAROL CHANNING: The thrill is the teamwork. You've got a Vincent van Gogh in each department: set designer, costumer, lighting person, director, choreographer, composer, lyricist, and on and on.

ALVIN COLT: I have often been asked to write a book about my backstage experiences. It could be called *Fitting Room Secrets.* But I never have. I don't think the world is interested in who has soiled bra straps or doesn't wear underwear.

My whole point of view has always been, If it's in the script, it should be on their back. In *Fanny,* Ezio Pinza played a former seaman, a working man in rather rough clothes. But on one special occasion, he had to be very dressed up. So I made him a gorgeous Sunday-going white suit, and the contrast was stunning. My first Broadway show, *On the Town,* was not a very spectacular show for costumes. But Nancy Walker, who played a lady taxi driver, was perfect in a taxi-yellow suit with a black-and-white checkered blouse. Right away the audience related the outfit to New York cabs.

Tina Louise wasn't too happy about a magenta color I picked out for her in *Li'l Abner,* because she had red hair. I changed it to tangerine. Lucille Ball's red hair became an issue in *Wildcat.* Her character called for very rough jeans, boots, brightly colored shirts, but all coordinated with her famous red hair. At one point Ronny de Mann, the hair designer on the show, said to Lucy, "I think I'm going to give you a hair rinse."

"What do you mean, a hair rinse?"

"Well, nobody really has hair that red."

"I do," said Lucy. And that was all there was to it.

When I designed the costumes for Eva Le Gallienne in *Mary Stuart* and *Elizabeth the Queen,* I was so fortunate in having the master artist Karinska to execute them. Both were fabulous, even though each weighed a ton. After one of our final fittings, Miss Le G. asked me if I could come up with something for her to wear in her dressing room. At the time I thought it a rather odd request, but as Miss Le G. was such a great actress and dear, dear person, Karinska whipped up a beautiful wine red velvet peignoir.

After each performance, Miss Le G. would greet her guests in the peignoir, but still in her full Queen Elizabeth makeup, wig, jewels, crown, and neck ruff. "My dear," she would say, "one mustn't break the illusion."

It would take her several hours to get out of all this. Then you'd see this little old woman emerge from the dressing room with her little Yorkie, Nana, tucked under her arm, and not for one minute would you think that a few hours before, this person had been Queen Elizabeth.

Costume designer Alvin Colt poses with sketches of just a few of his many creations.

IT HAPPENED ON BROADWAY

That extraordinary designer Irene Sharaff was working on *Candide* while I was working on *Li'l Abner*. The costumes for both shows were being made in Karinska's shop at the same time. Typical of Irene, she would sit there in the workroom, resplendent in black from huge hat to spike heels, watching that no one worked on anything but her clothes. But the minute Irene left, all the beautiful *Candide* costumes would be put aside, and out from under the tables would come Dogpatch. *Li'l Abner* would come to life from from five to ten o'clock every night.

How could anyone ever top what Irene did with the costumes in *The King and I*? What detail she put into them! When I was in Bangkok and visited the palaces and museums, I realized Irene really did her homework.

Costume designer Irene Sharaff in her ubiquitous black hat.

Costume designer Florence Klotz: "I planned on being married and having a lot of children. It didn't happen. I got this, and I never left. It hooked me."

FLORENCE KLOTZ: I was assistant costume designer for *The King and I* and saw all those gorgeous fabrics Irene imported from Thailand. While she was off in Philadelphia with an overlapping show, *A Tree Grows in Brooklyn,* I was alone in New Haven with Gertrude Lawrence, Rodgers, and Hammerstein. This was my first Broadway show, and it was a little frightening. Whenever there was a problem I'd run back to the hotel and call Irene. One call was made after I saw Gert bow to the king with her backside to the audience. Her skirt with its enormous hoops flew up, and to my amazement, I realized she wasn't wearing the proper period underwear.

HOWARD KISSEL: Good actors know the right undergarments change the way they walk. The last time *My Fair Lady* was revived on Broadway, they re-created the original costumes, but the women didn't know how to walk in them. In 1912 women walked very differently from the way they do now. You cannot walk in costumes the way you walk in jeans at the grocery store.

FLORENCE KLOTZ: The youngsters of today do not know of a girdle or a bra. In designing the costumes for *Showboat,* I had to put foundations on people who had never worn them. I had to explain that they must sit and stand as people of the period. If they felt constricted, that's the way it had to be.

Showboat goes from 1884 to 1927, and during that time everything changes: hair accessories, the silhouette of the costume, sizes of foundations and bustles, shoes. I designed everything, from the elaborate gowns to the jewelry, the buttons and buttonholes, the ties and suspenders. All my costumes are made specifically for each show. They are done in muslin first, then cut in material I choose and stitched together by hand. They're lined, inner-lined. Each performer I costume is individually fitted. I'm not a Seventh Avenue designer who makes beautiful clothes for a six-foot person who weighs a hundred pounds. I have to work with all kinds of bodies. If they have flab under their arms, they get sleeves. If their busts are too small, we pad.

Today the younger designers use a lot of nylon and drip-dry. But I still use silk. It does what you want it to do. What we're losing, though, are the people who have the skills to make the kinds of costumes I want. Their children don't want to be tailors, embroiderers.

ALVIN COLT: We used to have what was called the dress parade. Before a show went out of town, the director, producers—whoever was involved—would come to the costume shop and see everything on the actors in the sequence of the show. Every shoe and earring had to be in place. The hairdressers would be there. Everyone knew how they were to look. Unfortunately this is not done anymore. It costs too much, and there never is enough time.

FLORENCE KLOTZ: Your eyes will always go to red, which is why there is a lady in red in all of my shows. In *Follies* it was Alexis Smith. In *The Little Foxes* it was Elizabeth Taylor. In *Showboat* Magnolia is dressed in a beaded, very vivid red gown when her father sees her in Chicago after so many years. Glynis Johns told me she couldn't wear red in *A Little Night Music* because she's blond and fair skinned. I designed not just a red dress but one with many reds in it. She wore it the first time and the audience went, "Mmmmmm."

Opening night of *Follies,* I remember standing in the back while the spotlight fell on a very tall person in a black-and-white beaded outfit. Stephen Sondheim was beside me. He said, "I know what you're thinking."

I said, "Yeah, Florence Klotz did that."

And he said, "Yes. It will take a long time before you know that you are her."

Costumes by Florence Klotz for *Kiss of the Spider Woman* (1993).

I planned on being married and having a lot of children. It didn't happen. I got into this, and I never left. It hooked me.

JULES FISHER: I have always been intrigued with the way natural light was used in the theater of ancient Greece. They started a play at midday and went on until the sun went down. While today we can make use of a tremendous amount of lighting technology, if it's properly done, an audience shouldn't notice it. When you watch *Hamlet* you aren't thinking about the moonlight coming in the window. You're involved with what he's saying.

Oftentimes the quality of the light tells the story: the time of day, the weather, whether sun is streaming through the window. It can also help you appreciate what the actor is feeling, what the playwright wants you to feel. Any engineer can put a spot on someone. Lighting is not about function. It's much more about the mood and the emotion that the playwright and the director are trying to create. Our job is to support their poetic direction.

The first play I did on Broadway was *Spoon River Anthology*. It was unusual in that all the characters were dead. Each one sat on a stool and came forward to read a poem. There was very little interacting. From a lighting perspective, it was a chance for me to create a new world.

In *Hair* I used all kinds of light to create different moods and feelings. It was performed on a bare stage with very elemental means. The design was wonderful, because it was so simple. It had all kinds of 1960s icons: an Elvis statue, an Indian statue. I incorporated hints of the psychedelic lighting coming out of Fillmore East and rock-and-roll concerts. It wasn't sunlight coming into a room, but burbling colors, like the purple that people might experience coming out of a psychedelic trip. I was able to light the nude scene with a film image of a bed of flowers, a pattern projected straight down. All the actors were lit in this kind of ghostly but inviting pattern.

A collage depicting different wars was done under a flickering single strobe light, which made it very scary. Using a strobe light was not original; they were in every disco. But in a collage of war scenes, the effect was startling. Images of brutality were thrust into the audience's face ten times a second.

Over the past fifteen years, the trend has been toward the use of more sophisticated equipment. Where lighting was once controlled manually,

Lighting is not about function. It's much more about the mood and the emotion that the playwright and the director are trying to create.

now somebody touches a button. Computers are used to regulate sources of light, enabling us to have infinitely repeatable control. Robotic lights move, follow a person onstage. Lights can swing to one side and change in color and intensity, in form, in degree of softness or hardness.

There is reliance on visual technology. Whole sets lift up, drop down, and twirl in imitation of movies. If it's necessary to tell the story, if there's a purpose for the stage lifting up and revolving, fine. But if the story can be told simply, beautifully, without the over-reliance on technology, do it that way. Great theater still depends on the playwright and the actor—the words.

• • • • •

MANNY AZENBERG: Neil Simon has always said, "I want to make the audience laugh and cry within ten seconds, to show just how close those emotions are."

LINDA LAVIN: Neil Simon writes about family conflicts, the hidden secrets and the dynamics of resentment that come from guilt and shame and things unspoken, and the humor that comes from all of that. It's especially powerful to those of us whose parents and grandparents come from the Old World. They know about survival through humor. I come from that kind of a family: people who are funny and angry and driven and passionate.

CAROLE SHELLEY: Neil Simon can see immediately if you have something that he wants to use. He will take it, rework it, and use it. Vice versa: If you need something he has, he will take it from his inside and pass it on to you.

MANNY AZENBERG: In *Brighton Beach Memoirs,* there's a scene where the son sneaks into the kitchen and takes a cookie. The mother's standing with her back to him. She never turns around. The kid walks out of the kitchen, and the mother says, "Put the cookie on the table."

The first performance, the audience exploded with laughter. I didn't remember that as a funny line. So I said to him, "Did you know that was that funny when you wrote it?"

And he said, "Yeah."

He actually does know.

Broadway Bound is not one-half the success of *Brighton Beach Memoirs,* but in terms of the human experience, it is much more truthful.

Great theater still depends on the playwright and the actor— the words.

LINDA LAVIN: Neil Simon had cast every part in *Broadway Bound* except the role of his mother. I was told he was interested in talking to me about it. I read the play, and I knew the part was right for me. The mother was the center of the family, a strong, beautiful character who also had hidden dimensions of darkness. I noticed that by the second act she had disappeared, and the play was turned over to her son. But that was fine. The conflict the mother had with her husband was in the first act, and that was the scene I was really drawn to.

I was living in California. Neil came out to see me. We met at the Beverly Hills Tennis Club. I sort of dressed in character; he was in his tennis whites. We had a lovely breakfast, English muffins and coffee.

He knew my work from *Last of the Red Hot Lovers,* but I worried that he might think I was too identified with the character of Alice in the television series. "Maybe you don't want Alice to be your mother," I told him. "That might be the downside, but it might also be the upside, mightn't it?"

Playwright Neil Simon has always said, "I want to make the audience laugh and cry within ten seconds, to show just how close those emotions are." Here he is with Anita Gillette and Judd Hirsch rehearsing *Chapter Two* (1977).

He said, "Well, it might."

Later I read for him and the director, Gene Saks. Then they started talking about the play. Finally I said, "You know, I have to go home and make dinner. Am I going to be doing this?"

And they said, "Oh yes. Rehearsals start in late July."

MANNY AZENBERG: A few months before we went into rehearsal for *Broadway Bound,* we all got together to read the play. We were into the second act, and at that moment, I hated it. I asked the stage manager to give me a script so I could see how long the scene was. Neil noticed. He took the yellow pad I had on my lap and wrote me a note: "Don't worry. I know how to fix it."

Afterward we went out to have a bite to eat. Neil asked what we thought. Gene Saks said there was something wrong with the second act. I said I missed the mother in the second act. Neil said, "Give me two weeks."

LINDA LAVIN: Neil told me, "I'm going to write you a monologue. I want you to see her when she's happy." Soon after, I received twelve pages of script. It was the scene where the mother dances with her son as she recalls the highlight of her youth, the time she danced with George Raft.

Doing it was a soaring experience. It felt right. There are times in your life when your work and your life come together. Everything you are and everything you know come together in a burst of creation. That's what happened for me in *Broadway Bound*.

MANNY AZENBERG: Linda got the scene that won her the Tony. I got the note scribbled on a piece of yellow paper that says, "Don't worry. I know how to fix it." I put it in a frame and hung it on my office wall.

CAROLE SHELLEY: Neil was responsible for bringing me to America. I was the Pigeon sister with the odd voice in *The Odd Couple*. I did it in the play, the movie, the television series. But I also played Neil's mother on the national tour of *Broadway Bound*—an Englishwoman playing a Brighton Beach Jewish mother. I walked around stooped, my hands in my sweater. She got bone-deep in me. I couldn't get rid of her, couldn't get rid of the woman, even after the play was over.

LINDA LAVIN: If you do a joke in a Neil Simon play more than three times and it doesn't work, it's out. Neil gave me a wonderful joke: The mother has finished cleaning. The boys, being writers, write on little pieces of paper. They start looking for one, and they say, "Ma, where's that piece of paper that had that joke?"

"I threw it out."

Jerome says, "You threw it out? It was really important. I wanted it."

And the mother says, "If I kept everything you threw out, I'd have a cellar full of liver."

We did it, but the audience turned into an oil painting. "Maybe it's the way I did it," I said to Neil.

He let me try it a few more times; same reaction. "It's one of those things we thought was funny, but it just doesn't work," he said.

MANNY AZENBERG: There are few jokes in *Broadway Bound;* most of them are organic funny lines. But at the very end of the play, the mother describes the immigration process to her son. "You know, when my mother, your grandmother, came into the harbor and passed the Statue of Liberty, the men were praying, the women were crying. You know why, don't you?"

And the son says, "Sure, freedom, coming to the United States."

"No," the mother says. "They took one look at that face and said, 'That's not a Jewish face. We're going to have problems.'"

In *Lost in Yonkers,* Bella gets up and describes how she meets this guy. The family is outraged. They're hysterical. The brother says, "What does he want from you?"

And Bella screams, "He wants me. And I want him. And I want to have his baby. Please, Mama, let me have the babies."

And the audience is laughing and crying at the same time.

● ● ● ● ●

ERIC STERN: "Fuck the music. Sing the words," Jule Styne used to say. Of course, he cared passionately about the music, but he knew that unless the words—that is, the action of the drama—were clear, you might as well go to a concert. Jule would see an actor perform his music, and he'd adjust it. He was so unprotective of himself, so comfortable with other people's opinions. He was the ultimate collaborator.

MAURY YESTON: Two days after *Nine* opened, I got a call from Jule Styne: "Kid, I want to talk to you." He gave me all kinds of advice. I played the score for one of my early shows for Alan Jay Lerner. "You know," he said, "Oscar Hammerstein used to have me drop over every once in a while so he could give me advice. You do the same."

"Fuck the music. Sing the words," Jule Styne used to say.

Tommy Tune called me when he was having trouble with *Grand Hotel.* "I have a room with a piano at the Ritz Carlton in Boston. Come and save the show." Robert Wright and George Forrest, two beloved gentlemen of the theater who wrote the songs for the original movie version, were in town. I took them to lunch, we hit it off splendidly, and I grabbed an oar. Wright and Forrest said that meeting me reminded them of their meeting with Cole Porter, who lent them a hand when they were young. I'm very mindful of this great Broadway tradition of passing advice from generation to generation.

FREDDIE GERSHON: Frank Loessor did not just write *How to Succeed, Guys and Dolls,* and all those things. He helped get the financing for *Kismet;* he introduced Richard Adler and Jerry Ross to George Abbott, helped them do *Pajama Game* and *Damn Yankees.*

The thrill of teamwork on a Broadway show: Performers, producers, composer, lyricists, et al. for *On the Twentieth Century* gather around the piano.

For years Meredith Wilson had tried to get *The Music Man* produced. People said, "It's too hokey. Who cares about Iowa?" But Frank Loesser believed in the show and kept getting him auditions. Finally, he got Kermit Bloomgarden to listen to the score. Kermit brought in Moss Hart, with Kitty.

Moss could not bear listening to unsophisticated material, barbershop quartets and the like. Kitty realized Meredith Wilson was becoming dispirited, so she became a very good audience, and he worked to her. The next day Moss Hart said, "Mr. Wilson, would you give me the privilege of being the producer of your musical?"

ERIC STERN: When you create a show you create it around your cast. I've seen the best of them, and I mean the best of them, write and rewrite a song to fit a play the minute they see the play performed. Fifty percent of what happens in a show happens in rehearsal. The composer and the lyricist tailor the material to what they see people doing as they play the roles.

LEN CARIOU: There was a scene in *A Little Night Music* that called for me to do a kind of eleventh-hour song, but Stephen Sondheim was having a problem writing it. We rehearsed everything around it until there was nothing left to rehearse, and he still hadn't written the song.

Hal Prince, Glynis Johns, Hugh Wheeler, and I were in the rehearsal room working on the scene with the missing song. I said, "I don't think my character should say this because of the changes we've made. We have to find some other language." They all agreed. We improvised a bit, changed the scene into something new, and called Stephen down to see it.

"Thanks very much," he said. "I think that is going to help me. I think I'm finally going to get my song."

About three days later he came in. "I have the new song," he said, sitting down at the piano. I was licking my chops. But Stephen looked up at me and said, "Sorry, Len. Because of all the changes, it isn't your song anymore. It's Desiree's."

And he went on to play, "Isn't it rich? Aren't we a pair . . ."

I just stood there. "Send in the Clowns" was the song Sondheim was supposed to be writing for me.

Glynis Johns had never sung in her life. She had no vocal training. But she had a quality in her voice, and Stephen tailored it for her, very simple, very short phrases. I still think her version of "Send in the Clowns" is the best ever.

TED CHAPIN: Sondheim was writing songs for *Follies* even as rehearsals were going on. As production assistant, I was kept busy taking sheet music from him and bringing them to the music copyists. We were in Boston when they decided to expand "Can that Boy Fox Trot?" because Yvonne De Carlo, playing the part of a faded movie queen, was going to sing it. The song ended up being longer but not better. It had to be changed. "What is this four-note range that Yvonne has again?" Steve asked. And off he went. A couple of days later he handed me a lyric page: "I'm Still Here."

Fourteen changes were made to the lyrics of that song. They are as subtle as "I got through *three* commercials, and I'm here" changed to "I got through *five* commercials" because "through three" is hard to sing. A couple of days later he changed it to "I'm almost through my memoirs, and I'm here."

LEN CARIOU: I was with Stephen in his apartment, and he played "The Ballad of Sweeney Todd." He said, "Do you know the 'Mass of the Dead' in the Catholic Church?"

I said, "Yes, I'm a Catholic."

He played the first line of the mass, and then the melody to "Attend the tale of Sweeney Todd . . ."

It was the notes of the mass in reverse. That was a little conceit of Stephen's. I'm sure nobody knows half of them. He has his own private humor.

* * * * *

ERIC STERN: As conductor, I stand in a trench in a no-man's-land separating the audience from the stage. Life in the pit is a strange kind of insanity. You're somewhere between a disciplinarian and a cheerleader, working with overqualified musicians, trained to concertize, who are playing the same thing night after night. There's a Zen to it, a mind-set that you ride like a current. There are times when you and the orchestra are all together on a big hovercraft, just gliding along. There are times when the orchestra is just thirty cranky, angry people.

There's a good deal of humor in the pit, note passing and hand signals, eye and body language. For some shows, you have time to catch up on your reading. There are two huge sections in each act of *Carousel* where the orchestra does nothing. In *Les Mis,* however, you never put down your stick.

The audience is on the back of my neck, and every now and then I'll

> *As conductor, I stand in a trench in a no-man's-land separating the audience from the stage. Life in the pit is a strange kind of insanity.*

overhear a conversation. Once, at the beginning of a second act, a woman in the third row said, "This is the most awful thing I have ever seen."

Her daughter cried, "Mother, the conductor can hear you."

"Don't worry, darling," the mother said, "it's not his fault."

I try to never make it my fault. I put myself in the place of someone in the fifteenth row on the side who has scrimped for six months to take his girlfriend to see the show. I look for a moment, a different turn of phrase, a chord that sounds better if I throw my hand this way rather than that. I try to find a new joy once a week.

SUSAN STROMAN: Dance propels the plot forward; dance and direction have to be seamless. Time and place have to be evoked. *Crazy for You* takes place in the 1930s, a time when people danced together and in up-tempo. Ballroom dance styles were created, tap was popular, Charleston steps were left over from the 1920s. People danced because they were in love; sometimes dancing made them fall in love. The look was Art Deco. All that found its way into my choreography. And then we were lucky. The Gershwin estate allowed us to open up the music for dance. We turned "Embraceable You" into a comedy number. That was taking a big chance.

Casting is one of the hardest parts of the process. Five people have to agree. The girls in *Crazy for You* had to be Follies girls, all over five foot eight. The fellows had to look like normal guys.

HOWARD KISSEL: Casting is instrumental to helping you understand the play. If you cast it right, as soon as the actor steps on the stage, you get certain impressions that help you understand what the play is about.

"Dance propels the plot forward," says choreographer Susan Stroman, pictured here working up a number for *Big* with a young dancer.

In the Arthur Miller play *Broken Glass*, the part of a middle-aged woman was played by Amy Irving. A woman who looks that young and that good? This was 1938. A middle-aged Jewish woman living in Brooklyn in 1938 did not go to the gym. She wouldn't look like Amy Irving. The miscasting distorted the play.

LEE ROY REAMS: I knew Hal Prince saw me as a song-and-dance man. So when I auditioned for *Phantom*, I wanted to wear a mask. They wouldn't permit it.

Hal said, "My god, I didn't know you could sing like that."

I said, "For twenty years you never let me audition for you. How could you know whether I could sing?"

I still didn't get the job.

DOLORES GRAY: It took eight weeks before I could get an audition for the London production of *Annie Get Your Gun*. They sent Bea Lillie over from England, they sent Gracie Fields. No deal. Finally it was my turn. I wore a little black suit and a little flowered hat. I tried to play things down.

Richard Rodgers had produced the show with Oscar Hammerstein. "I'm sorry to ask you to sing, Miss Gray," he said. "I have seen you in *Are You with It?* but, frankly, I don't remember your voice."

"I do understand, Mr. Rodgers," I said. "Everyone was looking instead of listening, because I wore almost nothing."

And he said, "Touché."

I had sung about twelve bars of an Irving Berlin number, "How Deep Is the Ocean?", when he said, "That's fine, Miss Gray. Please come back at about twelve-fifteen, before the matinee tomorrow. I'll have almost everybody here."

I wore flat shoes, a brown sweater and skirt. I pulled my hair back with a little piece of ribbon, and I didn't wear any makeup. I had seen the show four times in a row and I knew it backward and forward, but I was scared.

After the audition Richard Rodgers and Oscar Hammerstein took me backstage to an office and called London. "We have just found Annie," they said.

FREDDIE GERSHON: We were sitting in the darkened Shubert Theater on a Monday morning, drinking Irish coffee from Sardi's, auditioning actors who had responded to an open call. Outside it was snowing, freezing cold. Mandy Patinkin had tried out for the Che Guevara role and just took over the stage. But we still needed someone to play the title role, Evita.

Then a young woman came onstage in a sweatshirt and dungarees, her hair tied up in a bun. She had arrived in New York on the red-eye from

I stepped back from the moment and just looked around the room. This was what I had always dreamed of.

California but was stuck out in the airport for hours because of the snow. Before a dispirited Tim Rice and Andrew Lloyd Webber, she crossed to the upright piano and took the page turner's chair. Standing behind it, with her hands gripping the top of the chair so tightly that her knuckles gleamed white, Patti LuPone sang "Don't Cry for Me, Argentina." And in front of your eyes, on an empty stage, with no sets, with no special lighting, she was transformed. Tim Rice said to me, "I'm hearing my words for the first time."

SCOTT ELLIS: I auditioned over and over again until I got a part in *The Rink*. I was one of six guys with Liza Minnelli and Chita Rivera. We sat in a circle and read the script while Kander and Ebb sang through the score. I stepped back from the moment and just looked around the room. This was what I had always dreamed of.

My whole life turned on that one audition. If I hadn't gotten *The Rink,* I would not have met Kander and Ebb, I would not have directed *Flora, the Red Menace,* my first show off Broadway, nor *Steel Pier* on Broadway.

Susan Stroman, David Thompson, and I came up with the idea for *Steel Pier* and brought it to Kander and Ebb. We couldn't get the rights to the movie *They Shoot Horses, Don't They?* So we created our own story.

I sat down with the actors and gave them all books, and we discussed the environment of dance marathons in Atlantic City. Then we read through some of the scenes and talked about the characters. My training was in acting, and that gave me a language to use with actors about intentions and obstacles and through-line and objective. I feel the most important thing a director can do is create an atmosphere of exploring and being able to fail. I'm not a director who says, "You do this."

JERRY ZAKS: I am a control freak. I hate stuff that's messy. I admire when stuff can be messy and still have an effect on me. That's a different school of directing.

JANE SUMMERHAYS: Jerry Zaks worked me into *Lend Me a Tenor*. I was off book when I went in, knew the lines, knew the role cold.

Jerry said, "We're going to get used to the words," and for the next three hours I underwent the most intense rehearsal I ever had. If I started to flag he would say, "Stay with me. Stay with me." We went through the entire play; we analyzed what was going on in the head of the character. "This is why you are doing it," he said. I asked questions. We tried it again, word by word. Intentions. Pace. Everything was orchestrated down to the beat.

"Don't think about it," Jerry said. "Do it. Do it. Cut out all the air spaces. If the audience has time to think about it, you've lost them."

JERRY ZAKS: There is such an emphasis on telling the truth as taught by the Actors Studio, by Sanford Meisner, that actors are afraid to do things with size and style, lest they be perceived as being too big. They are afraid to masquerade, afraid of being false. British actors are less apologetic about making externals real, about using props and gesture and voice to make a character. Real, for us, has gotten to mean small, earnest. One of the greatest fallacies ever foisted upon an acting student is the need to maintain constant eye contact. Take any scene in life and see how often people are really looking each other in the eyes.

One of the hardest things about directing is knowing when you have started to tell your own story at the expense of the author's story. Because, as Oscar Wilde said, you fall in love with your babies. Larry Gelbart wanted me to cut a bit of business in *A Funny Thing Happened on the Way to the Forum.* "Kill your darlings," he said. He was right. But it was hard.

I had seen Phil Silvers do *Forum* in 1972. I remember him getting a big laugh with a courtesan on his lap, down left. I remember Nancy Walker working a little harder than she had to. But it was funny. I stood in the back and laughed out loud a lot. Years later I read the script and thought it as funny a script as I'd read in my life. I had to do it.

TONY WALTON: When I signed on to do *Forum* with Jerry Zaks, I got my ancient portfolio out to give him an idea of the designs I had made for the original 1962 production. The first thing that emerged was a little rough drawing suggesting a three-dimensional, sculptural, and carved clown-town set. The look I had ultimately settled on was more flat and vaudevillian. Jerry looked at the drawing. "You mean that was your absolutely first instinct? Why don't we go with that?"

The 1996 production of *Forum* was a sort of *Twilight Zone* experience. I had started afresh with new costume sketches, and all through the fittings—especially for the gorgeous courtesans—I was conscious of my twenty-something self watching this grizzled geezer mucking about with his original designs, and I could feel him saying, "What on earth do you think you're doing?"

"Well," mumbled my current self, "I hope we've learned a little something in thirty-five years, young fella. After all, we've collaborated with talents such as Willa Kim, Pat Zipprodt, and William Ivey Long—among others. I certainly hope *something* has rubbed off!"

JERRY ZAKS: The notion of casting *Forum*—Nathan Lane was the obvi-

Set and costume designer Tony Walton had a twilight zone-type experience working on the 1996 production of *A Funny Thing Happened on the Way to the Forum* as he had done the sets and costumes for the original production in 1962.

ous choice to play Pseudolus—staging it, having Tony Walton design it, all were totally nondaunting and exhilarating. What I lost sleep over was "Comedy Tonight," the song that saved the show originally.

We wanted to do our own version but didn't know what we wanted it to be. Then I thought how the whole point was that this evening was being presented by a group of actors who perform both comedy and tragedy but are much more comfortable with comedy. Somewhere I had the image of seeing Nathan's face in reaction to this situation.

I said to Tony, "Here's my idea. They're singing, 'Open up the curtain, open up the curtain . . .' The curtain goes up, only it's tragedy, a scene from *Medea*." Tony went crazy; he had so much fun with that.

I went to the producers. "We'll get as big a laugh as has ever been heard on a Broadway stage."

Producers! "Uh, how much will this curtain cost? How much will the scenery cost? Are we going to only use it once?"

We don't know. Nobody knows. All you do is follow your heart.

We did it, and it got us five laughs. The company sings, "Open up the curtain . . . ," and the curtain rises on a frantic, wailing scene from *Medea.* The curtain comes down: first laugh. Nathan doesn't move; he stands frozen at the curtain: second laugh. Nathan does a slow take-out at the audience as if to say, *What was that all about?*: third laugh. Nathan starts to say something and goes back to the curtain: fourth laugh. Nathan comes back out to the audience with a sheepish smile. In previews this didn't get a laugh. Nathan added an apologetic giggle: fifth laugh.

Everything in my production of *Forum* was structured to within an inch of its life. That earns you the right to discover happy accidents. Nathan ad-libbed. He would use latecomers all through the evening: "Oh, you've missed the opening number. Wait a minute, I'll do it again." And he'd do the whole thing in thirty seconds.

At the end of the play when he yelled, "The plague! The plague! Run for your lives." He'd point to the latecomers. "Not you. You came in late."

The lights would come down on *Forum,* and I'd hear this roar. It was almost sexual—forgive me, it was the roar of people who had been satisfied in a big way. After my internist saw the show, he wrote me a letter: "You're as much of a healer as I am."

I've done so much comedy, and it never fails. I hear the sound of laughter, and I hear the sound of people falling in love.

I went to the producers. "We'll get as big a laugh as has ever been heard on a Broadway stage."

• • • • •

FREDDIE GERSHON: We had recorded the score for *Evita,* and the album soared. It was a huge, huge hit. As a musical play, however, it had no form or substance. It was just this record album.

And then Hal Prince got involved, and *Evita* was invented. It was Hal who transformed a four-hour concert piece into a coherent two-hour musical play. How do you tell the story of the five-year rise of Juan Perón from colonel to general to dictator? Hal Prince told it in two minutes, in a number with a group of men playing musical chairs. The last man in the last chair is Perón.

How do you tell the story of the five-year rise of Evita, who screwed her way to the top? Hal Prince told it in two minutes, in a number with a revolving door. A cheap-looking woman goes through a revolving door on the arm of an undistinguished man. When she comes around, she's better dressed and on the arm of a more important-looking man. She keeps going through the revolving door, each time emerging better dressed, better coiffured, with bigger jewels and more glamorous furs. On the last go-around, she emerges on the arm of a general, who introduces her to Perón.

• • • • •

JAMES HAMMERSTEIN: Josh Logan directed *South Pacific,* a two-and-a-half-hour musical, in a four-, five-day run-through. It would have taken another director three weeks. He had everybody running. In *Mr. Roberts,* he redirected a scene with twenty-seven people onstage in twenty-five minutes. Tearing us all apart, he changed everybody's business. He took a piece of business I invented and gave it to another actor.

Logan was a manic-depressive. When you got him on the way up, you could feel him throwing his energy to the actors. You could feel his nerves vibrating. "I direct a scene totally honestly," he said. "If it doesn't work I put nerves underneath that scene. If it still doesn't work, I go to the author and say, 'Rewrite it.'"

George Abbott—actor, writer, director, producer—died at the age of 107. He had his last hit when he was 96. He was austere, honest, objective. You would refer to him as "Misterabbottsir"—one word. After

George Abbott, if you worked for another director, you had too much free time.

I was stage manager for *Damn Yankees*. We were on the road. Gwen Verdon stops the show with "Whatever Lola Wants." Ray Walston comes out afterward. He's supposed to say, "What a flop!" which always gets a tremendous laugh. But this time he takes his handkerchief and hits it on the ground three times in imitation of Lola. There's a deathly hush, and he dies like a dog.

At the note session, Abbott, like usual, shows no emotion. He gives notes like he's reading the telephone directory. Then he comes to Walston. "Oh, Ray, try hitting your handkerchief on the ground five times instead of three."

Well, of course, it stopped the show.

HOWARD KISSEL: Abbott would say, "Walk three steps downstage. Pause. Say the line." That was mechanical. And yet, they knew if they took three steps downstage, they'd get the laugh.

ELAINE STRITCH: "Mr. Abbott," I said during a rehearsal for *On Your Toes,* "I'm so bored coming into the room with high heels, a mink stole, a bag and gloves, taking them off, and throwing my fur scarf on the sofa and saying, 'Hello, darling.'"

"Get an umbrella," he said.

On my lunch break, I ran over to Saks and got the tightest, chicest umbrella. And after that, I never played a scene in that show without my umbrella. It was magic. Anytime I got mad at anybody, I raised the umbrella. Everyone was scared to death of me.

BARRY NELSON: George Abbott had no patience for actors who asked why they had to walk upstage instead of downstage.

HARVEY SABINSON: At a production meeting, the designers were explaining the set. "We're going to use a Persian rug here; the carpet will be green with floral patterns . . ." Mr. Abbott let them go on for a while until finally, looking very bored, he said, "Hold it, hold it. Just tell me one thing: Where are the doors?"

JOHN KANDER: Opening night, if the show was a hit, Mr. Abbott would have a glass of wine, dance with his favorite chorus girl, and celebrate. If the show was a flop, he'd have his glass of wine, dance with his favorite chorus girl, and say, "Well, this time it didn't work."

• • • • •

OPPOSITE PAGE

At the rehearsal of *Fiddler on the Roof:* (left to right) lyricist Sheldon Harnick, producer Hal Prince, and director/choreographer Jerome Robbins (1964).

MORTON GOTTLIEB: My uncle Jacob Oppenheimer owned the Lyric Theater on Forty-second Street, and when I was five years old, I saw the Marx Brothers in *Cocoanuts* there five times. After each performance I went backstage and told Groucho how to improve his act. I guess being a nervy kid equipped me to become a producer.

My producing partner was Helen Bonfils, the richest woman in America. She owned the *Denver Post* and one-third of the land in Denver. We began with Noël Coward's *Sail Away.* Helen put in $400,000, which was a lot of money for a musical then. But I saved her $100,000 by getting $50,000 from the Cunard Line for putting their name on the hats of the chorus guys and $50,000 from American Express for using their name. I was always very cheap.

I put my experience to good use in 1966 when I brought *The Killing of Sister George* over from England. I convinced the Shuberts to let me have the Belasco Theater and pay no rent until we recouped our investment. It had been open only one night in the past two years anyway. I made a deal to pay all the operating costs, and I got the cooperation of the union to do the one-set play with just three house stagehands.

No one thought it had a chance here because it was about lesbians. The critics panned it, but that didn't stop us. Since there was a lot of curiosity and we kept the costs way down, we ran through the season. We got our money back, and we paid off. The following season the play toured all across America, with Claire Trevor playing the lead. We were a big hit, and we did it all with pennies.

LEE ROY REAMS: Everyone thinks to be in the theater you have to have such an ego. I think you have to have a lack of ego to be up there. You're constantly receiving rejection, constantly being judged and criticized. To succeed, you have to be passionate about your work. And it's that commitment that makes us so verbal and indulgent in the craft.

BARRY NELSON: Many players do not go on in the business because they don't have the resilience. They have the sensitivity, but they can't take the blows.

LEN CARIOU: Actors are like athletes. They must work or they atrophy pretty quickly.

BETTY BUCKLEY: Doing *Sunset Boulevard,* my entire life was about maintenance: a voice teacher once a week, physical therapy twice a week, a trainer every day for one to two hours, massage therapy a few times a week, manicures, pedicures. When I'm in a show, I'm in constant training.

SHIRLEY VERRETT: You don't know what work is until you've been on Broadway: exercising, yoga classes, keeping the body in shape. I rehearsed more for *Carousel* than I ever did in the opera; we had rehearsals every day. Nicholas Hytner kept saying, "Repetition, repetition. Seventy-five times a day. Repeat, repeat, until you can recite it when you're brushing your teeth."

I always knew that one day I would make the switch from the opera world to Broadway. And sure enough, one day Roz Starr, the celebrity sleuth who had been following my career for years, called my management and made the introductions that got me into *Carousel*. I had always loved the music. The story was so sad, and in the 1994 revival, it was even sadder. That was what made me get into it, it had the dramatic vitality I sometimes found lacking in opera.

It was quite a change, coming from a world where I was always the star, where tickets were sold by my name, to a part that had me come onstage about five times, with not much to say and only two major songs to sing. Broadway was a different kind of life for me. But I began to find a life within that life.

I tried to fit in, not to do anything operatic. I even tried to keep "You'll Never Walk Alone" simple. A lot of people coming from the opera would say, "This is what I can do; I'll blast the roof off." But I understood it was part of the play, and I wanted to be an ensemble player. It was not until two months after opening night that I took chances, started to play with things, do things with my body, change an accent on a word when singing, take a breath in a different place.

ELAINE STRITCH: As I am in the autumn of my life, I am finally able to say that it is the work that satisfies. It is in the moment. A movie star doesn't hear a "Bravo" from the seventh row. I have gone back and forth from musical theater to straight plays. One year I did Noël Coward's *Sail Away,* and the next year I did *Who's Afraid of Virginia Woolf?* I went straight from *Showboat* to *A Delicate Balance.* It's a kick for me to do everything.

Still, I must admit that preparing for a play is such a difficult adventure that every time I wonder why in God's name I choose to do this. It's my version of nine months of a difficult pregnancy: morning sickness and evening tears, misunderstandings, a long, long trip.

BARRY NELSON: The first couple of weeks are deadly, with everybody

Broadway was a different kind of life for me. But I began to find a life within that life.

learning the lines, bumping into one another. There's always doubt about whether the show has any chance of success.

ELAINE STRITCH: You're up in your hotel room, and you say, "I'll never be able to do that again." And then you slap your knuckles, and you get up, and you get dressed, and you vocalize, and you get some exercise, and you put on a nice-looking rehearsal outfit, and you get over there. Surprise, surprise, everybody goes, "Yea!"

HOWARD KISSEL: Bob Whitehead, the last of the great producers, told me the way Zoe Caldwell prepared for *Master Class*. She got to the theater at five-fifteen. She then took off her clothes and slowly put on each article of clothing, from the bottom up, as if it was Maria Callas's clothing. By seven-thirty, a half hour before the curtain, when she would go to greet the other actors, she was in the character of Callas.

JANE SUMMERHAYS: The house opens. The squawk box goes on: "Ladies and gentlemen, a half hour!" You start gearing up. Sometimes there's fatigue. You think, How am I going to do this? Then you hear sounds of the theater filling up, the orchestra warming up, and you perk up. Before you know it, there's the five-minute call, and then the overture.

JERRY ZAKS: Openings are your springboard. We had three openings for *Anything Goes* before I realized that I'd had two too many. What we kept was a scratchy recording of Cole Porter singing, "In olden days a glimpse of stocking . . . ," in the dark. The record would fade out, and the orchestra would swell up: "NOW HEAVEN KNOWS . . ." Goose bumps.

CAROL CHANNING: Onstage, you just have to tell the absolute truth about the character you are playing. You hope you communicate it, and you hope it comes back like a tennis ball. If you're listening to the sound of your own voice, nobody else is. The audience knows, and they freeze on you.

ELAINE STRITCH: Onstage, nothing is as important as truth, nothing. As soon as you lie, they know it.

BARRY NELSON: The fun for me is knowing what the other person is saying and what my character would be thinking at that time. On the stage you get the chance to do all that, to analyze and build a part, to react, to contribute something no one else can—not the author, not even the director.

DOLORES GRAY: You must keep it fresh every night. People pay a lot of money, and you've got to give them your best. You better be good or else you can get the hell out of the business.

Onstage, nothing is as important as truth, nothing. As soon as you lie, they know it.

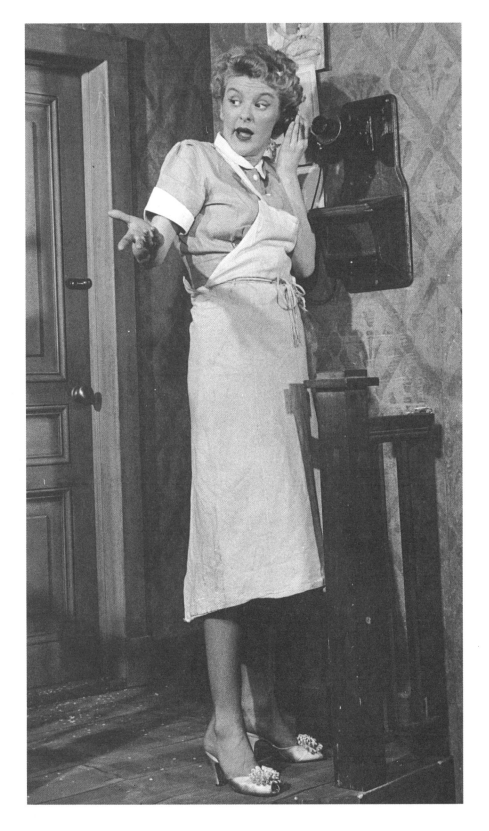

An original and true "Broadway Baby," Elaine Stritch pictured here in *Bus Stop*.

Sometimes the audience is just leaden. And you walk off the stage and say, "Well, we broke our little butts tonight but they didn't get it." But when they've liked it, the curtain calls are the thrill of a lifetime. Every time.

JOAN FONTAINE: Performing on Broadway is confining, demanding, relentless, day in and day out. You have to go on, whether you have a cold or are exhausted or your husband has just left you. While I was in *Tea and Sympathy,* I didn't dare read a book or see a movie. I had to concentrate completely on the character so that no other character would come into my ken and dilute my performance.

CAROL CHANNING: All I want to do is keep working. I don't know anyone in the theater who doesn't. Theater people never stop to realize how much they have surmounted. When Alfred Lunt died and they dimmed the lights in theaters all over the world, Lynn Fontanne told me, "Alfred would have been amazed." I knew what she meant. When you're doing a job, you're totally unaware of how it stands in relationship to the rest of the world.

Never for a split second did I think how wonderful it was to be on Broadway. What I thought was, I've got a job to do here, and I'm going to lose the audience any second unless I communicate this marvelous show to them. It's a big, big responsibility.

LOUISE LASSER: Sandy Meisner was right. It's not when you feel like doing it. It's when you don't. That's the craft.

ELAINE STRITCH: I was standby for Ethel Merman in *Call Me Madam.* "Standby" is a chic way of saying "understudy." All I had to do was call in every night: "Is Ethel all right?" She always was.

Then I was offered the part of Melba Snyder, the newspaper reporter, in the 1952 revival of *Pal Joey.* I always wanted to play Melba because she gets to sing "Zip, " a knockout, stop-the-show song. I went to Leland Hayward, the producer of *Call Me Madam:* "If Ethel gets sick, my first respects will be to you."

He said fine.

I went to Jule Styne, who was coproducing *Pal Joey* with Richard Rodgers: "If Ethel gets sick, I'll have to go over to her theater and do her part."

He agreed.

We rehearsed. We rehearsed. We were going to go on cold in New York. Then Richard Rodgers comes in, sees a run-through, and says, "We have to go out of town."

I get a driver. We time the ride from New York to New Haven. The "Zip" number performs at 10:00. At 7:30, I go to Ethel Merman's dressing room, knock on the door. She says, "Get outta here." I get in the car at twenty-five of 8:00. Twenty-five of 10:00 I arrive at the theater in New Haven, go in the back door all made up. Get out onstage, sing "Zip! Walter Lippmann wasn't brilliant today / Zip! Will Saroyan ever write a great play?"

For a week, it was: Knock on the door. "Get outta here."

Get in the car. New Haven. "Zip! Walter Lippmann . . ."

Get in the car. Back to New York.

Next night: Knock on the door. "Get outta here."

Get in the car. New Haven. "Zip! Walter Lippmann . . ."

Get in the car. Back to New York.

Next night: Knock on the door. "Get outta here."

Get in the car. New Haven. "Zip! Walter Lippmann . . ." It was like a Sondheim song.

Then it's opening night in New Haven, and there's a snowstorm the likes of which you have never seen. I call Ethel. "Get outta here," she says.

No driving through this snowstorm. I get on the 7:30 train to New Haven, but it sits in Penn Station. I've blown it. This is the disappointment of my life, having my understudy go on for me in a big musical like *Pal Joey*.

Finally, at 8:15, we pull out of the station. I put on my makeup on the train, have a couple of brandies to fortify myself. We arrive in New Haven at 10:01.

I go out carrying my little suitcase. There's a line waiting for cabs. I get into a car. I don't know whose car it is. It could've been Jack the Ripper's. I say to the driver, "I have to go the Shubert Theater right now, pronto."

He says, "You're crazy."

"I haven't got a gun," I tell him. "But if I had one, I'd put it in your back. Take me to the Shubert Theater."

He drives me to the theater. "Write your name down on this piece of paper," I tell him. "You've got tickets for *Pal Joey* tomorrow night."

I get out of the car. I'm wearing a fur coat, a Dior suit, and boots. All pretty good for the part, except for the boots. I walk through the stage door. I can hear Helen Gallagher singing, "In the flower garden of my heart . . . ," from the song that precedes my entrance.

It's not when you feel like doing it. It's when you don't. That's the craft.

My understudy is in the wings. I say, "Give me your shoes." She wore a nine, I wore a seven. I looked like Minnie Mouse. Who gave a shit?

I walk out and say, "Hello." Suddenly I'm Melba the reporter. I sit down with Harold Lang, play the scene, sing "Zip," get eighteen curtain calls.

I was twenty-something. At that age, what's the trick? I had energy up the wazoo.

More than thirty-five years later, I'm playing Parthy in *Showboat,* and a twenty-something woman who's in a scene with me passes by my dressing room. "Oh, Miss Stritch," she says, "I'm not going on tonight."

OPPOSITE PAGE

At home in an empty theater,

George Abbott enjoys a moment

of repose.

"What's the matter, dear?"

"I have a headache."

"Oh, I'm so sorry. But why aren't you going on?"

"I'm confused," she says.

"I'll say you are," I tell her. "Let me straighten you out. You don't stay out of a Broadway show because you have a headache. You go on with your headache, and you know what? I promise it will go away."

After the performance, she comes by my dressing room again. "You were right; I feel terrific."

End of story.

BARRYMORE
THE LIFE
THE NEW MUSICAL
3-TIME WINNER!
BEST MUSICAL
1997 DRAMA DESK AWARD • 1997 OUTER CRITICS AWARD • 1997 DRAMA LEAGUE AWARD

11 | EPILOGUE: THE PERPETUAL INVALID

FRED GOLDEN: My wife and I saw the film of *Mr. Roberts* on television. And when it was over, we had a drink and talked about the time I did the advertising for the play. Of all the shows I worked on, *Mr. Roberts* remains my favorite. I was at every one of the rehearsals. I got to know Leland Hayward, Josh Logan, Henry Fonda.

That night I couldn't fall asleep. Early the next morning I got out this little book I had kept with the names of all the people from *Mr. Roberts*. I thought I'd call a couple of them, tell them I had just seen the movie, reminisce with them about the time we worked together on the play. Only, as I went down the list, I realized everyone had passed on. There was no one left.

KITTY CARLISLE HART: I regret the fact that my era, with Moss and George and all the others, is gone. You want to reclaim their work because there's really nothing that can replace them. The longer we get away from them, the more illustrious they become. They seem to me like the French impressionists of the theater.

JOHN LAHR: Broadway is the nostalgia for a theatrical universe that no longer exists. The real theater, the theater that takes us further into ourselves and into the world, hasn't happened on Broadway for thirty years.

SHIRLEY HERZ: Broadway has become a theme park. You have Garth Drabinsky with big megamusicals and his two new houses, you have Disney at the New Amsterdam, and something is lost. New York isn't a four-o'clock-in-the-morning town anymore. They can put up all the signs they want. It was more fun to see a broken bulb and know that there was life behind it.

HARVEY SABINSON: Houses are dark year in and year out. Unproductive theaters like the Belasco are carried by productive ones like the Imperial and Majestic. There will never be another free-standing legitimate theater built in New York.

I walk around now and pass a parking lot on Forty-eighth Street where the Windsor Theater used to be. That's where my brother had his first show. Up the block was the Playhouse Theater, where the League of New York Theaters had its offices many years ago. So much is gone.

ROBERT WHITEHEAD: For about a century the structure of the American commercial theater functioned within predictable boundaries. Costs, ticket prices, audiences all seemed to stay within reasonable dimensions. There were many productions; theater was a generative force. Then in the 1960s that started to change. Costs began rising, ticket prices began climbing, and production lessened, particularly of straight, serious plays.

Film and television, with their economics and wild production schedules, came into play. In the early days of film, the theater reacted by becoming more important in terms of comedy, but later on actors saw they could make more money from movies and television than they could from the stage. The theater gradually began to lose its audience to half-hour sitcoms. Theaters stood empty, and there was a strange desolation in the land.

HARVEY SABINSON: When I started, in the postwar years, there were seventy-five to eighty-five openings a year. Today if we have thirty, it's a great season.

ROBERT WHITEHEAD: There are no longer enough failures on Broadway. If there were thirty-five or forty failures a season, it would mean fifty-five plays had been produced. It is only out of a platform of a lot of work that the great successes emerge.

Forty years ago *Master Class* would have been part of the season. Now it stands out. Its commercial and creative success is very rare in today's theater, as it is essentially a serious and tragic play, and the time that we're living in is not hospitable to plays of that nature.

JOHN LAHR: Occasionally a play like Tony Kushner's *Angels in America,* the great triumph of the commercial theater, gets on. And that almost didn't come in.

CLIVE BARNES: *Angels in America* was first done at Britain's National Theater, then it moved to the West Coast. Dramas come to Broadway in a very circuitous way.

HOWARD KISSEL: Broadway has become the showcase; it is no longer the innovator. It is the end stop rather than the beginning. Where once most plays started on Broadway and went out into the world, Broadway

Broadway has become the showcase; it is no longer the innovator.

has become the final stop on a journey that might begin in a workshop downtown and then go to Seattle or Chicago and then come back. Theater has been decentralized.

FOSTER HIRSCH: Broadway no longer has any real connection to what is going on today. It has become some sort of island because it can only appeal to a certain economic group or tourists, for whom things go in one ear and out the other. The market for plays with issues has very much diminished. Compare the current lineup to any year in the 1930s, when there was a real commitment to plays with an ideological structure.

HARVEY SABINSON: I remember when creative producers generated ideas for shows and got writers to write them. My brother had one backer for *Finian's Rainbow,* and it cost $250,000 to produce.

FOSTER HIRSCH: There used to be one or two names over the title: Feuer and Martin, David Merrick, Alex Cohen—a producer whose voice counted for something, whose taste meant something. Now you have fifteen names.

FREDDIE GERSHON: I was at a rehearsal where a bathing suit manufacturer wrote notes to Tommy Tune telling him what to incorporate or delete. Tommy Tune? Give me a break. These people are highly presumptuous, ungifted, cocktail-party producers.

Some of them are better at it than others. Some of them have learned and have gotten much better. Some of them are heirs to large fortunes, and the theater needs the money. But the truth is generally that they are dilettantes playing at a game.

LEE ROY REAMS: There are still some people, like Cameron Macintosh, who are doing interesting things. But overall the single producer—like David Merrick, who had the power to do what he wanted to do—has been replaced by the conglomerates, the money people.

JOSEPH TRAINA: The increasing corporate influence detracts in small ways from the experience of theatergoing. Shows are much larger, more difficult to manage, especially in the old facilities. Amenities are lost; the public is not treated as well.

LEE ROY REAMS: The musicals of Fosse and Champion had a consistency because there was one person in control. They told the composer, the costume designer, the set designer what they liked or did not like. Nowadays everyone gets a percentage. The composer can say, "Oh really, you don't like my song. It's not your job to like it. It's your job to stage it." The star can say, "I won't do that!" The set people, the costume people—they all have the power to do what they want.

On the other hand, we still have the most talented people, women who can belt, sing softly, sing character, handle operatic material. But they don't have the image of an Ethel Merman or a Mary Martin, because no one has written a vehicle for them. If needed, a television or Hollywood name will be put into a show to sell tickets. The star of a Broadway show today is the director or the writer, the composer or the lyricist.

BETTY BUCKLEY: It was Michael Bennett who, in *A Chorus Line,* conceived the ensemble musical where everyone was recastable. And the talent is not necessarily nurtured here, as it is in opera. People like Patti LuPone, Bernadette Peters, and myself are really blessed in that we have made our own stamp in this day of the ensemble musical.

Which is why I am grateful to Andrew Lloyd Webber for writing *Sunset Boulevard,* which required a leading lady with prowess. Glenn Close got the job because she could sell tickets, and given that musical theater is not really her forte, she really did an incredible job. It was difficult taking over from her. Because of the competition set up in the press and the nature of the diva personality of the role itself, I was thrust into what felt like a competitive environment with women I really respect. I'm a great fan of Glenn Close, Patti LuPone, Elaine Paige. We're like thoroughbreds in a Norma Desmond race.

FOSTER HIRSCH: It doesn't matter who's playing in *Les Mis, Miss Saigon.* It's the show you go to see, not the star. A star like Julie Andrews might return for a particular vehicle, but that's not a Broadway career. Generally speaking, there aren't enough shows to sustain Broadway careers any longer.

LEE ROY REAMS: Still, everyone wants to be a star right away. That's not how it was when I first came to New York, and you started out as a dancer or a singer in a chorus and worked your way up. There used to be twenty shows casting at any given time. Today we're lucky if we get one show that's not precast and prearranged by casting agents whom we can't even get in to see because supposedly everybody knows our work.

We were trained to project; we sang with those big voices, no microphones. There was an energy in hearing that. Now we are totally in the charge of that man who dials your voice up and down. Many singers don't have the volume, and many dancers don't have the extensive training. They're more athletic and aerobic, but there's a loss of artistry and discipline.

We were trained to project; we sang with those big voices, no microphones. There was an energy in hearing that.

I believe in revivals. They're our legacy. But getting new people to write new shows has become so hard, going through the process of trying to sell an idea. No one wants to take a chance. It takes millions and millions of dollars to get a show on; the union costs, the fabric costs—it's horrendous. Everyone screams at the price of the tickets. But how else can you pay for all of that? You have this incredible net to make every week.

JAMES HAMMERSTEIN: We're not becoming opera, are we? We're not pricing ourselves out of business, are we?

MARTY JACOBS: Once, if a show opened and ran four months, it was wonderful. Today that doesn't even begin to pay its expenses. Even if a show is a hit, writers have to wait a year or so before they see any money. Meanwhile they can write a terrible television show and get a lot of money up front.

LEE ROY REAMS: Unless you are a megahit and become a tourist attraction, you can't make money. *Beauty and the Beast* personifies the tourist attraction Broadway has become. You have the Disney name. You can bring your children—and thank god you can, because maybe those are going to become the people who are going to sustain the audience.

HARVEY SABINSON: You can rent a machine that translates a show into in German, French, Portuguese, Spanish, Japanese. That's great for the tourist trade, but it doesn't move the theater forward.

LEE ROY REAMS: In the old days we saw everything, whether it was a hit or a miss. We went to see the next Bob Fosse show, the next Gower Champion show, the next David Merrick production. We went because it was part of our heritage.

HOWARD KISSEL: Up to the 1960s, New Yorkers went to the theater all the time. These days they go for a birthday, an anniversary—if then—or because they have to entertain people from out of town.

JOSEPH TRAINA: After the initial rush, your normal theatergoers are the tourists and people who are used to going to amusement parks, the circus, the movies. They've been raised on television, and they're very casual. They'll sit on the arms of the chairs, put their feet up on the seats, throw their coats and jackets on the railings.

MANNY AZENBERG: My generation and maybe the next one will have a recollection of theater on the order of Peter Brook's production of *King Lear,* Lee J. Cobb in *Death of a Salesman,* Laurence Olivier in *The Entertainer,* Paul Scofield in *A Man for All Seasons*—if you didn't see them, you missed something that is not repeatable. We'll remember seeing the early Osborn plays, those of Tennessee Williams, Arthur Miller, William Inge, and Edward Albee. But the generation after that will think of theater the way we think of vaudeville. They may go every so often to see theme-park, event theater: *Phantom II, Les Mis III,* or revivals of musicals they've heard of.

ROBERT WHITEHEAD: Strangely enough, when the musical theater was at its most exciting and most expressive of us as a country, our theater had a kind of world influence. A lot of plays were being done, and out of them grew the great musicals. But then the volume of productions went down, down, down, until there was practically nothing. And when the serious plays began to disappear, the great American musicals began to disappear. One fed off the other.

So some people went to England and brought over musicals to fill in the vacuum. Extravaganzas. They looked after the commerce.

HOWARD KISSEL: The Andrew Lloyd Webber shows and the like fulfill many people's idea of what an evening in the theater is supposed to be: spectacle, constantly changing panoramas, theater as a movie. The average person doesn't know that something should happen to him while he's watching a play. He gets beautiful stage pictures, and he thinks he's gotten his money's worth.

To someone brought up on the brilliance of American musicals, the music of these shows is nothing. To someone whose idea of a great lyricist is Alan Jay Lerner or Lorenz Hart, the lyrics of these shows are appalling. But to an audience that doesn't know anything beyond Bob Dylan, there's nothing wrong with the music or the lyrics. These audiences wouldn't know what to make of even a secondary musical of the 1950s, like *Pajama Game,* which in terms of lyrics and music puts all these shows to shame.

The Broadway musical had a tremendous, galvanizing energy. The audience would get this fabulous performance and erupt in applause. That energy would fuel what happened next, and at the end of the evening, you were exhilarated. My feeling is that at the end of an evening of spectacle theater, you're enervated. You just want to get out of there and go home.

Look at the reviews for *Cats.* Not one was enthusiastic. Has that had any effect? The bulk of the public, they see a set go up, go down, and they're very happy. The public has no sense of history; it's all *now.* They get it from television. It's now, and it's over, and we go on to the next thing.

Very often when friends ask what they should see, I urge them to find

My feeling is that at the end of an evening of spectacle theater, you're enervated.

a nice French restaurant. Because for $67.50 you can get an excellent dinner. Restaurants are the theater of our time.

CLIVE BARNES: The so-called British musicals are not musicals. They have music that people have heard before, though they may not realize it. They have a story taken from a pop movie or *Madame Butterfly.* They have chandeliers, helicopters landing. As I said, and I was the first person to write it, you come out humming the scenery.

WARD MOREHOUSE III: Whether you think his music is derivative or not, Andrew Lloyd Webber gives people what they want. He is the Ziegfeld of his day.

JOHN LAHR: In the sung-through musical that Sondheim pioneered and that Andrew Lloyd Webber popularized, the narrative function has been taken away from the playwright and given to the songwriter. You listen to a song in a completely different way than you listen to a scene. Auden makes the point that rhyme makes any statement acceptable, gives it authority. Distinctions really aren't possible. "April, May, and December" sounds right if the rhythm is working. When you hear a song, you are enchanted; the root of the word *enchant* is the same as the French word for "song"—*chanson.*

The musical increasingly is not telling a narrative story. Its telling is through song, and song is not sufficient to establish character; it cannot carry the burden of psychology and situation. You need prose and plot. With all he's given the musical, Sondheim, by deconstructing it, has taken it narratively to a place where it can't function.

ERIC STERN: Much of the sung-through musical is declamatory, and as a result, it's lost the dynamic. The heart is gone. We are told what to think and what to feel. The great American musical was built on the foundation of letting a character speak for himself. We were so good at doing that, but we seem to have lost the knack.

CLIVE BARNES: Like the French or Viennese operetta, the Broadway musical, as we knew it, is virtually dead. The guts were knocked out of it when Lennon and McCartney chose not to write a musical. Why should they have done a show that closed in Philadelphia when they could do ten pop concerts and make a fortune?

JOHN KANDER: Back in 1966, as I was unpacking in my hotel room in Boston, I heard "What use is sitting alone in your room . . ." on the radio. It was only the first preview of *Cabaret,* and already the title song was a hit.

But I think that was about the last year that Broadway show tunes regularly became huge popular hits. It's not that wonderful songs are no longer being written. It's just an indication that the music world has changed.

FREDDIE GERSHON: Even "Memory" never went more than the top twenty on the *Billboard* charts. People don't identify contemporary pop music with the Broadway stage. Do you think that someone who likes hip-hop and rap music is going to relate to "Old Man River"?

MARY ELLIN BARRETT: When the guitar replaced the piano as the principal instrument of accompaniment, it changed the nature of popular music. But there's obviously a hunger for the old-time show tunes, which may explain why there are so many revivals.

ERIC STERN: Now I sound like one of those old geezers who lick their chops and say we're going to hell in a handbasket. But one does miss a kind of literate pleasure in the theater these days. It's not about the words anymore. It's about a sensory rush that we get from fog or a big sensuous chord from an orchestra.

I guess I'm a white elephant. I came rushing into an industry that is not there anymore. Mind you, I have a wonderful job. I worked with Jule Styne on two original scores. As musical director, I watched Charles Strouse put the score of *Rags* together. I watched Stephen Sondheim put together original scores. I worked with Cy Coleman, who is remarkable; Comden and Green. I love being here. I don't want to sound cranky. I don't think we're on the road to ruin. We're just changing.

We Americans created musical theater, and we did it better than anybody else. We gave a gift to the world. But if those days are over, we'll move on to other things.

BERNARD GERSTEN: There are really two Broadways. There is the Broadway of the long-running imports like *Cats* and *Les Mis* and the American revivals like *Damn Yankees* and *Forum*. And there is the other Broadway: the not-for-profit theater, the Royale and Tony Randall's National Actors Theater, the Roundabout, Lincoln Center Theater. The encroachment of the nonprofit theater has been a source of irritation for some and great solace for others. But in New York City it represents the bulk of original producing initiative. The theater would be a much sorrier, sadder, less vigorous place without it. The two most heralded shows of the 1996 season, *Bring in 'Da Noise, Bring in 'Da Funk* and *Rent*, began their lives in small off-Broadway institutional theaters. They evolved, worked out their

*I don't think
we're on the
road to ruin.
We're just changing.*

kinks, attracted the fancy of the public and critics, and moved to larger houses on Broadway.

ROBERT WHITEHEAD: The not-for-profit will never fully realize its responsibility until it gets money through legislation. What happened here, happened in England: The theater began to disappear in the West End. But there was some force inside the nation that made them feel it was time to have a subsidized theater, what they call now the Royal National Theater. Today a lot of the best things on Broadway come from the West End. Both Broadway and the British theater are living off the British taxpayer.

FOSTER HIRSCH: What drama is developed originally for Broadway? Almost none. Life begins in the regional theaters. But somehow to have a success in the regional theater is not enough; the goal is to bring it to Broadway.

You can't give up on Broadway. When you think it's all over, something wonderful will come along. It still is the final imprimatur of success.

RICHARD KILEY: Broadway is the perpetual invalid, badly wounded and dying. Yet it always comes back, albeit in a different form.

FOSTER HIRSCH: Hal Prince continues to have a sustained Broadway career, which is unusual for today. Many of the best musicals over the past quarter century have his stamp on them—the dark musicals, the anti–R & H musicals, the vehicles with social and political commentary, like *Kiss of the Spider Woman,* which is set in a South American prison. You could say he is the Bertolt Brecht of the American musical theater.

CLIVE BARNES: Sondheim's *Sweeney Todd* was the first of the bizarre musicals. It is great comedy, great drama, and some very beautiful songs of the kind of melodic lyricism that you don't find except when you go back to the older generation of George Gershwin, Richard Rodgers, Jerome Kern, Burton Lane.

I have complaints about Sondheim, but he is one of the finest American composers, period, and also the best lyricist we've had since Ira Gershwin or Cole Porter.

GEORGE C. WOLFE: Theater should be reflective of all the different dynamics of what is happening in America. That is what was so interesting and wonderful about the 1996 season. There was a new musical, *Bring in 'Da Noise;* a revival, *The King and I;* a serious drama, *Buried Child;* a light comedy, *Moon over Buffalo.* It was one of the healthiest years in a very long time because of the proliferation of the different voices. Given the size of this country, there should be a full range of works on Broadway.

FOSTER HIRSCH: The 1996 revival of Edward Albee's *A Delicate Balance* made me hopeful. Here was a revival of great play originally produced about thirty years earlier that got wonderful reviews and a decent run. It's a very demanding play, with lots of dialogue that requires you to listen in a way we're not used to listening in this era of spectacle shows. Its success means there is still a desire for that kind of theater. The glitter can come back. There have to be concessions. Unions, producers—everyone has to concede to make it possible for people to put on shows.

HOWARD KISSEL: *Molly Sweeney* was an enthralling play of recent years, and really quite amazing when you think about it. The characters barely moved; they never addressed each other, but there was continuous talk. The play described a painful odyssey, an odyssey that was quite different from what you'd expect. *Oh, this blind woman will learn to see; it will be a wonderful thing.* It turned out not to be so wonderful.

This is a work that stays with you for a long time, as does Jason Robards's performance in it. There are certain people—and I think Jason Robards is one of them—who come to life in the theater.

PAUL LIBIN: *Angels in America* was a seminal event in theater in the 1990s—the whole intertwining of politics in America, the crisis in the homosexual community, the Rosenberg thing, the Roy Cohn thing, the conflict over AIDS: Is it God's punishment or a disease?

ERIC STERN: When we talk about why the theater is not quite as vibrant as it could be, we are overlooking our losses because of AIDS. It is not a small matter that a good deal of the talent pool of this art form is not growing into maturity. Apart from the personal tragedy, it is a cultural tragedy.

MERLE DEBUSKEY: The Broadway theater has been absolutely magnificent in attempts to make things better for those who are afflicted with AIDS. That is the sharpest focal point in the theater ever; people are gathered together on this issue like nothing before.

ELAINE STRITCH: Broadway continues to be a small town. The old saying "There are no small parts, just small actors" still rings true here. Your whole part might be "Hark, I hear the cannon," and you still get respect. In Hollywood, if you have a small part, you're nobody. I was in a very successful television series, *My Sister Eileen.* For six months I ate lunch every day at the Brown Derby. Then *The Perry Como Show* opened opposite us, our ratings fell, and we were canceled. The day the story about it appeared in the *Hollywood Reporter,* I went to the Brown Derby, and I couldn't get a table. That's Hollywood.

Compare that treatment to what you'd get from Vincent Sardi and old man Sardi. They've never, never shoved an actor of any quality or status in the back, no matter what that person was doing at the time.

JOHN LAHR: In Hollywood they sit around and dream up movies and television programs. It's a group mind. But the wonderful thing about theater is that you have individual voices penetrating the culture, having a discussion, an argument, trying to make us see different things in language. The role of theater is to open the heart, edify the mind, make us imagine a future. And when it's good, the theater gets you closer to the real heart of the moment, which is a thing I love.

HARVEY SABINSON: The basic idea for reclaiming the theater district and redoing Times Square comes from the League of New York Theaters. We were the prime movers in the attempt to get the government to do something with this great economic resource in the heart of New York City that no other city in the world has. We got the word out in the "I Love New York" campaign and helped bring in tourists.

PAUL LIBIN: All the research confirms that one of the reasons tourists are coming to New York City is to see a Broadway show. They're not coming to see something that's dying.

Insiders are always talking about the day's sales: how many people bought tickets and what the value of that is. Some ask, "How many groups were in that number?" as if groups are some kind of alien theatergoer. Or they ask, "How much was TDF [Theater Development Fund, which offers reduced price tickets] yesterday?" as if that makes a difference. Or they'll say, "The only people who went to that play were Hadassah parties." What the hell does that mean? I love everybody who goes to see a Broadway show—just for the fun of it, as the slogan says.

MICKEY ALPERT: Admittedly the theater has changed. It's gotten smaller. There are fewer theaters. In my time, probably a dozen were torn down and never replaced. The Uris, now the Gershwin, is new. The Minskoff and Marriott Marquis are new. But once there was the George Abbott, the Morosco, the Helen Hayes, the Bijou, the Empire. All gone.

Straight plays have moved from 1,000- to 1,200-seat theaters to theaters that seat 500. The audience dies off a little every year. Kids don't go.

And when it's good, the theater gets you closer to the real heart of the moment, which is a thing I love.

They can't afford it. There are so many alternatives; they're not interested.

But Broadway is bigger and healthier than ever. It doesn't die, it changes. I hate to hear people say it was better. It wasn't better; it was different. Was Frank Sinatra better than the current pop singer? He wasn't. He was the singer of your generation.

It's become a different business. *Fiddler, Dolly!, My Fair Lady* ran three or four years. So did *Crazy for You,* which is nowhere as important a show. *A Chorus Line* ran for fifteen years. *Cats, Phantom* will go beyond that. Less is done, but it's more profitable than ever.

ERIC STERN: Wags say in another ten years there will simply be three producers on Broadway, and none of them will be in New York. It's becoming more and more corporate and global. But this little ten-block area remains the place where plays are up and running, where tourists and new audiences come, where love of theater is created. Broadway is a metaphor for theater in New York City; it will continue to reflect who we are, and I don't mind if it's a repository for some lost sensibility.

JERRY ZAKS: I really don't give a damn about debates. I don't worry about whether or not the theater is dying. That's for critics and intellectuals. I'm inside it, I'm too busy working. I am trying to make it happen on Broadway.

CURTAIN CALL

Many people helped make this collective memoir possible:

The members of the Broadway community, who treated us with such grace and warmth, were so generous of their time, and so willingly shared with us the stories of their lives in the theater;

Those who helped us gain access to the interviewees: Roz Starr, celebrity sleuth extraordinaire; Fred Golden, a dear man and new friend, who also provided memories and encouragement; Mike Hall, the same whirling dervish who guided us through our first oral history and who got us off to a "flying start" with a well-placed newspaper plug; Mickey Alpert, our first interviewee, who set us in the right direction; and Price Berkley, who, through his *Theatrical Index*—frequently and appropriately described as "the Bible of the professional theater throughout the country"—was an invaluable source for fact checking and information on the theater scene;

Monique Bell, Doris Blum, Sam Crothers, Terrie Curran, Margo Feiden, Bert Fink, Nicole Harman, Stephanie McCormick, Michael Milton, Brooks McNamara, Martin Richards, Tabby Sardi, Susan L. Schulman, Bruce Stapleton of *Playbill,* Ron and Howard Mandelbaum of Photofest, and Tony Walton, who gave us suggestions, information, materials, permissions, and the gift of their valued time;

Our agent, Don Congdon, who provided the support and counsel we have come to expect from him, and our new editor, Walt Bode, who provided intelligent and tasteful feedback in a manner marked by gentleness and tact.

How fortunate we were to enjoy the support and friendship of so many.

MYRNA & HARVEY FROMMER
Lyme, New Hampshire, 1998

PICTURE CREDITS

INDEX